EC Law

■ EUROPEAN LAW SERIES ■

Series Editor:

PROFESSOR JOHN A. USHER

EC Law in the UK

CHRISTINE BOCH

Europa Institute
University of Edinburgh

LONGMAN

An imprint of **PEARSON EDUCATION**

Harlow, England · London · New York · Reading, Massachusetts · San Francisco
Toronto · Don Mills, Ontario · Sydney · Tokyo · Singapore · Hong Kong · Seoul
Taipei · Cape Town · Madrid · Mexico City · Amsterdam · Munich · Paris · Milan

Pearson Education Limited
Edinburgh Gate
Harlow
Essex CM20 2JE
England

and Associated Companies throughout the world

Visit us on the World Wide Web at:
http://www.pearsoned-ema.com

First published 2000

ISBN 0-582-35716-0 PPR

British Library Cataloguing-in-Publication Data

A catalogue record for this book is available from the British Library

Set in Sabon 10/12pt
Typeset by Land & Unwin (Data Sciences) Ltd, Bugbrooke, Northants
Printed in Great Britain by Henry Ling Ltd, at the
Dorset Press, Dorchester, Dorset.

Contents

General Editor's Preface

The Longman European Law Series is the first comprehensive series of topic-based books on EC Law aimed primarily at a student readership, though I have no doubt that they will also be found useful by academic colleagues and interested practitioners. It has become more and more difficult for a single course or a single book to deal comprehensively with all the major topics of Community law, and the intention of this series is to enable students and teachers to 'mix and match' topics which they find to be of interest: it may also be hoped that the publication of this Series will encourage the study of areas of Community law which have historically been neglected in degree courses. However, while the Series may have a student readership in mind, the authors have been encouraged to take an academic and critical approach, placing each topic in its overall Community context, and also in its socio-economic and political context where relevant.

Community law by its nature may be capable of applying and being invoked at the national level, and most Community law is administered by national authorities within each Member State. The availability of national remedies therefore forms an essential element in the proper application and enforcement of Community law. The relationship between Community law and national law is a subject on which much has been written, but it remains an area of continuing development particularly with regard to the question of remedies. I am particularly grateful to my colleague Christine Boch for writing on EC law in the UK from the refreshing perspective of a French-trained lawyer living in Scotland.

John A. Usher

Preface

In the Community legal system, individuals, lawyers and national courts are all conscripted into the task of enforcing Community law. Most of the time, individuals rely on Community law before national courts in order to obtain a benefit for themselves. Yet although they do not act to secure enforcement of Community law for its own sake, individuals also advance the Community interests as the vigilance of individuals serves to detect breaches of Community law which the Community machinery could not detect. The vigilance of individuals also alleviates the tasks of the Commission in ensuring that the Member States comply with their Community obligations. As will be seen throughout the book, Community law has been invoked in the UK in a variety of – very inventive – situations, which may be categorised into two subheadings: the shield and the sword. On the one hand, Community law is invoked against an individual, a company, or a public body to force them to comply with Community law in preference to national law. On the other hand, Community law is invoked to resist an application of national law allegedly incompatible with Community law. Of course individuals, lawyers and national courts will not be involved in the enforcement of Community law if they are not all well-informed about its potential. All too often, Community law either suffers from legal racism or is perceived as the subject one may choose to specialise in or not, or as the *chasse-gardée* of big commercial law firms. But Community law is neither of these. It is not foreign law, but an integral part of the legal systems of all jurisdictions in the UK, and it can be made relevant to any area of legal practice.

This book aims to familiarise readers with the possibilities for legal redress before the UK courts when rules of Community law are violated. It is believed this is best done by focusing on case law, and as far as practicable on case law involving the UK courts. In this way, the role played by lawyers and litigation in the shaping of the Community legal system will become apparent. The book however does not purport to show which way the case law could and should develop, and therefore academic work in this area will not be examined at any length.

The position of the individual in Community law is focused upon. It is a litigant's perspective, and a narrow one since it will only study judicial remedies before UK courts. Thus, alternative non-judicial redress such as Parliamentary questions and petitions or complaints to the Ombudsman, all of which can play an important part in securing individuals' protection against certain violations of Community law, will not be discussed. The limited rights of individuals or companies to bring proceedings before the Court of First Instance will not be discussed either.

It is almost trite to say that in the Community, legal integration is much more developed than political integration, and that a picture of the Community which places litigation at centre stage and concentrates on enforcement issues gives a rather distorted image of the reality of daily life in the Community. Certainly for the UK, some of the troublesome years in its (ever) awkward relationship with the Community have also been the years where major legal battles were fought in the UK courts. Thus, not long after John Major trumpeted on his government's great achievement at Maastricht regarding opting-out of Community social policy, the House of Lords was reviewing the validity of primary UK legislation, namely the Employment Protection (Consolidation) Act 1978 against a superior Community law norm. Yet, if the book may give the impression that Community law is a powerful weapon, the reality it describes is just the tip of an iceberg. Unfortunately, non-compliance with the law of the Community by all those who are supposed to respect it, remains all too frequent.

The UK legal structure is characterised by an unusual feature in a unitary state: a plurality of legal systems and therefore differences in current practice between England and Wales, Scotland, and Northern Ireland. For reasons of convenience, the book will be phrased in terms of English law, although where Scottish cases are discussed, Scottish terminology is used. However, these legal systems are not my own, and the book does not purport to offer a British view on the Community, but rather a Community lawyer's view of the ways in which a particular Member State accommodates Community requirements. I have used throughout the numbering of the EC Treaty which will be changed once the Treaty of Amsterdam enters into force on the 1st May. The case law and the literature quoted or discussed throughout the book naturally uses pre-Amsterdam numeration. A table of equivalence will show the new numbers for the provisions referred to in this book.

I owe thanks to many people who in very different ways made this book possible. Pierre-Charles Amilhat convinced me to go to Bruges to learn some Community law, Judge David Edward enabled me to exercise my freedom of worker's right, Professor Hector MacQueen always offered help and advice, Professor John Usher gave me the opportunity to write this book, and Peter Cullen made constructive criticisms of some chapters of the book. All responsibility for the views expressed and the mistakes made is, of course, mine alone.

The task of completing this book was eased with the help of Laurence. My children bore the loss of many hours when they might have expected my company. In recognition of the burdens which this task has imposed upon them, I dedicate this book to my family.

Christine Boch
February 1999

Abbreviations

AC	Appeal Cases
Admin LR	Administrative Law Report
All ER	All England Law Report
Bull EC	Bulletin of the European Communities
CA	English Court of Appeal
CAP	Common Agricultural Policy
CDE	Cahiers de Droit Européen
CFI	Court of First Instance
CH	Chancery Report
CMLR	Common Market Law Reports
CMLRRev	Common Market Law Review
ConsLJ	Consumer Law Journal
CrimLR	Criminal Law Review
ECHR	European Convention of Human Rights and Fundamental Freedoms
ECJ	European Court of Justice
ECLR	European Competition Law Review
EJIL	European Journal of International Law
ELJ	European Law Journal
ELR	European Law Review
EPL	European Public Law
EU	European Union
HL	House of Lords
ICLQ	International and Comparative Law Quarterly
ICR	Industrial Cases Report
ILJ	Industrial Law Journal
JEL	Journal of Environmental Law
LJIL	Leiden Journal of International Law
LQR	Law Quarterly Review

MJECL	Maastricht Journal of European and Comparative Law
MLR	Modern Law Review
OJ	Official Journal of the European Communities
QB	Queen's Bench
RTDE	Revue Trimestrielle de Droit Européen
SLT	Scots Law Times
WLR	Weekly Law Report
YEL	Yearbook of European Law

Table of Cases

TABLE OF CASES

TABLE OF CASES

TABLE OF CASES

Table of Legislation and Treaties

Table of Equivalence

TABLE OF EQUIVALENCE

Previous Numbering	New Numbering	Previous Numbering	New Numbering
Art 100a	Art 95	Art 148	Art 205
Art 100c	repealed	Art 150	Art 206
Art 102a	Art 98	Art 151	Art 207
Art 103a	Art 100	Art 152	Art 208
Art 104a	Art 102	Art 155	Art 211
Art 104b	Art 103	Art 157	Art 213
Art 105	Art 105	Art 158	Art 214
Art 105a	Art 106	Art 163	Art 219
Art 109	Art 111	Art 164	Art 220
Art 109a	Art 112	Art 166	Art 222
Art 109e	Art 116	Art 167	Art 223
Art 109f	Art 117	Art 168a	Art 225
Art 109j	Art 121	Art 169	Art 226
Art 109k	Art 122	Art 170	Art 227
Art 113	Art 133	Art 171	Art 228
Art 118	Art 137	Art 173	Art 230
Art 118a	Art 138	Art 175	Art 232
Art 119	Art 141	Art 177	Art 234
Art 126	Art 149	Art 178	Art 235
Art 127	Art 150	Art 179	Art 236
Art 128	Art 151	Art 184	Art 241
Art 129	Art 152	Art 185	Art 242
Art 129a	Art 153	Art 186	Art 243
Art 129c	Art 155	Art 189	Art 249
Art 129d	Art 156	Art 189a	Art 250
Art 130b	Art 159	Art 189b	Art 251
Art 130d	Art 161	Art 189c	Art 252
Art 130e	Art 162	Art 190	Art 253
Art 130r	Art 174	Art 191	Art 254
Art 130s	Art 175	Art 193	Art 257
Art 137	Art 189	Art 198	Art 262
Art 138	Art 190	Art 198a	Art 263
Art 138a	Art 191	Art 198c	Art 265
Art 138b	Art 192	Art 203	Art 272
Art 138c	Art 193	Art 204	Art 273
Art 138e	Art 195	Art 209a	Art 280
Art 140	Art 197	Art 215	Art 288
Art 141	Art 198	Art 220	Art 293
Art 144	Art 201	Art 228	Art 300
Art 145	Art 202	Art 228a	Art 301
Art 146	Art 203	Art 232	Art 305

TABLE OF EQUIVALENCE

Previous Numbering	New Numbering
Art 235	Art 308
Art 237	repealed
Art 238	Art 310

Treaty on European Union

Previous Numbering	New Numbering
Art A	Art 1
Art B	Art 2
Art C	Art 3
Art D	Art 4
Art E	Art 5

Previous Numbering	New Numbering
Art F	Art 6
Art F(1)	Art 7
Art J.1	Art 11
Art J.5	Art 15
Art J.8	Art 18
Art K.1	Art 29
Art K.4	Art 32
Art K.6	Art 34
Art K.7	Art 35
Art K.9	Art 37
Art K.12	Art 40
Art K.14	Art 42
Art L	Art 46
Art O	Art 49

■ CHAPTER ONE ■

Identifying Community law

The EEC Treaty is quite unlike any of the enactments to which we have become accustomed . . . It lays down general principles. It expresses its aims and purposes. All in sentences of moderate length and commendable style. *But it lacks precision.* It uses words and phrases without defining what they mean. An English lawyer would look for an interpretation clause, but he would look in vain. All the way through the Treaty there are gaps and lacunae. These have to be filled by the judges, or by regulations or directives. It is the European way . . . Seeing these differences, what are the English courts to do when they are faced with a problem of interpretation? They must follow the European pattern. No longer must they argue about the precise grammatical sense. They must look for the purpose and intent. They must divine the spirit of the Treaty and gain inspiration from it. If they find a gap they must fill it as best as they can . . .[1]

This chapter discusses a selection of actions that involve a Community dimension, in order to demonstrate the breadth of impact of Community law, and how wide-ranging Community law arguments can be. Beforehand, a description[2] of the sources of Community law is required. What are Community rights, where do they come from, and who are they for?

In the aftermath of the Second World War, a number of bodies and institutions were set up with similar titles. And today, there are at least four fields of law often confusingly referred to as 'European Law':[3] the law of the European Convention of Human

---

1. *Bulmer v Bollinger* [1974] 2 CMLR 91, per Lord Denning. Emphasis added.
2. Sources are being dealt with comprehensively in J. Usher, *EC Institutions and Legislation* (Longman, 1998).
3. Edward and Lane, *European Community Law: An Introduction* (Butterworths, 1994) para. 1.

Rights and Fundamental Freedoms; the law of the European Communities; the law of the European Union; and the law of the European Economic Area. In this book, the terms European law, European Community law, or Community law will be used interchangeably to refer exclusively to the law of the European Communities,[4] a subset of the law of the European Union.[5]

The Treaty of Maastricht or 'Treaty on European Union' introduced a 'three pillars' structure. The three Communities remain in existence as components of the central pillar (the first pillar), the side pillars are on the one hand Common Foreign and Security Policy (the second pillar), and on the other Co-operation in the fields of Justice and Home Affairs (the third pillar). The Treaty on European Union introduced 'citizenship'. This was largely inspired by the concern to bring the Union closer to its citizens and to give expression to its character as more than a purely economic project. This concern is also reflected in the removal of the word 'economic' from the Community's name and by the introduction into the EC Treaty of a range of activities and policies transcending the field of economy.[6] The Treaty of Maastricht provided for a future revision process which began in March 1996 and concluded with the signing of the Treaty of Amsterdam on 2 October 1997.[7] This new treaty will only enter into force once ratified by the 15 Member States.[8] It provides for a renumbering of EC Treaty provisions (see Table of Equivalence, p. xxx); it 'communautarises' a part of the third pillar by inserting a new title on 'Visas, Asylum, Immigration and other Policies relating to the free movement of persons in the EC Treaty'. 'Police and Judicial Co-operation in Criminal Matters' remains an intergovernmental matter.[9]

Primary sources

The sources of Community law are contained in the constitutive or 'founding Treaties' establishing the three Communities; in the

---

4. The European Coal and Steel Community (ECSC), the European Community (EC) and the European Atomic Energy Community (EURATOM).
5. Edward and Lane, *op. cit.*
6. Case C-274/96 *Criminal proceedings against H.O. Bickel*, opinion of Jacobs, AG, para. 23 [1998] ECR I-7637.
7. OJ 1997 C340.
8. 1st May 1999.
9. See Usher, *op. cit.*, Chapter 1, for a detailed account of the revision.

Treaties revising the founding Treaties, notably the Merger Treaty of 1965, the Budgetary Treaties, the Single European Act and the Treaty on European Union; in the Treaties of Accession (which provide for the accession of new Member States), and in protocols, conventions, and acts ancillary to the founding Treaties and the Treaties of Accession. The Preambles to the Treaties have legal force; and disregarding them as mere '*Euro-waffle*'[10] would be unwise. The European Court of Justice (ECJ) has in a number of landmark decisions made express reference to the Preamble when interpreting substantive provisions of the Treaty and deciding on their effect.

A second category of primary sources of Community law comprises international agreements by which the European Union is bound. These consist of agreements with one or more third countries or international organisations, concluded either by the Community and the Member States together or by the Community itself in exercise of its external relations powers. These agreements include agreements such as GATT (which predates the foundation of the EEC), the Treaty establishing the European Economic Area (EEA), and 'Association Agreements', notably the Lomé Convention with the African, Caribbean and Pacific (ACP) countries; and the 'Europe Agreements' with some of the countries of former Eastern Europe. On occasions, UK courts may be faced with questions regarding the effects of such agreements. Thus, in *Polydor*,[11] the Court of Appeal asked the ECJ whether the Portuguese Association Agreement had the effect of allowing parallel imports from Portugal.

The final category of primary sources are the general principles of law.[12] They have been developed by the ECJ, as part of its general duty to ensure that the law is observed.[13] They derive from the constitutions of the Member States, or from international agreements, such as the European Convention on Human Rights and Fundamental Freedoms (ECHR), to which the Member States, but not the Community, are parties.[14] With regard to the ECHR, it must be borne in mind that the ECJ only finds inspiration from it,

---

10. John Major, *The Times*, 3 November 1992.
11. *Polydor Ltd v Harlequin Record Shops Ltd and Simons Record Ltd* [1980] 2 CMLR 413; and also Case 270/80 [1982] ECR 329.
12. See Usher, *General Principles of Law* (Longman, 1998).
13. Article 220 EC.
14. Opinion 2/94 [1996] ECR I-1759.

and that there is a real possibility of diverging interpretations between the Luxembourg and Strasbourg Courts.[15] The general principles of law include principles of 'administrative justice' such as legal certainty and proportionality; and principles 'aligned with British concepts of natural justice'.[16] Primary sources take precedence over derived legislation; accordingly, challenges to the validity of legislation in conflict with primary sources can be mounted before national courts.[17] The general principles of law are a source of Community law and as such must be observed by the Community institutions when they legislate, but also when they administer Community law. General principles of law can be relied upon in litigation where the validity of Community legislation is questioned; equally, executive action by the Commission can be challenged if it can be shown to be in breach of the general principles of law.[18] Where Member States act as agents of the Community, by interpreting or applying Community law or administering Community policies, they, similarly, are constrained by the general principles of law.[19] Member States must also observe general principles of law when they are derogating from the free movement provisions.[20]

Legislation made under the Treaty

The EC Treaty defines the powers of Community institutions and provides for the constitutional framework under which the body of Community legislation is being made. Legislation made under the Treaty consists of regulations, directives and decisions.

Article 249 EC provides that 'a regulation shall have general application. It is binding in its entirety and directly applicable in all the Member States.' A regulation 'being essentially of a legislative nature'[21] has general application in that it contains general and

15. R. Lawson, 'Confusion and Conflict? Diverging Interpretations of the European Convention of Human Rights in Strasbourg and Luxembourg' in R. Lawson and M. de Blois (eds), *The Dynamics of the Protection of Human Rights in Europe* (Kluwer, 1994), p. 219 at 252.
16. Edward and Lane, *op. cit.*, p. 65.
17. See further Chapter 11.
18. See further Chapter 11.
19. Case C-2/92 *R v MAFF, ex parte Bostock* [1994] ECR I-955.
20. Case C-260/89 *ERT v DEP* [1991] ECR I-2925.
21. Cases 16 & 17/62 *Confédération Nationale des Producteurs des Fruits et Légumes v EEC Council* [1962] ECR 471.

abstract provisions, and has legal effects extending to an indeterminate group of persons and to a multiplicity of circumstances described in general terms. Being binding in its entirety, a Member State is not entitled to apply the provisions of a regulation in an incomplete or selective manner and thus exclude those parts which it considers to be contrary to certain of its national interests.[22] Regulations take effect in all Member States either 20 days after their publication in the Official Journal or at a later date specified in the text. In exceptional circumstances[23] a regulation may take effect retrospectively. In the criminal sphere, regulations cannot operate retroactively.[24] Although, in theory, as soon as they come into force regulations are 'directly applicable in all the Member States', in practice, they often require some further action in the Member States. Whatever degree of intervention is needed, Member States must ensure that the Community nature of the regulation is clear, and that its substance is in no way altered.

A directive is binding on each Member State as to the result to be achieved within a prescribed period, but leaves the Member States the choice of form and methods for attaining the objectives set at Community level. This discretion is on occasion severely curtailed by precise and detailed provisions. Even where Member States enjoy genuine discretion, this is closely supervised by the ECJ. The use of administrative practices, which by their nature may be changed according to the whim of the authorities and which lack appropriate publicity, is not acceptable.[25] The provisions of a directive must be implemented with unquestionable binding force and with the specificity, precision and clarity required in order to satisfy the requirement of legal certainty.[26] This requirement is difficult to fulfil when the directive itself is ambiguous.[27] The practice of annexing the text of the directive to national provisions designed to implement it is now commonplace.

The obligation of result laid down in directives varies greatly, depending on the content, or type of directive. Some directives require Member States to set up procedures, others may impose obligations on Member States to provide information to the

22. Case 128/78 *Commission v United Kingdom* [1979] ECR 419 428–9.
23. Case 108/81 *Amylum v Council* [1982] ECR 3107.
24. Case 63/83 *R v Kirk* [1984] ECR 2689.
25. Case 160/82 *Commission v The Netherlands* [1982] ECR 4637, para. 4.
26. Case C-59/89 *Commission v Germany* [1991] ECR I-2607, para. 24.
27. See further Chapter 3.

Community institutions or to notify them of a proposed course of action such as the introduction of new technical regulations. Some directives require Member States to grant exemption from VAT, others oblige them to introduce or modify substantive provisions governing legal relationship in the private sphere. In practice, this means that when directives come before national courts a variety of issues may arise, *inter alia* checking that Member States have set up adequate procedures which offer the guarantees required, or substituting a legally perfect provision in a directive for a provision of national law, or deciding which effects to attach to the non-observance of an obligation to notify standards or provide the relevant information, or deciding whether the sanctions attached to a failure to comply with the obligations laid down in the implementing legislation will secure proper compliance with the directive. The fact that there are different types of directives also implies that questions as to whether or not, and in which circumstances, individuals may be recognised as having an interest in ensuring that Member States comply with these different directives, will vary.

According to the text of Article 249 EC, the addressees of directives can only be the Member States. As far as individuals are concerned, this means that rights and obligations can only be brought into being by the national measures that implement the directives and *not* by the directives themselves. In other words, Article 249 provides that directives can only reach individuals through the medium of national legislation. 'Wherever a directive is correctly implemented, its effect extends to individuals through the medium of the implementing measures adopted by the Member States concerned'.[28] Where a directive is not implemented in national law, the rights and obligations therein are not readily available.[29] Where it is implemented, Community law appears in the national legal systems 'disguised' as national law. It follows that it is necessary to check whether or not there is a directive which covers the situation under consideration. When a UK statute or statutory instrument implements a Community directive, it is useful first of all to check whether the Community directive has been properly implemented. If not, then it may be challenged, and

[28.] Case 8/81 *Becker* [1982] ECR 53, para 19.
[29.] Although various routes are available to individuals: see Chapter 5. Also see S. Prechal, *Directives in European Community Law: A Study on EC Directives and their Enforcement by National Courts* (OUP, 1995).

6

what may have seemed like a simple plea of guilty or a fair dismissal, might well become a plea of not guilty or a claim for unfair dismissal.

It is important to appreciate that directives lay down two separate obligations for Member States. Alongside the obligation to implement the directive – sometimes referred to as 'black-letter implementation' – Member States have an obligation to ensure that the objective which the directive intends to achieve is actually met – 'implementation in practice'. Community law requires Member States, and, insofar as they are organs of the States, their national courts and tribunals, to ensure the exercise and effective control over compliance with the provisions of the directive and with the national legislation intended to put it into effect.[30] In other words, Member States must not only transpose directives properly, they must secure their effective application and enforcement. So, for example, full implementation of Article 7 of the Package Travel Directive,[31] requires Member States to adopt, within the prescribed period, all the measures necessary to provide purchasers of package travel with a guarantee that, as from the time limit for implementation, they will be refunded money already paid and be repatriated in the event of the organiser's insolvency. Full implementation is not secured if the national legislature has done no more than adopt the necessary legal framework for requiring organisers by law to provide sufficient evidence of security.[32]

Directives are not only sometimes implemented imperfectly, they are often implemented belatedly, or not at all.

> It is central to the coherence and unity of the process of European construction that each Member State should fully and accurately transpose into national law the Community Directives addressed to it within the deadlines laid down therein.[33]

The Community is beset with a pathology of non-compliance, an acute problem in relation to directives, where poor or bad implementation at times seem to constitute the norm. This is also true of the United Kingdom, despite its good record in relation to formal

---

30. Case 222/84 *Johnston v Chief Constable of the RUC* [1986] ECR 1651, para. 13.
31. Council Directive 90/314 on package travel, package holidays and package tours; OJ 1990 L158/59.
32. C-178/94 *Dillenkofer v Germany* [1996] ECR I-4845.
33. TEU, Final Act, Part III: Declarations, Declaration No 19, 'Declaration on the Implementation of Community Law.'

transposition, and claims have been pursued successfully in order to secure proper, effective application and enforcement of directives.[34]

Enforcing directives raises different sets of issues. National courts may be called upon to play different roles, at different points in time,[35] in ensuring that Member States comply with the obligations laid down in directives. In cases of alleged wrongful implementation, national courts might need to refer the matter to the ECJ in order to ascertain the full extent of the Community requirement. In cases of established wrongful implementation, national courts' duties will change. In the absence of implementing measures, i.e. without the medium of national law, to what extent can directives reach individuals, and to what extent can individuals insist on effective application of Community directives? Questions will also arise, depending on factual circumstances, as to the title and interest of individuals and other legal persons to challenge implementing legislation as failing to achieve the required result. Flowing from this are issues of whether a potential litigant ought to challenge United Kingdom-wide implementing legislation in the English or in the Scottish courts where title and interest is viewed differently.[36] The various duties of national courts in giving effect to directives and the different techniques developed by the ECJ and available to individuals to enforce directives will be considered later.[37]

'Soft law'

In the Community there are rules of conduct which, although without legally binding force, may nevertheless have important practical effects since they offer guidance as to the interpretation and scope of application of Community law. This 'soft law' takes a multitude of forms; from acts explicitly recognised by Article

---

34. See Chapter 7.
35. Compare Case C-129/96 *Inter-Environnement Wallonie ASBL and Région Wallonne* [1997] ECR I-7411 and Case C-230/97 *Criminal proceedings against Ibiyinka Awoyemi*, [1998] ECR I-6781 with Case 148/78 *Ratti* [1979] ECR 1629.
36. C. Himsworth, 'No Standing Still on Standing', Chapter 9 in Leyland and Woods (eds), *Administrative Law Facing the Future* (Blackstone, 1997), at 206–8.
37. See Chapter 5.

249 EC, namely recommendations[38] and opinions as well as declarations, *action programmes, communiqués* and resolutions of Community institutions. Other official documentation may assist. This includes notices, communications and other statements of policy issued by the Commission; as well as answers to parliamentary questions in the European Parliament.[39] In the UK, reports such as those of the House of Lords' Select Committee on the European Communities provide useful information as to new developments which can be expected, and as to the different issues surrounding the implementation of particular Community instruments.

Case law as a source of law

The extent to which the case law of the ECJ is a source of law deserves some attention. The European Communities Act 1972 s 3(1) expressly provides:

> that any question as to the meaning or effect of any of the Treaties and of Community legislation, must, if not referred to the European Court, be decided in accordance with the principles laid down by, and any relevant decisions of, the European Court.

Which decisions of the ECJ can be regarded as relevant and binding on the UK courts? A preliminary ruling under Article 234 is binding on the referring court, but what exactly is its broader effect on other courts in the same national legal system and on the domestic courts of other Member States? Community rules have to be interpreted so as to have the same effect in every Member State[40] and the function of Article 234 is to secure uniform application and interpretation. Therefore, preliminary rulings are designed to have a wider impact than just on the referring national court. The ECJ indicated in *CILFIT*[41] that a reference may be made in future cases in which the same question of interpretation arises again or to which the ruling is capable of applying, even by

---

38. Case C-322/88 *Grimaldi v Fonds des Maladies Professionnelles* [1989] ECR 4407.
39. In *Three Rivers DC v Bank of England* [1997] 3 CMLR 429 Clarke J even had regard to an opinion from ECOSOC.
40. Case 81/87 *R v HM Treasury, ex parte Daily Mail* [1988] ECR 5483.
41. Case 283/81 *CILFIT v Ministry of Health* [1982] ECR 3415.

a court which would otherwise be obliged to refer. In *ICI*,[42] it was made clear that a declaration of invalidity of Community legislation may be relied upon by other national courts. In addition, the ECJ makes frequent reference to 'consistent and well-established case law'; and has attached important practical consequences to such a body of case law. Hence, in relation to State liability for breaches of Community law, characterisation of breaches of Community law has been made in the light of the ECJ's earlier case law. In *Brasserie du Pêcheur*,[43] the ECJ held[44] that the German *Biersteuergesetz*, prohibiting the marketing of beer containing ingredients other than water, hops, malt and yeast, as Bier, found to contravene Article 28 of the Treaty in 1987, could not be regarded as an excusable error, since the incompatibility of such rules was manifest in the light of earlier decisions of the Court, in particular *Cassis de Dijon* (1979),[45] and *Vinegar* (1981).[46] Therefore, 'consistent and well-established case law' ought, in general, to be studied with particular attention. Still, it should be borne in mind, that there is no such thing as a doctrine of binding precedent as understood in the UK. The ECJ is not formally bound by previous rulings, although in practice, like any other court, it rarely departs from previous decisions. National courts are bound by a previous ruling of the ECJ,[47] but no national court is precluded from making a reference if it wishes the ECJ to reconsider a previous ruling on the interpretation of a specific provision;[48] and, on three occasions, the Court expressly overruled a previous decision.[49]

---

42. Case 66/80 *International Chemical Corporation v Amministrazione delle Finanze dello Stato* [1981] ECR 1191.
43. Cases C-46/93 & 48/93, [1996] ECR I-1029.
44. At para. 59.
45. Case 120/78 *Rewe-Zentrale v Bundesmonopolverwaltung für Branntwein* [1979] ECR 649.
46. Case 193/80 *EC Commission v Italy* [1981] ECR 3019.
47. See *Perkins* where the High Court considered itself bound by *Grant* [1998] IRLR 508.
48. The English courts have sent no less than four references on the Sunday trading legislation: Case 145/88 *Torfaen Borough Council v B & Q plc* [1989] ECR 3851, Case 306/88 *Rochdale Borough Council v B & Q plc* [1989] ECR 6457, Case C-304/90 *Reading Borough Council v Payless DIY* [1992] ECR I-6493; Case C-169/91 *Stoke-on-Trent v B &Q plc* [1992] ECR I-6635; whilst the French (Case C-312/89 *Conforama* [1991] ECR I-997) and Belgian courts (Case C-332/89 *Marchandise* [1992] ECR I-1027) sent questions raising the same issues.
49. C-10/89 SA *CNL-Sucal NV v HAG GF AG (Hag II)* [1990] ECR I-3711, Case C-267–8/91 *Criminal proceedings against Keck and Mithouard* [1993] ECR I-6097, Case C-394/96 *Brown v Rentokil* [1998] ECR I-4185.

Judgments of the Court, collegiate decisions, are terse, cryptic and with little indication of the reasoning on which they are based.[50] The Opinions of Advocates General are more akin to the style of legal writing of the United Kingdom bench. The task of an Advocate General is to 'make, in open court, *reasoned submissions* on cases brought before the Court of Justice, in order to assist the Court in the performance of the task assigned to it'.[51] The usefulness of Opinions is twofold. Where the ECJ departs from it, the Opinion can be regarded as a dissenting opinion, and may be invoked as a persuasive authority in subsequent cases to try to convince the Court to reconsider previous rulings. Where the ECJ followed it, an Opinion may be the best guide to the reasoning of the Court. 'Although not binding upon the Court, they are a source of Community law.'[52]

Like any legal system, Community law has its unique features which must be taken on board. The next section will remind lawyers that when using Community law they must be aware of its specific character.

The notable features of the Treaty

It is a *framework treaty*, in that it merely provides general principles as guidelines for the attainment of Community objectives. The details are left to be worked out by the institutions at a later date, although the level of treatment given to the different subjects varies. Furthermore, whilst matters dealt with under the Treaty are wide-ranging, progress in some areas has been more satisfactory than in others. This uneven level of performance in terms of development of policies can also be traced through the enforcement of Community law, some aspects of Community law being enforced more effectively and efficiently than others.

The Community Treaty lays down the foundations of the most comprehensive existing framework for international co-operation. This is in fact linked to the *dynamic nature of the integration process*. If the powers attributed to the Community are defined in sectoral terms, *inter alia* agriculture, transport, environment,

---

50. Steiner and Woods, *EC Law*, 5th ed. (Blackstone, 1996), p. 26.
51. Art 222 EC Treaty, emphasis supplied.
52. Edward and Lane, *op. cit.*, p. 31.

health and safety and consumer protection, they have to be understood in functional terms, i.e. by reference to the objectives[53] to be achieved. In the progress towards the realisation of these objectives, the Community influences national substantive policy areas. The Community can limit national autonomy even in spheres not formally transferred to the Community[54] when national policies act as a barrier to integration or threaten the achievement of one of the objectives of the Community, as will be illustrated through case law. The dynamic character of the Community can also be seen in the Community legal order. All general provisions of Community law and in particular the provisions of the Treaty, must be interpreted in a evolutionary way,[55] a technique which, at first, surprised English judges:

> The European Court, in contrast to English courts, applies teleological rather than historical methods to the interpretation of the Treaties and other Community legislation. It seeks to give effect to what it conceives to be the spirit rather than the letter of the Treaties; sometimes, indeed, to an English judge, it may seem to the exclusion of the letter. It views the Communities *as living and expanding organisms and the interpretation of the provisions of the treaties as changing to match their growth.*[56]

The UK courts now seem better accustomed to the ECJ's 'dynamic role appropriate to the construction of a living constitution',[57] and to the need for different interpretation techniques.[58]

A law of solidarity

Today, the implications of the reasons for setting up the Community seem forgotten, if not the reasons themselves. But to create the conditions for peaceful co-existence implies that membership of the Community carries with it acceptance of a duty of solidarity, and acceptance that integration is meant to bring about

---

53. Article 2 EC.
54. See e.g. linguistic policies in Boch, 'Language protection and Free Trade: The Triumph of the Homo McDonaldus?' (1998) 4 European Public Law 379.
55. Case 283/81 *CILFIT v Ministry of Health* [1982] ECR 3415.
56. Lord Diplock in *R v Henn and Darby* [1981] AC 850, emphasis added.
57. Lightman J in *R v Secretary of State for Defence, ex parte Perkins* [1997] 3 CMLR 310 at 328.
58. *Ibid.*

interdependence. The obligations undertaken by the Member States are not just to each other, they are obligations to the Community. 'The Member States have undertaken certain far-reaching obligations not simply on a reciprocal basis, but primarily towards the new collectivity they set up'.[59] This duty of solidarity provides the background to the enforcement of Community rules.

> In permitting Member States to profit from the advantages of the Community, the Treaty imposes on them the obligation to respect its rules. For a State unilaterally to break, according to its conception of national interest, the equilibrium between advantages and obligations flowing from its adherence to the Community brings into question the equality of Member States before Community law and creates discriminations at the expense of their nationals. This failure in the *duty of solidarity accepted by Member States by the fact of their adherence to the Community* strikes at the very root of the Community legal order.[60]

Moreover, in the Community, under no circumstances may a Member State unilaterally adopt, on its own authority, corrective or protective measures designed to obviate any breach by another Member State of rules of Community law.[61] Thus, full and effective enforcement of Community rules in the different Member States and appropriate sanctions for breach of Community law are not only in the interests of the Community but also in the interests of the Member States, given that the Community does not tolerate retaliation as an acceptable response to breach by Member States of their Community obligations. Assurance that Community obligations are fully observed in all the Member States also serves the interests of individuals and companies, for they ought not to be deprived of the rights and benefits which integration is meant to bring about.

The autonomy of Community law

The autonomy of Community law with regard to national legal systems, a principle originally designed as a defensive mechanism

---

59. Donner (1974) 11 CMLRev 127 at 128.
60. Case 128/78 *Commission v United Kingdom* [1979] ECR 419, para. 12 (emphasis added); see also Case 39/72 EC *Commission v Italy* [1973] ECR 101 at 116.
61. Case C-5/94 *R v MAFF, ex parte Lomas* [1996] ECR I-2553, para. 20.

to protect the identity of Community law from the incursions of national laws,[62] has led the ECJ to construct a Community meaning for many Community concepts. 'Public policy',[63] 'worker', 'court or tribunal' are just some of the Community concepts independent from domestic definitions. The Community interpretation attached to these concepts is also based on the need to ensure the uniform application of Community law. As the Court explained in *CILFIT*:[64]

> it must be borne in mind that Community legislation is drafted in several languages and that the different language versions are all equally authentic. An interpretation of a provision of Community law thus involves a *comparison of the different language versions*. It must also be borne in mind, even when the different language versions are entirely in accord with one another, that Community law uses *terminology which is peculiar to it*. Furthermore, it must be emphasised that *legal concepts do not necessarily have the same meaning in Community law and in the law of the various Member States*. Finally, every provision of Community law must be placed in its *context* and interpreted in the light of the provisions of Community law as a whole, regard being had to the objectives thereof and to its *state of evolution* at the date on which the provision in question is to be applied.

The provisions of the EC Treaty must be interpreted according to the general objectives set out in Article 2, and in order to determine the overall purpose of regulations and directives, the ECJ will have regard to their preambles. Certain Treaty provisions, such as the principles of non-discrimination or free movement of goods, are regarded by the ECJ as fundamental to the aims of the Community. The scope of the prohibition laid down in Treaty provisions is interpreted broadly; conversely, the scope of the power to derogate from these provisions is subject to judicial control and is strictly and narrowly construed.[65]

---

62. R. Kovar, 'The relationship between Community law and national law', *Thirty Years of Community Law* (Luxembourg, 1983) at p. 110.
63. Case 41/74 *Van Duyn* [1974] ECR 1337, para. 18.
64. Case 283/81 *CILFIT v Ministry of Health* [1982] ECR 3415 at 3430, emphasis added.
65. Case C-328/91 *Secretary of State for Social Security v Thomas* [1993] ECR I-1247, para. 8.

Community law and individuals

'As the Court of Justice has consistently held, the Communities Treaties established a new legal order . . . the subjects of which comprised not only the Member States, but also their nationals'.[66] In the Community legal system, individuals can lay claims to individual rights which national courts must protect. The Treaty is not only concerned with relationships between States, it affects relationships between individuals. First, some Treaty provisions such as Articles 37, 43, 49, 80, 81, 230, expressly grant rights to, or impose obligations on, individuals. Secondly, many Articles, although addressed to Member States, affect individuals' interests as obligations may be imposed on them or rights may be created for their benefit. Thus, actions claiming equal pay from private employers can be brought under Article 141 EC; Article 28 EC can give rise to rights enforceable by a company against another company:[67] the holder of industrial property rights in a product who distributes or consents to the distribution of that product in a Member State is prohibited by virtue of Article 28 EC from objecting to the importation from other Member States of goods marketed by himself or with his consent elsewhere in the Community.

'Community law has the habit of emerging in unlikely corners'[68]

In this section, a selection of actions[69] involving a Community dimension, will illustrate the breadth of impact of Community law. The Community legal order is in constant evolution, the dynamic extension of the aims and objectives of the Community is reflected in the far-reaching ambit of Community law. Community law arguments arise in all kinds of legal proceedings – commercial, administrative, financial, social – and in criminal cases. British lawyers have displayed real inventiveness in bringing cases with no *prima facie* link with Community law within the material scope of

66. Opinion, 1/91 [1991] ECR I-6079.
67. Case 15/74 *Centrafarm v Stirling* [1974] ECR 1147, para. 15; Case 119/75 *Terrapin v Terranova* [1976] ECR 1039, para. 4.
68. Lord Mackenzie Stuart, *The European Communities and the Rule of Law*, 29th Hamlyn Lectures (1977) p. 1.
69. Brought before or originating in the UK courts or involving UK nationals.

the Treaty. Establishing connections with Community law points does not always succeed. However, even where it does not, it may pay dividends. All throughout the Community, traders breaching rules limiting their commercial freedom have sought to defeat such national regulatory frameworks by – sometimes abusive[70] – reliance on Community law. In this way, rules relating to Sunday trading[71] were challenged in England and Wales. The argument that they breached Article 28 EC was farfetched in the extreme; yet it won a partial victory from the ECJ[72] before ultimately failing,[73] and in any event, from a purely commercial perspective, had the effect of permitting clients to continue trading on Sunday for a number of years pending the final outcome.

Arguments involving the concepts of indirect discrimination as developed by the ECJ in relation to Article 141 EC and the Equal Pay and Equal Treatment Directives brought within the scope of Community law the precarious status of part-time workers,[74] and have been recognised and applied by the House of Lords.[75] United Kingdom courts were also persuaded to intervene in relation to pregnancy issues,[76] even before the adoption of the Pregnancy Directive.[77]

The *Daily Mail* sought to transfer its central management and control to the Netherlands for tax purposes and applied for judicial review of the Treasury's refusal to acknowledge its right to change residence without consent. It sought a declaration that it would not be required to obtain Treasury consent[78] alleging that

70. Cases C-267 & C-268/91 *Keck and Mithouard* [1993] ECR I-6097, para. 14; J. Steiner, 'Drawing the line: Uses and Abuses of Article 30 EEC' (1992) 29 CMLRev 749.
71. Shops Act 1950.
72. Case 145/88 *Torfaen Borough Council v B & Q plc* [1989] ECR 3851, in which the Court indicated that in some circumstances, a prohibition of Sunday trading might infringe Article 30.
73. Case C-169/91 *Stoke-on-Trent City Council v B & Q plc* [1992] ECR I-6635; and even then the non-application of Article 30 to the Shops Act 1950 was decided not on the ground that the matter fell outwith the scope of Community law, rather that the Court found that the *purpose* of the Sunday trading rules was *compatible with Community law*.
74. See *inter alia* Case 171/88 *Rinner-Kühn v FWW Spezial-Gebäudereinigung* [1989] ECR 2743; Case C-33/89 *Kowalska v Freie und Hansestadt Hamburg* [1990] ECR I-2591.
75. *R v Secretary of State for Employment, ex parte EOC* [1995] 1 AC 1.
76. C-32/93 *Webb v EMO Air Cargo Ltd* [1994] ECR I-3567.
77. Directive 92/85, OJ 1992 L348/1.
78. Section 482(1)(a) of the Income and Corporation Taxes Act 1970 prohibited companies resident for tax purposes in the United Kingdom from ceasing to be so resident without the consent of the Treasury.

Articles 43 and 48 EC precluded the Member State of origin from making the right to transfer its central management and control to another Member State subject to prior consent.[79]

A decision by the Chief Constable of Sussex not to provide live-stock exporters with full-time police protection against animal rights protesters, but to limit that protection to two days a week, was challenged on the grounds *inter alia* that it violated Article 29 EC.[80] Article 29 EC prohibits quantitative restrictions on exports and measures having equivalent effect, but Article 30 EC provides that such restrictions may be justified on grounds of public mor-ality, public policy or public security. The Chief Constable therefore had to justify the extent of police protection, which he successfully achieved by demonstrating that his decision was based on the need to make the best use of available resources.

A decision of the Royal Navy to discharge one of its servicemen in pursuance of the policy of the Armed Forces to discharge any person of homosexual orientation is not contrary to Article 2(1) of the Equal Treatment Directive;[81] although Article 5(1) of the same directive precluded dismissal of a transsexual for a reason related to 'gender reassignment'.[82] An employer's refusal to allow travel concessions to a person of the same sex with whom an employee has a stable relationship, where such concessions are allowed to a worker's spouse or to the person of the opposite sex with whom a worker has a stable relationship outside marriage, does not con-stitute discrimination prohibited by Article 141 EC or the Equal Pay Directive.[83] The Treaty of Amsterdam provides for the inser-tion of a provision[84] which, once the new Treaty enters into force, will confer express legislative competence on the Community to take appropriate action to eliminate various forms of discrimina-tion, including discrimination based on race, ethnic origin, religion or belief, disability, age or sexual orientation. Given that the ECJ has unequivocally indicated that it is a matter for the Council – and not for the ECJ – to make this extension in Community rights,[85]

---

79. Case 81/87 *The Queen v HM Treasury and Customs and Excise Commissioners, ex parte Daily Mail and General Trust* [1989] ECR 5483.
80. *R v Chief Constable of Sussex, ex parte International Traders Ferry Ltd* [1997] 2 CMLR 164 (CA), confirmed in the House of Lords [1998] 3 WLR 1260.
81. *R v Secretary of State for Defence, ex parte Perkins* [1997] 3 CMLR 310.
82. Case C-13/94 *P v S and Cornwall County Council* [1996] ECR I-2143.
83. Case C-249/93 *Lisa Grant v South-west Trains Ltd* [1998] 1 CMLR 993.
84. This new Article 6a EC will be renumbered as Article 13 EC.
85 Case C-249/93 *Grant v South-West Trains Ltd, op. cit.* fn 83, para. 48.

challenges of policy on such grounds in judicial review proceedings would be best brought under the Human Rights Act.[86]

The Human Fertilisation and Embryology Authority's discretion to authorise the export of sperm must be exercised in conformity with Community law. The Authority cannot refuse to allow the export of sperm without proving that the breach of Article 49 EC which it would entail is justified. A recipient has the right to be treated in another Member State with her husband's sperm unless there are good public policy reasons for not allowing this to happen.[87]

A decision of the Secretary of State for the Environment designating the Medway Estuary and Marshes as a Special Protection Area (SPA) for birds, but excluding part of the Lappel Bank, a decision based on the need to expand the industrial facilities of Sheerness and safeguard the future of the town as a port, was held to be unlawful. By virtue of Article 4(1) or (2) of Directive 79/409 a Member State may not when designating an SPA and defining its boundaries, take account of economic requirements as constituting a general interest superior to that represented by the ecological objective of the Directive.[88]

The establishment and operation of lotteries is an economic activity falling within the scope of Article 49 EC.[89] The seizure by HM Customs and Excise of advertisements and application forms for a lottery organised in Germany for distribution to United Kingdom nationals was challenged as breaching *inter alia* Article 49. However the concerns of social policy and prevention of fraud pursued by the UK legislation on lotteries,[90] were accepted as valid justification.

Article 12 EC prohibits discrimination on grounds of nationality 'within the scope of application of this Treaty', a concept capable of encompassing a variety of issues. This provision is breached

---

86. *R v Secretary of State for Defence, ex parte Perkins*, per Lightman J, considering *R v Ministry of Defence, ex parte Smith* [1996] IRLR 100, at p. 558C–H per Bingham MR.

87. *R v Human Fertilisation and Embryology Authority, ex parte DB* [1997] 2 CMLR 591 (CA).

88. C-44/95 *R v Secretary of State for the Environment, ex parte Royal Society for the Protection of Birds* [1996] ECR I-3805.

89. C-275/92 *HM Customs and Excise v Gerhart Schindler and Jörg Schindler* [1994] ECR I-1039.

90. Section 1(ii) of the Revenue Act 1898 in conjunction with Section 2 of the Lotteries and Amusements Act 1976, before their amendment by the National Lottery etc. Act 1993.

where British nationals possessing no residence or assets in Germany, having brought proceedings before a German civil court against a company established in Germany for payment of the purchase price of goods supplied, are required by the competent German court, on application by the defendant, to furnish security for costs pursuant to the German Code of Civil Procedure.[91] Indeed such a rule:

> falls within the scope of the Treaty within the meaning of the first paragraph of Article 6 and is subject to the general principle of non-discrimination laid down by that Article in so far as it has an effect, even though *indirect*, on trade in goods and services between Member States. Such an effect is liable to arise in particular where security for costs is required where proceedings are brought to recover payment for the supply of goods.

In a number of areas such as, *inter alia*, equal pay, equal treatment and working conditions, Community law touches matters which concern solely Britain and the people in it. Thus health and safety legislation can be enforced by a British employer against a British employee in a British firm. In other fields, 'activation of Community rights' is necessary. Such activation flows from the exercise of freedom of movement. Thus, where a married woman who is a national of a Member State has exercised Treaty rights in another Member State by working there, enters and remains in the Member State of which she is a national for the purposes of running a business with her husband, Community law entitles her spouse (who is not a Community national) to enter and remain in that Member State with his wife.[92] However, a non-Community national who is married to a Community national does not enjoy any of the rights of free movement of the latter unless and until the latter has moved out of their home country into another Member State and as it were 'activated' their Community status, or where there is some other factor connecting the family with a situation governed by Community law.[93] It remains to be seen how the

---

91. C-323/95 *Hayes v Kronenberger GmbH* [1997] ECR I-1711. For other challenges to measures of civil procedure involving overt or disguised discrimination on grounds of nationality, see Case 22/80 *Boussac* [1980] ECR 3427; Case 20/92 *Hubbard v Hamburger* [1993] ECR I-3777.
92. Case C-370-90 *R v Immigration Appeal Tribunal and Singh, ex parte Secretary of State for the Home Department* [1992] ECR I-4265.
93. *R v Secretary of State for Home Affairs, ex parte Tombofa* [1988] 2 CMLR 609.

courts would deal with situations where it would be alleged that the 'activation' has been triggered by an oblique motive.

Finally, Community law has an even more far-reaching, pervasive, incidental influence. First, given the requirement to make effective remedies available for breach of Community law, United Kingdom courts have been encouraged to make available the same remedies in a purely national context.[93] In England,[94] senior judges have pointed to divergence from EC law as a justification for changing domestic law both in matters of procedure[95] and on questions of substantive law.[96] Secondly, Community general principles and methods of interpretation which domestic courts had to apply when giving effect to Community law, including those derived from the ECHR,[97] are now discussed in the context of claims based on domestic law.[98] This indirect reception of Community law into national law often takes the form of the importation of a principle or technique from one legal system through another, courtesy of the case law of the ECJ. So, for example, the German principle of proportionality adopted and adapted by the ECJ as a means of controlling arbitrary actions by the Community institutions was then applied by national courts reviewing actions of national authorities in a Community law context, before being discussed in purely domestic situations.[99]

---

94. For two explicit references to EC law as the reason to adapt the remedy more generally, see *M v Home Office* [1994] AC 377; *Woolwich Equitable Building Society v Inland Revenue Commissioners* [1993] AC 70.
95. But not in Scotland, see *McDonald v Secretary of State for Scotland* 1994 SLT 692, although the decision might need to be reconsidered in the light of *Millar and Bryce Ltd v Keeper of the Registers of Scotland* (see Boch 'Interim Remedies against the Crown Revisited' 1997 SLT 165).
96. *M v Home Office*, [1992] QB 270, 360G–307A (Lord Donaldson MR).
97. *Woolwich Equitable Building Society v I.R.C.* [1992] 3 WLR 366 at 395–6 (Lord Goff), *R v Independent Television Commission, ex parte TSW Broadcasting Ltd* [1996] EMLR 291.
98. Even before incorporation: *R v Secretary of State for the Home Department, ex parte Brind* [1991] 1 AC 697.
99. Usher, *General Principles of Law, op. cit.* at p. 155.

CHAPTER TWO

UK courts: United Kingdom courts or Community courts?

Even though the Treaty of Rome has been signed, it has no effect, so far as these courts are concerned, until it is made an Act of Parliament. Once it is implemented by an Act of Parliament, these courts must go by the Act of Parliament, and then only to the extent that Parliament tells us.[1]

The Treaty of Rome is the supreme law of this country, taking precedence over Acts of Parliament. Our entry to the Community meant that (subject to our undoubted, but probably theoretical right to withdraw from the Community altogether) Parliament surrendered its sovereign right to legislate contrary to the provisions of the Treaty on the matters of social and economic policy which the Treaty regulated.[2]

However intellectually stimulating and politically and academically interesting speculation about the loss of sovereignty or otherwise may be, the reality is that the European Communities Act affirms the existence of an ultimate rule of recognition for the EEC and at the end of the day, the real test of this is the attitude of the courts, officials and private persons in the UK.[3]

Why are UK courts involved in the protection of Community rights? What role do they assume when enforcing Community rights? Where does the duty come from – the European Communities Act 1972 or Community law as 'a new legal order'?

---

1. *McWhirther v Attorney General* [1972] CMLR 882 at 886.
2. *Stoke-on-Trent City Council v B & Q* [1990] 3 CMLR 31, per Hoffmann J.
3. *Pigs Marketing Board v Redmond* [1979] 3 CMLR 118. Armagh Magistrates' Court per Mr W.B. McIvor at 121, para. 17.

21

Community law as a new and distinct legal order

Soon after the EEC Treaty came into force, the ECJ had to examine the relationship between the new legal order and the national legal orders. In so doing, it denied the Member States the classic sovereign right – recognised in public international law – to determine the method by which and the extent to which an international treaty can penetrate their legal systems. The Court emphasised both the autonomy of Community law and its uniqueness and specificity. Community law is not an extension of national law, nor can it be equated with public international law.

> The objective of the EEC Treaty, which is to establish a Common Market, the functioning of which is of direct concern to interested parties in the Community, implies that this Treaty is more than an agreement which merely creates mutual obligations between the contracting States . . . . . . the Community constitutes *a new legal order of international law* for the benefit of which the States *have limited their sovereign rights*, albeit within limited fields . . . independently of the legislation of the Member States, *Community law* . . . not only *imposes obligations on individuals* but is also intended to *confer* upon them *rights* which become part of their legal heritage.[4]

> By contrast with ordinary international treaties, the EEC Treaty has created its own legal system which, on the entry into force of the Treaty, became an integral part of the legal system of the Member States, and which their *courts are bound to apply* . . . The integration into laws of each Member State of provisions which derive from the Community, and more generally the terms and spirit of the Treaty, make it impossible for the States, as a corollary, to accord precedence to a unilateral and subsequent measure over a legal system accepted by them on a basis of reciprocity. . . . the law stemming from the Treaty, an independent source of law, *could not*, because of its special and original nature, *be overriden by domestic provisions, however framed*, without being deprived of its character as Community law and without the legal basis of the Community itself being called into question.[5]

These leading cases, introducing what in the literature is referred

---

4. Case 26/62 *van Gend en Loos v Nederlandse Administratie der Belastingen* [1963] ECR 1. Emphasis added.
5. Case 6/64 *Costa v ENEL* [1964] ECR 585 at 593. Emphasis added.

22

to as the concepts of direct effect and primacy, regulate the relationship between the newly created legal order and the national legal orders. They also provide a striking illustration and application of the interpretative methods of the ECJ. The obligation on national courts to apply and give priority to Community law in the domestic legal order is a prerequisite to the proper functioning of the Community legal order. Without such an obligation, Community rules would lose their significance, as they would be subordinate and lack utility. In subsequent cases, the ECJ relied again on the special nature of Community law to explain to – and convince – national courts that no national provision, of whatever kind, could override Community law. In *Internationale Handelsgesellschaft,*[6] the Court reaffirmed the supremacy of Community law even in the face of 'fundamental rights as formulated by the Constitution' of a Member State or the 'principles of a national constitutional structure.' By 1978, it was a logical and inescapable conclusion that:

> every national court must, in a case within its jurisdiction, apply
> Community law in its entirety and protect rights which the latter
> confers on individuals and must accordingly set aside any
> provision of national law which may conflict with it, whether prior
> or subsequent to the Community rule. Accordingly, any provision
> of a national system and any legislative, administrative or judicial
> practice which might impair the effectiveness of Community law
> by withholding from the national court having jurisdiction to
> apply such law the power to do everything that is necessary at the
> moment of its application to set aside national legislative
> provisions which might prevent Community rules from having full
> force and effect are *incompatible* with those requirements which
> are the very essence of Community law.[7]

The power to set aside national provisions which conflict with Community law or hamper its immediate application, cannot be reserved to a special court. In the UK, the significance of *Simmenthal* is that any court, whether supreme or at first instance, whether a creature of statute or otherwise has jurisdiction to apply Community law,[8] including the power to suspend the application of an Act of Parliament.[9]

---

6. Case 11/70 [1970] ECR 1125 at 1134.
7. Case 106/77 *Simmenthal* [1978] ECR 629 at 644.
8. *Shields v E Coomes (Holdings) Ltd* [1979] 1 All ER 456.
9. See further the *Factortame* saga, fn 19 below and Chapter 6.

By declaring that certain provisions of Community law create rights for individuals, being rights one might expect national courts to protect, the ECJ placed the burden of ensuring the uniform and effective application of Community law on national courts. Each and every national court or tribunal is called upon to measure the compatibility of national legislation with Community law: 'every national judge is considered to be a Community judge and is empowered to question the Community validity of national law'.[10] Essentially, the Community law element present in a given dispute confers power, rather than the position of a court or tribunal in a given hierarchy. In a very real sense, every court or tribunal is transformed, for these purposes, into a kind of constitutional court, irrespective of whether such a court already exists in the same jurisdiction. Every 'judge', whether of high judicial office or at the bottom rung of the ladder, becomes a constitutional judge with the power to review the conformity of any provisions of national law, *whatever its rank and nature*, with the Community 'constitution'. So, the Chairman of an Industrial Tribunal becomes a constitutional judge who can review the compatibility of sections of UK primary legislation with Community law.[11] Community law changes the traditional distribution of responsibilities between the different levels of jurisdiction in the Member States. For example, in circumstances where a court of first instance, having sought a ruling from the ECJ, delivers its decision, this would be binding on superior courts within the domestic appellate structure, in so far as it is based on the ECJ ruling. Yet all UK courts would have the right to seek another ruling on the same issue.[12] Community law empowers each and every national judge, and lower courts have proved to be the most prolific users and most loyal allies of the ECJ.[13] The implications of the Court jurisprudence are far-reaching. Each court or tribunal in the Member States is a guardian of the supremacy of Community law. Still, the

10. Curtin, 'The Decentralised Enforcement of Community Law Rights, Judicial Snakes and Ladders' in D. Curtin & D. O'Keeffe (eds), *Constitutional Adjudication in European Community Law and National Law* (Butterworths, 1992) p. 34.
11. *Marshall v Southampton & South West Hampshire Health Authority* [1988] 3 CMLR 389.
12. Although the ECJ now invites national courts to extrapolate principles from its case law: see *R v Secretary of State for Defence, ex parte Perkins* [1998] IRLR 508.
13. See the Annual Commission Reports on the Application of EC Law.

logic of primacy has created numerous challenges for national courts. For national courts coming to terms with the requirements imposed by the ECJ is a step-by-step process, as these requirements themselves evolve as the Community legal system matures.[14]

The ECJ is not concerned with the national arrangements by which a treaty can produce effects for individuals. The national perspective is obviously rather different. The domestic constitutional and institutional arrangements governing the reception of treaties can hardly be ignored by national courts. The regulation of the internal effect of rules of international law is determined by national law and not by national courts. Accordingly, Community law has effect in the UK because the UK Parliament has so enacted, and if Parliament were to change the law, then the courts would have to follow that will. The ECJ can only pronounce on the effect Community rules ought to have within the national systems, following its vision of what the Community legal order requires. It falls outside its jurisdiction to rule on the effect that Community law ought to have according to national law.

With primacy and direct effect, the decentralised system of enforcement of Community law is put in place. Enforcement by national courts is undoubtedly the strength of the Community legal system, as Member States are very unlikely to defy their own courts. It is also a double-edged sword, as national courts may not always feel they are in a position to enforce Community law or abide by the Community requirements. In other words, whatever the ECJ may say about the desired effect of Community law in the national legal order, whatever steps it may have taken to influence the workings of the national judicial systems, it remains the position that it must be accepted, applied and followed by national courts. National courts are subject in all Member States to various constraints imposed by judicial codes, practices and national constitutions.

To understand why in the UK the ECJ requirements are not always met, it is necessary to look at the rules enabling UK courts to recognise Community law. Yet one feature must be stressed at the outset; UK courts were placed in a more comfortable position than those of the six founding Member States. First, by the time of British accession, the concepts underlying the Court's vision of the requirements of the Community legal order had already been

---

14. See Chapter 6.

developed. At the time of *van Gend en Loos*,[15] some Member States could argue that the ECJ had elaborated the obligations undertaken by them in a way that involved a transformation of their nature, going well beyond what the Member States had thought they had undertaken, but the fact that the EEC Treaty was different from any other international law treaty had been clearly set out in the Commission's papers on negotiation of Accession Treaties. The doctrine of primacy of Community law as elaborated by the ECJ was well understood by the British Government at the time when membership negotiations started.[16] In fact, the claim to primacy was known and understood well enough to be relied upon in proceedings aimed at preventing entry into the Community.[17] So whilst the European Communities Act is sometimes described as 'a masterpiece of writing designed to minimise political controversy',[18] UK accession took place in full knowledge of the rules. As Lord Bridge acknowledged in *Factortame*:

> if the supremacy within the European Community of Community law was *not always inherent* in the EEC Treaty it was certainly *well established* long before the United Kingdom joined the Community. Thus, whatever limitation of its sovereignty Parliament accepted when it enacted the European Communities Act 1972 was entirely voluntary . . .[19]

Secondly, if courts in the UK had no power to review the validity of UK law,[20] there are no separate constitutional courts with exclusive jurisdiction to pronounce on the validity of national legislation, a fact which has caused particular problems in other jurisdictions. In any jurisdiction, courts may have difficulty establishing the basis upon which to refuse applying provisions of domestic law in conflict with provisions of Community law. Yet, in jurisdictions with a constitutional court the problem is more

---

15. See fn 4 above.
16. C. Munro, 'The UK Parliament and EU Institutions – Partners or Rivals?' in E. Smith (ed), *National Parliaments as Cornerstones of European Integration*, (Kluwer, 1996) p. 86.
17. *Blackburn v Attorney General* [1971] 2 All ER 1380; *McWhirther* [1972] CMLR 882; C. Munro, *Studies in Constitutional Law* (Butterworths, 1987), p. 128.
18. S. Weatherill and P. Beaumont, *EC Law*, 1st ed. (Penguin, 1993), p. 317.
19. *R v Secretary of State for Transport, ex parte Factortame* (No 2) [1991] 1 AC 603 at 658, emphasis supplied.
20. Although the view expressed in *Pickin v British Railways Board* [1974] AC 765 has been clearly superseded by *R v Secretary of State for Employment, ex parte Equal Opportunities Commission* [1995] 1 CMLR 391.

acute. Indeed, if the refusal is based on the constitution, it then becomes a question of the constitutionality of the domestic legislation which ought to be left to the constitutional court.[21]

How did the UK reconcile the doctrine of parliamentary sovereignty with the transfer of apparently sovereign powers to the European Community? How did the UK accommodate itself to a substantial and continuing influx of law, the substance of which derives from outside Parliament and the application of which is likely to depend upon legal principles and practice somewhat alien to the existing legal system?

European Community law in the UK: The European Communities Act 1972

The Bill which became the European Communities Act 1972[22] was passed by a majority of eight, although in the previous general election the Conservatives had acquired a majority of 43, thereby signalling the start of the intra-party disunity over Europe which has persisted ever since.[23]

Community law was incorporated into UK law by the ECA, 'an Act which to the connoisseur of statutory drafting methods, must appear to be a collector's piece.'[24] A new source of law was recognised and a great volume of new law created for the UK by two short sections. It provides, in effect, that rights arising from the Treaty are 'enforceable Community rights' to be applied and enforced as part of the law of the UK. As Sir Geoffrey Howe pointed out at the time:

> Community law has not been incorporated into or made identical with our own domestic law. Our courts are simply required to give direct effect to Community law *according to its own nature.*[25]

Section 2(1) provides:

All such rights, powers, liabilities, obligations and restrictions from

21. C. Boch, 'Home Thoughts from Abroad' in *In Search of New Constitutions*, Hume Papers on Public Policy (EUP, 1994) pp. 28–52.
22. Hereafter ECA.
23. Munro, *op. cit.* at p. 83.
24. Scarman L.J. (1973) 24 NILQ 61.
25. Quoted by J. Usher, *European Community Law and National Law: the Irreversible Transfer?* (Allen & Unwin, 1981), p. 61.

time to time created or arising under the Treaties, and all such remedies and procedures from time to time provided for by or under the Treaties, *as in accordance with the Treaties* are without further enactment to be given legal effect or used in the United Kingdom shall be recognised and available in law, and be enforced, allowed and followed accordingly; and the expression 'enforceable Community Right' and similar expressions shall be read as referring to one to which this subsection applies.

This section unquestionably expresses the will of Parliament to make UK law subject to Community law in the area of Community competence. By this provision, Parliament informed judges that Community law must be accepted on the terms it is made. Whether the right, power, liability, obligation or restriction is enforceable depends on Community law. The specific nature of Community law is acknowledged, and the Act does not purport to transform its character; what, as a matter of Community law, is Community law, will be law in the UK.

Section 2(2) provides for the implementation of future legal obligations by Order in Council or Regulations. This section deals with the enactment of subordinate legislation to put into effect Community obligations which so require. It also provides for the enactment of subordinate legislation for the enjoyment of Community rights. One of the obligations which must be included within the scope of this subsection[26] is the obligation under Article 10 EC Treaty 'to facilitate the achievement of Community's tasks'. Given the ambit of what may fall within the Community sphere, the powers conferred by s 2(2) are very wide, in spite of the limits set out in Schedule 2 to the Act on what can be the subject of such subordinate legislation.[27] If such a 'Henry VIII clause' which confers power to legislate by way of Orders co-extensive with that of Parliament, is not specific to the ECA, the increased sphere of influence and growth of the power of the Executive at Parliament's expense constituted the biggest impact on internal constitutional arrangements following Accession.[28] Arguments based on section

---

[26]. L. Collins, *European Community Law in the United Kingdom*, 4th ed. (Butterworths, 1990), p. 114.

[27]. For example, Schedule 2, paragraph 1(2) does not include the power to make any provision imposing or increasing taxation.

[28]. P. Birkinshaw, 'European Integration and UK Constitutional law' (1997) 3 European Public Law 57.

2(2) were used on at least two occasions. In *Duddridge*,[29] in an application for judicial review of the decision of the Secretary of State for Trade and Industry declining to issue regulations restricting the electro-magnetic fields from electric cables, an unsuccessful argument was attempted to the effect that the Secretary of State had, by virtue of section 2(2), an obligation under European Community law to apply the precautionary principle and to interpret his statutory powers and duty so as to accord with Community law, namely Article 174 EC. In the *EOC* case,[30] the applicants sought, *inter alia*, an order of mandamus to compel the Secretary of State to exercise his powers under section 2(2) in order to rectify the breaches of Community law contained in the Employment Protection (Consolidation) Act 1978.[31]

In the UK, the major constitutional hurdle was how to ensure that the supremacy of Community law would not be abrogated by the doctrine of implied repeal through the operation of a later inconsistent statute. Indeed, according to the doctrine of parliamentary supremacy or sovereignty of Parliament, there are no entrenched laws and the provisions of an Act of Parliament will impliedly repeal any prior rule of law – which might include Community rules – with which they are inconsistent.[32] These principles apply to the ECA as well as any other statute, since technically, no hierarchy of law exists. The ECA did not affect the legislative competence of Parliament, it merely controlled the consequences of legislative activity by creating a duty of construction for courts. The Act denies effectiveness to legislation in conflict with Community obligations. By virtue of section 2(4), ' . . . any such provision (of any such extent) as might be made by Act of Parliament, *and any enactment passed or to be passed*, other than one contained in this Part of the Act, shall be construed and have effect subject to the foregoing provisions of this section . . . '[33]

In this section, primacy is reduced to a matter of statutory interpretation. The adoption by UK courts of canons of interpretation

---

29. *R. v Secretary of State for Trade and Industry, ex parte Duddridge* [1995] 3 CMLR 231, para. 58 (QBD), upheld in the Court of Appeal.
30. See fn 20 above.
31. J. Convery, 'State Liability in the UK after *Brasserie du Pêcheur*' (1997) 34 CMLRev 603 at 621.
32. Parliament has the right to make or unmake any law whatever and no person or body is recognised by the law of England as having a right to override or set aside the legislation of Parliament.
33. Emphasis added.

which at times may depart from the traditional orthodoxy is authorised by the ECA:

> In construing our statute, we are entitled to look to the Treaty as an aid to its construction; but not only as an aid but as an *overriding force*. If on close investigation it should appear that our legislation is deficient or is inconsistent with Community law by some oversight of our draughtsmen then it is our bounden duty to give priority to Community law. Such is the result of s.2(1) and s.2(4) of the European Communities Act 1972.[34]

Dressing up primacy as a rule of construction pays lip service to the doctrine. In addition, the solution to a possible conflict of norms rests on a comparison of the substance of a Community rule with the substance of a national rule. Yet the substance of a Community rule is not a matter for national judges. The proper legal response to a conflict between a statute and the requirements of Community law is that, rather than asking the question whether the later national legislation is inconsistent with the earlier Community rule, judges should consider whether it repeals or amends the statute by virtue of which the Community rule was transposed into UK law. Hence, the crucial question is whether the later legislation, in conflict with Community law, purports to amend or repeal the ECA. This approach was adopted by Lawton LJ in *Macarthys v Smith*:[35]

> Parliament's recognition of European Community Law and of the jurisdiction of the Court by one enactment can be withdrawn by another. There is nothing in the Equal Pay Act 1970 as amended by the SDA [Sex Discrimination Act] 1975 to indicate that Parliament intended to amend the European Communities Act 1972 or to limit its application.

In this way, judges are in effect accepting that the ECA is not an ordinary statute, for it cannot be repealed but by 'intentional and express repudiation'. It is of course always possible for the UK to enact legislation purporting to repeal the ECA, but this repudiation would mean that the UK no longer intends to remain in the Community.

Section 3(1) provides that:

---

34. *Macarthys v Smith* [1979] 3 All ER 325 at 329, emphasis supplied.
35. *Ibid.*, at 334.

for the purposes of all legal proceedings any question as to the meaning or effect of any of the Treaties, or as to the validity, meaning or effect of any Community instrument, shall be treated as a question of law (and if not referred to the European Court), *be for determination as such in accordance with the principles laid down by and any relevant decision of the European Court or any court attached thereto.* [Emphasis added]

Parliament thus informs judges that they must accept Community law, not only on the terms it is made,[36] but as interpreted by the ECJ. Parliament informs judges that the limits of what they can do are determined by the ECJ. Such a provision may not appear surprising in a legal system where case law is such a prominent source of law. It might also have been necessary in the light of the theory of precedent. Still, it remains a central provision, and one which goes further than any other national incorporating provision, for UK courts are bound by the Treaty, the legislation made under it, and also by the judge-made law. It is also, interestingly, a section which contradicts the others. By giving the European Court case law the status of a formal source of law, it acknowledges the specific nature of Community law which precisely rejects the need for incorporation, and treats national arrangements for the incorporation of treaties as irrelevant. For the ECJ, direct effect and primacy mean that Community law penetrates the national legal order and becomes the highest norm in the national legal order without any need for incorporating legislation, as Community law is not dependent on national law.

Section 3(2) provides that:

> Judicial notice shall be taken of the Treaties, of the Official Journal of the Communities and of any decision of, or expression of opinion by, the European Court on any such questions as aforesaid; and the Official Journal shall be admissible as evidence of any instrument or other act thereby communicated of any of the Communities or of any Community institution.

The most widely publicised judicial consideration of the meaning and breadth of the 1972 Act was provided in the speech of Lord Bridge in *Factortame*:[37]

---

36. Section 2(1).
37. See further Chapter 5.

. . . Under the terms of the European Communities Act it has always been clear that it was the duty of a United Kingdom court, when delivering final judgment, to override any rule of national law found to be in conflict with any directly enforceable rule of Community law.[38]

An important issue for UK courts is what falls to be regarded as 'enforceable Community rights'. At present, the concept seems to be limited to situations where the Community right is embodied in terms which can be construed as having direct effect. However, it is *not* for UK courts to supply their own definition of the term 'enforceable Community rights'. Section 3(1) of the ECA requires that *all Community law* which can be enforced, by whatever means, has to be enforced. National legislation may be necessary to enable the courts as a matter of national law to recognise the Community rules; however, the substantive content of the rules and the different ways in which Community rules can be made available and enforced in the UK is *entirely* a matter of Community law. Community law is not created by national legislation. In the words of Sir Geoffrey Howe, Community law takes effect by virtue of an Act of Parliament, but not 'as if enacted thereby'.[39] It may be that in *Factortame*, given that protection was sought in relation to *merely putative Community rights*, the granting of interim relief was based on section 3(1) rather than on section 2(4).[40]

'An irreversible transfer'[41]

Sovereignty of Parliament can be defined as the absence of any legal restraint upon the legislative power of Parliament. However, as has been shown,[42] Parliament has never been competent to legislate upon any subject matter; Parliament was not born free, and 'the legislative history of the British Isles is one of transfers and one of delegation'.[43] Absence of legal restraint may also imply that, once Parliament has legislated, no court or other body has the

---

38. *R v Secretary of State for Transport, ex parte Factortame* (No 2) [1991] 1 AC 603 per Lord Bridge at 658 (emphasis supplied).
39. Usher, *op. cit.* at 33 and 34.
40. S. Weatherill and P. Beaumont, *EC Law*, 2nd ed. (Penguin, 1995) p. 373.
41. Usher *op. cit.*
42. J.D.B. Mitchell, *Constitutional Law* (Green, 1964).
43. Usher, *op. cit.* at p. 36.

power to review the validity of legislation. In this respect, belonging to the Community means accepting the existence of a higher norm against which to measure the compatibility of national legislation, and *all* British judges are, as a matter of Community law, empowered to do just that. The House of Lords has accepted that there is no constitutional bar to an application before the UK courts directly seeking judicial review of primary legislation alleged to be in breach of Community law.[44]

Furthermore, the enactment of legislation binding within the UK is no longer the sole concern of the UK Parliament. The UK's accession resulted in some transfer of sovereignty to the Community. As was quickly acknowledged, approximation of laws by directives 'causes an irreversible removal of legislative power from the United Kingdom Parliament . . . A Member State no longer has the powers it has transferred to the Community, including the power to affect individuals in certain areas of law'.[45] In the early 1980s, it was already possible to say that:

> the stage has now been reached where the current legal and political reality is that there has been a transfer of powers to the Communities . . . Whilst the political reality remains membership of the Community, such powers are unlikely in practice to be recovered, and at least to that extent the transfer can be regarded as irreversible.[46]

Whether the UK Parliament intended to refrain from exercising its own legislative powers rather than transfer its own powers in the area in which Community legislative powers operate seems immaterial, although the argument occasionally resurfaces.[47] The true debate nowadays focuses not on the existence of a transfer, but on its scope. The reality in the Community is that transfer appears to be a continuous process whose precise scope alters as the Communities develop.[48] Further, the Member States, in spite of their

---

44. *R v Secretary of State for Employment ex parte Equal Opportunities Commission* [1994] 2 WLR 409.
45. House of Lords Select Committee on the European Communities, in its report on the *Approximation of laws under Article 100 of the EEC Treaty* (Session 1977/1978, 22nd Report) p. 42; Usher, *op. cit.* at p. 36.
46. Usher, *op. cit.* at p. 84.
47. *R v Secretary of State for Foreign and Commonwealth Affairs, ex parte Rees-Mogg* [1994] QB 552 QBD, where the exercise of sovereignty is deemed arranged, rather than limited.
48. J. Usher, *EC Legislation and Institutions* (Longman, 1998), Chapter 5.

attempts, have little success in controlling the expansion of Community competences. For some Member States, the problem is no longer arguing about whether sovereignty is limited or transferred in the area of Community competences. Rather the problem is how effectively to limit – if not curtail – the expansion of Community competences. This debate, in turn, poses real problems for judges. British judges must be confident that the expansion of Community competence is acceptable within the British Constitution – quite a different thing from accepting that, in the spheres where it applies, Community law is supreme.[49]

Statutes owe their legal force in the final analysis to judicial recognition, and the ECA is no different in this respect. Judicial recognition of the ECA rests on the judges' belief that Parliament and the British people have chosen to join a supra-national entity, understanding and accepting the legal and political consequences of such membership.

> British judges sit to administer the British Constitution, they cannot give unconditional allegiance to the Community as a superior source of law unless they are confident that this is compatible with British constitutional commitment. As European integration deepens, there are more and more radical transfers of legal authority. For all practical purposes, the Sovereignty of Parliament is curtailed by continued membership. It is not merely the consequence of a rule of construction. *Factortame* represents a rational attempt to explore the boundaries of legislative sovereignty within the contemporary constitution – even if the decision is presented in largely technical terms with little serious attempts to articulate the constitutional considerations at stake.[50]

Identifying the boundaries of Parliament legislative sovereignty becomes tantamount to delimiting the proper scope of application of Community law. Such an issue has recently been the object of some debate in the context of the use of general principles of law in judicial review proceedings.[51] Laws J held[52] that

---

49. See Hoffmann J, *op. cit.* fn 2.
50. T.R.S. Allan, 'Parliamentary Sovereignty: Law, Politics and Revolution' (1997) 113 LQR 443 at 448.
51. *R v Ministry of Agriculture, Fisheries and Food, ex parte First City Trading Ltd* [1997] 1 CMLR 250; *R v Customs and Excise Commissioners, ex parte Lunn Poly Ltd and another* [1998] STC 649.
52. *R v Ministry of Agriculture, Fisheries and Food and Another, ex parte First city Trading Limited and Others* [1997] 1 CMLR 250, para. 40 at p. 268.

the duty to obey the Treaty is to be sharply distinguished from law which is made by a court of limited jurisdiction, such as the Court of Justice. The legitimacy of that law depends upon it being elaborated by the Court within the confines of the power with which it is already endowed. . . . Although (by virtue ultimately of the ECA) its decisions are as a matter of English law supreme, its supremacy runs only within its appointed limits.

Conclusion

The fact that Community law prevails over UK law seems nowadays well accepted. In spite of some conflicting messages,[53] the current attitude of the UK courts can be described as globally *pro-communautaire*. However, the basis for the rule that Community law prevails is not necessarily that put forward by the ECJ. While the specific character of Community law has been recognised and further enacted in the ECA, where Parliament clearly required judges to abide by the requirements of the Community legal order as determined by the ECJ, British judges have maintained that their acceptance of Community law was primarily based on national law. The fact that Community law takes effect only by virtue of a UK statute and on the terms of the statute renders it vulnerable, as the ongoing difficulties about the definition of 'enforceable Community rights' demonstrate; sometimes British judges are simply not prepared to accept that they have duties in relation to the whole *corpus* of Community law and not simply in relation to rights which cannot be construed as directly effective.[54] The precise legal status of the general principles of law, and thus the legitimacy of their application by UK courts, has been questioned, an occasion for UK courts, like national courts in other Member States, to signal that they are not prepared to abandon supervision over the exercise by the Community institutions of their powers.

Acceptance of Community law under the terms of the ECA has other knock-on effects as regards the practical implementation of Community law principles in the UK courts. For example, the consistent emphasis on the statutory nature of the gateway for

---

53. See further Chapter 8.
54. See Chapter 8.

35

Community law[55] explained the characterisation of the breach of the Treaty as a breach of statutory duty.[56] Compliance with all the requirements of the Community legal order involves recognising direct effect and primacy by giving precedence to directly enforceable rights over inconsistent UK legislation. However, it also requires that *all* judges in the UK ensure the full effect of provisions of Community law and protect *all rights* which persons enjoy under Community law, including those which cannot be effectuated directly.[57] The courts in the UK should therefore be reminded of the full consequences of section 3(1).

55. J. Shaw in P. Behrens (ed.), *EC Competition Rules in National Courts, Part I: United Kingdom and Italy* (Baden-Baden: Nomos, 1992) pp. 88–90.
56. *Garden Cottage Foods v Milk Marketing Board* [1983] 3 WLR 143.
57. Cases C-6 & 9/90 *Francovich & Bonifaci v Italy* [1991] ECR I-5357.

CHAPTER THREE

Obstacles to the enforcement of Community law

Citizens will be unable to enforce all their rights under the Community legal system before any national court within the Union unless those members of the legal professions involved in the administration of justice, i.e. judges, prosecutors and lawyers are sufficiently informed and trained to do so.[1]

The difficult question which the Community has to address, is whether the Member States are to be required to enable individuals to exercise their rights effectively, or enable groups to ensure that public and Community interests are protected, by spelling out objective criteria for determining who shall have the right to initiate proceedings, what remedies are to be available, and what financial and other support should be provided to make access to those remedies a reality.[2]

This chapter will discuss a selection of obstacles to the enforcement of Community law by national courts.

An examination of the case law involving Community law reveals a wide range of situations. Sometimes the issue is the incompatibility of a statute with a Community law provision, and the UK courts have to solve a conflict of norms. In other cases, the existence of the Community right has to be established, and the litigant will have to convince the judge to adopt Community methods of interpretation or to refer the matter to the ECJ for the substance of the Community right to be established with clarity. Given that, at the time of writing, a reference to the ECJ takes on average 21.4 months,[3] it is essential that litigants try to obtain protection in the

1. COM (97) 596 final, Amended proposal, Recital 5.
2. C. Vincenzi, 'Private initiative and public control in the regulatory process' in T. Daintith (ed), *Implementing EC Law in the UK* (Wiley, 1993) p. 273.
3. *European Court Statistics, Weekly proceedings* No. 36/39 at p. 45.

interim. In other cases, the substance of the Community right is not disputed; rather, the availability of a remedy from the national court to afford protection of the Community right is at stake. Access to judicial process is threatened, either through a finding of lack of title and interest, or because a limitation period has expired, or the form of process is held incompetent, or a plea of no jurisdiction is sustained, or the decision sought to be challenged does not fall within the category of reviewable acts. Furthermore, actions have been brought in the UK courts designed solely to challenge the adequacy of sanctions on a failure to give effect to a substantive Community right.

It is necessary to be aware that obstacles to the enforcement of Community law are not all of the same nature or gravity, and that, consequently, they will be solved with greater or lesser ease. Moreover, some obstacles are of only historical interest for they have long been overcome, or simply have never been encountered in the UK.[4] It is also important to recognise that *only some* of these obstacles are typical of the enforcement of rules which find their origin at Community level. One such difficulty is the fact that according to the text of Article 249 EC, rights and obligations created in a directive can reach individuals only through the medium of national implementing provisions. However, many obstacles to the enforcement of Community law also exist where the claims arise in a purely domestic context. Typical of these 'national obstacles' are the rules which govern judicial review in England.[5] The leave procedure is of considerable practical importance, as it empowers the court summarily to dispose of an application for judicial review without testing any of the evidence or legal submissions of the body alleged to have acted illegally; the scope of judicial review remains undefined: the question of which activities or which bodies are or should be amenable to judicial review is still unsettled. 'National obstacles' are often exacerbated by the Community dimension. One must also be aware that when litigants are trying to enforce Community law against the State, they do not necessarily face the same hurdles as are encountered by those who try to rely on Community law against another private party. The identity of

---

4. Such as, for some years, the German courts' resistance to the unconditional supremacy of Community law, *i.e.* refusal to accept the superiority of Community law over German fundamental rights.

5. C. Haguenau, *L'Application effective du Droit Communautaire en Droit Interne* (Bruxelles: Bruylant, 1995).

the persons against whom the Community-based claim is made can in itself constitute an obstacle to the enforcement of Community law. The rest of the chapter will explain why Community law suffers from its dependence on national solutions and will look in some detail at a selection of 'Community' and 'national' obstacles.

Where do these obstacles come from? Why are there national obstacles?

If the Community constitutes a new and independent legal order, it is also a dependent legal order in so far as it relies for its enforcement on the legal orders of the Member States. Whilst there is an important distinction between Treaty Articles, Regulations and Directives, the question of how a Community obligation becomes part of the law of the Member States is only *one* element in the chain of action necessary to ensure the effective operation of that particular Community obligation. Characteristic features of the Community legal system are its decentralised structures and mechanisms for the monitoring of the implementation, application and enforcement of rules. With a few exceptions,[6] the Community system is in the hands of national authorities, administrations and courts. Except in some specific fields where the Commission plays a direct role in ensuring that the Community obligations are observed, or where Community legislation has laid down specific remedies and procedures, compliance with Community obligations rests with national authorities, whose responsibility it is to secure payment of agricultural levies, take appropriate measures for the conservation of fishing stocks, etc. Once, through whatever legislative process, the Community obligations have acquired the force of law in the Member States, national administrations and courts still have a very important role to play. Community obligations need to be made operative in practice; national mechanisms for investigation, control and sanctions have to be relied upon or provided. The Community system needs the laws and authorities of the Member States to determine the procedures for the enforcement of Community law.[7] Thus the Community law origin of the national

---

6. See Chapter 11.
7. T. Daintith, 'The indirect administration of Community law' in T. Daintith (ed), *Implementing EC Law in the UK* (Wiley, 1995).

legal rule may be obscured. Besides, the availability and effectiveness of remedies to enforce the law are dependent upon national solutions, designed to protect national rights, and which may therefore not necessarily be well suited to the protection of Community-based rights.

Enforcement of Community law in the UK courts is dependent on access to courts; when secured, litigants will have to try to convince the court of the existence and availability of their Community rights, and/or convince it to refer the matter to the ECJ, so that the putative Community right be authoritatively established. They will also need to secure a remedy which does not fall below the minimum standard of protection with which a Community right is invested.[8]

Going to court

Often the predictability of gaining access to the courts may constitute the first obstacle for litigants trying to enforce Community law. The costs of litigation,[9] the conditions relating to the availability of legal aid, legal expertise or knowledge of EC law, the existence of enforcement agencies and the size of their budget, all have a significant bearing on the decision to pursue a claim. It should be recognised, however, that in the area of equal pay and equal treatment some of these obstacles have been greatly reduced in the UK by the existence of bodies such as the Equal Opportunity Commission from which financial and legal assistance may be available.[10]

Lack of knowledge or awareness of Community law

Many areas of legal practice have a Community flavour.[11] Apart from the well-known and commonly used 'euro-defences' in commercial and criminal matters, Community law impacts *inter alia*

---

8. See Chapter 6.
9. For a consideration of how access to justice in the field of commercial law can be severely impeded by the costs of litigation, see C. Winder, 'The cost of commercial litigation in England – a European perspective, and a look at the future' (1996) 4 European Review of Private Law 339.
10. L. Fletcher, 'Enforcement of Community sex equality law' in Hervey and O'Keeffe (eds), *Sex Equality Law in the European Union* (Wiley, 1996) pp. 173–8.
11. See above, Chapter 1.

on immigration law, social security, and health and safety. In this latter area, Community law influences manufacturing requirements regulating the working environment as well as standards of care in personal injuries cases. It is impossible to know how many cases involving a potential Community law point will never see it discussed. Proceedings in which Community rules are being ignored cannot be covered by systematic research, but it is likely that Community law points are often not argued, for lack of awareness. Studies have uncovered the fact that some law firms, mainly smaller ones, practising in fields of law with a high level of Community law content did not recognise the Community law implications.[12]

The study of Community law is a requirement for entry into both branches of the profession, and British judges have on many occasions listened to sophisticated, ambitious and inventive Community law arguments.[13] Employment and equal opportunities lawyers in particular have been quick to realise and exploit the fact that Community law is a very fertile source of new lines of argument. Yet awareness of the wide range of opportunities offered by Community law, and the use of these, seem to remain the remit of a few specialists. In fact, a quick perusal of the names involved in such litigation will reveal the names of only a handful of solicitors and counsels. 'According to the opinions of judges, the failure to make references is sometimes the product of the parties' and their legal advisers' lack of knowledge of Community law.'[14] This aspect is in no way particular to Community law; the same remarks have been made in relation to judicial review, where it has been observed that only a small minority of solicitors are likely to have any experience of handling judicial review cases.[15] Moreover, in social security appeals, in which legal representation of parties is rare, it must be expected that litigants themselves will be aware of their Community rights or that the chairman will raise a Community law point *ex proprio motu*.[16]

The lack of awareness is by no means peculiar to the UK, and

---

12. J. Lonbay, 'Basic competence in European Community law for all lawyers' (1993) 18 ELR 408 at 410.
13. See Chapter 1.
14. Bingham, 'The National Judge's View' in Andenas (ed), *Article 177 References to the European Court* (Butterworths, 1994), p. 45. This is also true of immigration appeals.
15. Sunkin, 'Trends in Judicial Review' [1993] Public Law 443.
16. See further Chapter 6.

the reality of the problem has prompted the Commission to make a proposal for a European Parliament and Council Decision – the *Robert Schuman Project* – to establish an action programme to improve awareness of Community law for the legal professions.[17]

Financial considerations

In the same way that prosecution rates and powers of enforcement depend on the financial resources and enforcement personnel at the disposal of the authority responsible for enforcement, the decision for an individual to pursue or not to pursue a Community claim will be heavily influenced by financial considerations, particularly given the existence in the UK courts – unlike in some of the other Member States – of the 'costs follow success' rule. Where such a rule applies – *i.e.* the loser pays – the risk of losing, even if minimal, becomes an important factor in deciding whether to embark upon litigation. It remains to be seen whether an argument would succeed to the effect that a factor to which significant weight should be attached in exercising a discretion in relation to costs is a right to an adjudication in a Community law context where the law is not straightforward, as opposed to the weight attached to success on the merits. The basis of such an argument could be the full and effective protection of a Community law right.

Financial considerations include *inter alia* the lack of availability of legal aid and the disproportion between the sums at stake and the cost of litigation. All of these considerations are evidently compounded where a reference to Luxembourg has to be made, and in turn induce a practical, and understandable, reluctance to refer.

> The cost of a reference to Luxembourg is substantial. In a huge dispute between large multinational companies that really does not matter, but in a modest dispute between private parties, one is reluctant to see the burden of costs increased in a way that might be quite out of proportion to the sum in dispute.[18]

Additional evidence is provided by the case of *Maxim's Ltd v Dye*,[19] in which Graham J refrained from ordering a reference

---

[17.] COM (97) 596 final. [18.] Bingham, *op. cit.*, fn 14.
[19.] [1977] 2 CMLR 410.

where one of the parties – and ironically the one who might have benefited from the reference – opposed it on grounds of expense:

> If however, the party does not feel able by reason of expense to agree to a reference what is the judge to do? He may well find it difficult to reconcile with his judicial oath a decision deliberately given in ignorance of the correct view of Community law . . . It is suggested that a procedure should be worked out as soon as possible whereby legal aid can be obtained to enable the judge to receive the help he needs from the ECJ.[20]

The question of legal aid is relatively simple in the case of an individual party;[21] however, no provision for legal aid is available when the party is a commercial entity. A small company cannot itself justifiably be asked to bear the costs of finding out what the relevant Community law is.[22] Given that an ECJ preliminary ruling is, for the parties, a step in the proceedings pending before the national court, the extension of a legal aid certificate should be available to cover the reference. Where legal aid is not available in the main proceedings, it is unavailable for the reference.[23] In *Venter v SLAB*[24] the First Division of the Court of Session held that excessive cost was a relevant consideration in refusing legal aid; whether such a decision may have had any influence on the low level of references from Scottish courts is unknown.

In special circumstances,[25] legal aid is available from the ECJ itself.[26] An application for legal aid can be made to the ECJ at any time, but the legal aid budget of the Court is small and amounts awarded are likewise small. In *Jenkins*,[27] Mrs Jenkins was supported throughout the proceedings by her trade union and the Equal Opportunities Commission; the defendant, Kingsgate, a small company not in a strong financial position, took the view that it could not be represented before the ECJ, and its application

---

20. Graham J in *Maxim's Ltd v Dye* [1977] 2 CMLR 410 at 417–18.
21. *R v Boucherau* [1977] 1 CMLR 269, DC.
22. *Maxim's Ltd v Dye, op. cit.*
23. Usher in Vaughan (ed), *Law of the European Community Services* (Butterworths, 1994), p. 581.
24. 1993 SLT 147.
25. See Case 152/79 *Lee v Minister for Agriculture* [1980] ECR 1495.
26. Rules of procedure of the European Court of Justice, Article 76; see R. Plender (ed), *European Courts Practice and Precedents* (Sweet & Maxwell, 1997), paras 16.01–16.27.
27. Case 96/80 *Jenkins v Kingsgate Ltd* [1981] ECR 911 at 932.

for legal aid to the ECJ having been turned down, no argument was made on its behalf.

The rights of individuals to take enforcement action on their own initiative is undoubtedly a necessary, but not a sufficient, condition for effective enforcement. If individuals are to secure the various benefits Community law intends to bring about, they need financial resources. Without financial means they will be barred from access to the judicial process and will be deprived of effective remedies.

Finding the appropriate forum and choosing the correct form of action

Being creatures of statute, industrial tribunals and the Employment Appeal Tribunal (EAT) have their jurisdictions specifically delimited by the statute conferring jurisdiction upon them; there was no reference to Community law in these statutes. The first English judicial response to this was that industrial tribunals had no jurisdiction to decide questions of Community law.[28] The EAT held that it was not open to a claimant before an industrial tribunal to seek to enforce her or his rights under Article 149 of the Treaty. Such a claim would have to be brought in the High Court as an independent claim to an 'enforceable Community right' with all the consequences involved, in particular in relation to costs.[29] Soon afterwards, these jurisdictional problems were resolved,[30] but they have on occasion resurfaced. In *Wright & Hannah*,[31] the Scottish EAT refused to uphold the argument that the industrial tribunal had no jurisdiction to entertain an application brought directly under Article 149 and Directive 76/207. (It had been argued that the industrial tribunal should not be considered the appropriate forum since the application raised issues of public law as it related

28. *Amies v Inner London Education Authority* (1977) ICR 308.
29. A. Lester, 'The Uncertain Trumpet, References to the Court of Justice from the United Kingdom: Equal Pay and Equal Treatment without Sex Discrimination' in H. Schermers (ed), *Experiences and Problems in Applying the Preliminary Proceedings of Article 177 EEC* (Asser Institute Colloquium on European law, 15th Session 1985), p. 28 (TMC Asser Instituut, 1987) pp. 164–94 at 167.
30. *Snoxell v Vauxhall Motors Ltd* (1977) ICR 700.
31. *Secretary of State for Scotland and Greater Glasgow Health Board v Wright & Hannah* [1993] 2 CMLR 257.

to a decision taken in the exercise of statutory powers; and therefore fell within the supervisory jurisdiction of the Court of Session.)

Choosing the correct forum in which to commence proceedings may involve drawing a distinction between a private and a public law matter, and can be quite difficult. The English Law Commission[32] has recognised that the procedural exclusivity principle has given rise to much case law on the boundary between public and private law rights, and even generated needless litigation over procedural issues, rather than dealing with the substance of the dispute.[33] Accordingly, it has recommended the transfer of issues or proceedings into or out of Order 53 RSC so as to avoid serious detriment to cases involving a combination of public law and private law issues.[34]

Having decided on a forum, consideration must then be given to the correct form of action or process. If choosing the right process is already a complex issue in the domestic context, something that is not peculiar to English law, then Community law complicates it further. Indeed, with the presence of Community law, the uncertainty and potential for litigation over procedural issues where private rights and issues of public law are intermingled is increased, and the same is true, in cases involving a properly constituted private law cause of action where it is necessary to decide whether or not a person should be prevented from raising a defence involving a public law issue. The matching of a domestic form of process with the enforcement of a Community law right can be problematic.[35] EC law does not fit in with classifications made for other, domestic, purposes. Community law confers rights and obligations in private and public law, irrespective of traditional national legal boundaries. Thus, EC law imposes obligations on bodies, whatever their nature, which perform public functions, in both public and private law. Furthermore, EC obligations which are clearly in the public sphere may yet give rise to rights in private law, and vice versa. Competition law is a good case in point: in *Garden Cottage Foods*,[36] an alleged breach of Article 82 by the Milk Marketing Board – considered to be acting as an

---

32. Law Commission, No 226: *Administrative Law: Judicial Review and Statutory Appeals*.
33. *Ibid.*, at 3.3.   34. *Ibid.*, at 3.7.
35. J. Steiner, *Enforcing EC Law* (Blackstone, 1995), pp. 66, 67, 98; Jacobs AG in Case C-312/93 *Peterbroek v Belgian State*, paras. 20–27.
36. *Garden Cottage Foods Ltd v Milk Marketing Board* [1984] AC 130.

undertaking, rather than as a public body in the exercise of its statutory powers – which caused damage to a private party gave rise to a cause of action in English law for breach of statutory duty.

Identifying the competent form of process may not always be straightforward, as many Community law-based claims do not conform to traditional domestic pigeonholes. Are the rights conferred by Community law to be classified as public law rights, a breach of which can only be established and sanctioned through proceedings for judicial review, or are Community rights to be regarded as rights in private law, breach of which by a public or private person has to be established and sanctioned by a private law remedy? Such uncertainty is common in the competition law field. Undertakings, whether under public or private ownership, are subject to the application of the competition rules laid down in Articles 81 and 82 EC Treaty. However, the Treaty also recognises that public undertakings or private undertakings to which Member States grant special or exclusive rights for the purpose of running services of general economic interest can, in well-defined circumstances, avail themselves of the normal application of the competition rules. Thus, Article 86(2) EC provides for the so-called 'public mission defence'. The competition rules are only applicable in so far as the application of such rules does not obstruct the performance, in law or in fact, of the particular tasks assigned to them. Illustrations of the difficulties encountered by litigants seeking redress for breach of Community competition rules is provided by the following situations. When the defender is a public body performing a public law function in breach of EC law, there seems to be little doubt that the appropriate form of process is an application/petition for judicial review. However, when public bodies perform a commercial activity, should the appropriate form of process be other than judicial review?[37] The Keeper of the Registers of Scotland, an executive agency, was considered to be

> in the relevant sense and for pertinent purposes an undertaking . . .
> The fact that an entity which is . . . a public officer charged with
> statutory responsibilities, may in certain circumstances be subject

[37.] *Millar & Bryce v Keeper of the Registers of Scotland* 1997 SLT 1000, annotated at 1997 SLT 165; and see also *West v Secretary of State for Scotland* 1992 SLT 636.

to the rules on competition, is evident from Article 90 EC. The critical issue is whether the entity in question is, in respect of the matters at issue, involved in an economic activity.

However, identifying the competent form of process to challenge the decision under review allegedly in breach of Article 82 was difficult. Are contractual decisions of the Keeper amenable to judicial review or are they to be challenged by private action? The petitioner argued that 'although a contractual mechanism had been employed, in substance what had occurred was an administrative step by the Keeper of a kind amenable to judicial review'. But this was not accepted: 'contractual decisions are not open to challenge in this form of process'. When the defender is a private body exercising public powers, should the action be based on a private law remedy or be subject to judicial review? At present no straight answers to these difficult questions are available, and gaps in the protection of Community rights might ensue.

The *EOC* litigation[38] provides another illustration of the forms of process conundrum. An ex-employee (joined to the proceedings by the EOC) brought a claim for judicial review of the Employment Secretary's refusal to introduce amending legislation to the Employment Protection (Consolidation) Act 1978. The individual applicant, who was directly affected, could not succeed in her application, as her claim was essentially a private law claim which should be brought in an industrial tribunal. On the other hand, the EOC – which the relevant legislation did not directly affect – was able to challenge by way of judicial review.

Restitution of sums unduly paid provides another illustration of the difficulties litigants may encounter;[39] first annulment of the imposition of the charge via judicial review must be obtained, then restitution through a private law action.[40] The Law Commission recommended that, as is the case for damages, the court may order restitution in judicial review proceedings provided such restitution would have been granted in an action begun by writ.[41]

38. *Equal Opportunities Commission v Secretary of State for Employment* [1994] 1 WLR 409.
39. Law Commission, No 226: *Administrative Law: Judicial Review and Statutory Appeals*.
40. Haguenau, *op. cit.*, fn 5, p. 389.
41. Law Commission, *op. cit.*, 8.5 p. 73.

The immediacy of the remedy

The importance of interim protection is well known. The delay in obtaining a remedy is a critical factor in deciding whether to proceed in the courts at all. In many cases involving Community law, notably in the competition and environmental law areas, it is important for plaintiffs to try to obtain an interim remedy at the commencement of proceedings. In the absence of a right to seek interim relief and a concomitant power on the part of the national courts to grant it, a case may be rendered nugatory. In this respect, the picture is pretty bleak. This may be due to the broad nature of the tests applied at this stage or to the perceived complexity of the Community law argument. Nevertheless, there is no reason why courts should not adjudicate on such issues at the interim stage, and it may be essential that they do so if an appeal is to be taken against the refusal of an interim order.

In the field of competition law there seems to be evidence to the effect that UK courts are generally reluctant to give plaintiffs their remedies as soon as possible, namely at the interlocutory injunction stage.[42] In the environmental law field, the insistence on a requirement of a cross-undertaking in damages prevented the Royal Society for the Protection of Birds from securing an 'interim declaration' regarding the legal impropriety of the decision to exclude the Lappel Bank from a special protection area.[43] Accordingly the development plan proceeded, with the result that when the decision of the Secretary of State was declared unlawful, the expansion of the Port of Sheerness was completed. Where a public authority is bringing law enforcement proceedings in the public interest, there is no requirement for a cross-undertaking in damages where interim relief is sought.[44] Given that this is so, and that enforcement of environmental matters could be regarded as being in the public interest, it has been suggested that the requirement of a cross-undertaking in damages be abandoned.[45] Community law will be of no avail to support such a claim as it

---

[42.] Tickle and Tyler, 'Community Competition Law, Recovering Damages in the English Courts. New Era? False Dawn!' in Lonbay and Biondi (eds), *Remedies for Breach of EC Law* (Wiley, 1997), p. 136.

[43.] *R v Secretary of State for the Environment, ex parte Royal Society for the Protection of Birds* (1995) 7 Admin LR 434.

[44.] *Kirklees Metropolitan Borough Council v Wickes Building Supplies Ltd* [1993] AC 227.

[45.] M. Fordham, 'Interim Relief and the Cross-Undertaking' [1997] JR 136.

does not seem to require taking such a step,[46] even though a gap in the effectiveness of Community rules ensues.

Time limits in which to commence proceedings

This is an area where Community law in the form of directives gives rise to particular difficulties. Where a Member State implements a directive badly, when does the time limit for lodging a claim start to run? Does it start to run from the date of the adoption of the defaulting implementing legislation, or does it start to run from the time where proper implementation has taken place? Individuals can only start legal proceedings if they are able to ascertain their rights. When can individuals reasonably be considered to be capable of ascertaining the content of their Community rights? When can individuals reasonably be expected to be aware of their Community rights, and should national limitations applicable to claims in arrears be opposed to a litigant where the Member State is the guilty party responsible for non-transposition of the directive?

The features of Community law

Like any legal system, the Community system has its unique features. First there is the obvious problem of language, which in the Community legal order goes far beyond 'the inherent features of language which create difficulties for lawyers'.[47] The Treaty exists in 12, *equally authentic* language versions, Community legislation in 11, and both contain many legal terms which are unfamiliar to most lawyers, including British ones. Thus, such a central concept as the *acquis communautaire*[48] is so elusive that, in many Treaty versions, it cannot be rendered in any language other than French.[49] Other legal terms may be familiar to British judges, yet

---

46. See Chapter 10.
47. W.A. Wilson, *Introductory Essays on Scots Law* 2nd ed. (Green, 1984), pp. 10–20.
48. The body of Community law, principles and judicial decisions built over the years. See Gialdino, 'Some Reflections on the *Acquis Communautaire*' (1995) 32 CMLRev 1089; also M. Howe, *Europe and the Constitution after Maastricht* (Nelson & Pollard, 1993), p. 65.
49. Boch and Lane, 'European Community law *au Pays du Tartan*' in H. MacQueen (ed), *Scots Law into the 21st Century* (Green/Sweet and Maxwell, 1996), pp. 253–64.

they have a different meaning in the legal orders of each Member State, and more importantly another, autonomous, meaning in Community law.

Then there is the nature of Community law. The opacity and ambiguity of Community law has been cited by Lord Templeman as both its strength and its difficulty.[50] The Treaty is a framework treaty and the legislation made under the Treaty is often of poor quality, 'patently ambiguous or even self-contradictory',[51] reflecting in part the political difficulties surrounding its adoption. The quality of Community drafting is the subject of significant renewed attention in the Community institutions, and among other steps, guidelines against which Community legislation must be measured have been adopted.[52] Community legislation needs to be worded clearly, consistently and unambiguously, following uniform presentation and legal drafting, so that it will be easier to implement by national authorities and easier to understand for economic operators and the general public.[53] Doubts have been expressed as to whether any significant improvement can take place:

> The quality problem of Community legislation is above all a matter of substance. Its imperfection is strongly related to the subject matter of the rules and the particularities of the Community's institutional structures.[54]

Moreover, in most instances the issue of subsequent application of, and compliance with, the rules arises only if and when the rules have to be enforced.[55]

The Community legal system owes much to the ECJ. British lawyers will be perfectly comfortable in recognising case law as an important source of law. As for the UK courts, they are instructed, by virtue of section 3(1) of the ECA, to follow the case law of the

---

50. *Duke v GEC Reliance Ltd* [1988] AC 618 at 641.
51. Warner, 'EC Legislation: the View from Luxembourg' (1982) Statute Law Review, p. 138.
52. European Council, 1992 Edinburgh Summit and subsequent resolution on the quality of drafting, OJ 1993 C166/1; see also T. Burns, 'Law Reform in the European Community' (1996) 16 YEL 243.
53. COM (98) 345, *Legislate Less to Act Better: The Facts.*
54. R. Barents, 'The quality of Community Legislation: Some Observations on EC Legislation in the Agricultural Sector' (1994) 1 Maastricht Journal of Comparative Law, p. 114; see also A.E. Kellermann, 'The Quality of Community Legislation Drafting, in Curtin and Heukels (eds), *The Institutional Dynamics of European Integration* (Kluwer, 1994), p. 251.
55. See Chapters 6 and 11.

ECJ. Nevertheless, one must be aware of some of the pitfalls existing in this area.

Cases should not be read as making a clear-cut distinction between *ratio decidendi* and *obiter dicta*: 'in each case, everything that is said in the text of the judgment expresses the will of the Court',[56] and should therefore be taken notice of, an advice specially relevant to preliminary rulings: 'English lawyers and English courts should beware of treating EC preliminary rulings on their facts as authorities for particular propositions and they should also be wary of distinguishing the cases on their facts'.[57] The operative part of an Article 234 judgment of the ECJ is in limited terms since it specifically answers the precise questions referred by the national court, yet in the main body of the judgment the ECJ also develops general principles of interpretation. An illustration is provided by the case of *Von Colson*.[58] In the operative part of the judgment, the Court held that it was 'for the national court to interpret and apply the legislation adopted for the implementation of the Directive in conformity with the requirements of Community law'. In *Marshall II*,[59] the Court of Appeal quoted this paragraph as authority to refuse to construe the Sex Discrimination Act 1975 in the light of the Directive: 'The Act of course predated Directive 76/207 and was not enacted to give effect to the Directive'. However, in the main body of the judgment, the European Court had indicated that 'in applying the national law and *in particular* the provisions of a national law specifically introduced in order to implement Directive 76/207, national courts are required to interpret their national law in the light of the wording and the purpose of the directive.'[60] In other words, the duty imposed on national courts did not simply apply to the legislation specifically adopted to give effect to the Directive – a point eventually clarified beyond doubt in *Marleasing*.[61]

---

56. Case 9/61 *Netherlands v High Authority* [1962] ECR 213 Roemer AG at 242; Case 112/76 *Manzoni v FROM* [1977] ECR 1647 1661–3.
57. J. Shaw, 'European Community Judicial Method: Its Application to Sex Discrimination Law' (1990) 19 ILJ 228 at p. 243.
58. Case 14/83 *Von Colson and Kamann v Land Nordrhein-Westfalen* [1984] ECR 1891.
59. Case C-271/91 *Marshall v Southampton and South West Area Health Authority* [1993] ECR I-4367.
60. Para. 26, emphasis supplied.
61. Case C-106/89 *Marleasing v La Commercial Internacional de Alimentación* [1990] ECR I–4135.

Case citation in the case law of the ECJ has been the subject of some academic analysis, which suggests that on occasion the status of previous decisions is obscured, a source of confusion for those who have the task of giving effect to Community law. Previous decisions are normally only cited by the Court in support of its argument; authorities pointing the other way are either rarely mentioned, sometimes departed from without explanation, or occasionally even presented by the Court as supporting the opposite line.[62] It is difficult for the Court to be absolutely consistent, as it has to adapt to rapidly changing circumstances.

> The ECJ takes account of the intervening social and other changes and evolving standards . . . in deciding how the law should be developed to meet changing needs and demands on it . . . The concern of the ECJ is to ensure that the law adapts itself to meet new problems.[63]

Furthermore, the Community legal order is dependent on national judges. They must make the best use of the resources available in their national legal systems so as to ensure that both procedural and substantive rights granted by Community law can be vindicated, but they must also be prepared to make constructive efforts. In this regard, it is important to remember that there is a substantial interaction between the ECJ and the national courts. In the same way that the European Court has influenced the workings of national courts, national courts too have influenced the ways in which the ECJ develops the Community requirements. The European Court must ensure that it always keeps the national courts on board, and that its authority is accepted by the national courts, as formally the relationship is one between equals.[64]

The ECJ has been under attack in the last couple of years: there has been much talk about curbing its competence, although this did not result in any Treaty amendments.[65] Against this background, the task of the ECJ is a difficult one. It must ensure its authority is accepted as naturally as that of national supreme courts although it is not in any way in such a hierarchical position

---

[62.] A. Arnull, 'Owning up to Fallibility: Precedent and the Court of Justice' (1993) 30 CMLRev 247–66.
[63.] *R v Secretary of State for Defence, ex parte Perkins* [1997] 3 CMLRev 310 per Lightman J.
[64.] See Chapter 4.
[65.] The Amsterdam Treaty even expands the European Court's jurisdiction.

– an aspect often forgotten when the Court's case law is put to the rigorous test of academic scrutiny.[66] The ECJ has further been criticised for not deciding questions referred under Article 234 EC in a manner which enables Community law to develop on the basis of intelligible and rational principles. However, the very division of function under Article 234 EC does not necessarily provide the best context in which to discharge such a function. Sometimes national courts themselves seek a correct answer in a given case, thereby preventing the ECJ from making rulings of general significance; and rulings on very specific questions generate further, still more specific, questions.[67]

Illustrations of the difficulties encountered by national courts are provided by the line of case law which tested the limits of Article 28 EC in the context of Sunday trading[68] and Sunday employment legislation. In *Torfaen*,[69] the Court held that the prohibition laid down in Article 28 did not apply to national rules prohibiting retailers from opening their premises on Sunday where the restrictive effects of such rules on Community trade did not exceed 'the effects intrinsic to rules of that kind', and further that 'the question whether the effects of specific national rules do in fact remain within that limit is a question for the national court'. As a result, courts in England and Wales took divergent approaches.[70] When answering references from other national courts[71] raising comparable issues,[72] the ECJ itself decided on the proportionality issue. This caused 'consternation'[73] and partly motivated the decision of the House of Lords to make a further

---

66. C.W.A. Timmermans, *Compliance with Judgments of International Courts* (Kluwer, 1996), pp. 118–19.
67. See the opinion of Jacobs AG in Case C-338/95 *Wiener S.I. GmbH v Hauptzollamt Emmerich* [1997] I-6495 para. 42.
68. The English and Welsh Shops Act 1950, section 47.
69. Case 145/88 *Torfaen Borough Council v B & Q plc* [1989] ECR 3851.
70. *Torfaen v B & Q* [1990] 3 CMLR 455 (East Gwent Magistrates); *B & Q v Shrewsbury and Atcham B.C.* [1990] 3 CMLR 535 (Shrewsbury Crown Court), an unsurprising result given that it involved weighing the interests pursued by the Sunday trading rules against the Community interests in ensuring the free movement of goods.
71. Case C-312/89 *CGT v Conforama* [1991] ECR I-997; Case C-332/89 *André Marchandise* [1991] ECR I-1027.
72. Legislation prohibiting employment on a Sunday.
73. Arnull, *op. cit.*, fn 62.

preliminary reference.[74] This yielded a clear response by the ECJ, which itself undertook to assess whether the Shops Act 1950 was proportionate to the legitimate aim of socio-economic policy that it pursued.

The tests of objective necessity and proportionality have to be applied in a variety of situations involving Community law arguments,[75] and UK judges have learnt new judicial techniques. They have had to make difficult value judgments, and sometimes even have had to rethink their role.

> The fact that the European Court has said a particular question is one for decision by the national court does not endow that court with quasi-legislative powers. It must confine itself within the area of judicial intervention required by the Treaty and not trespass on questions which are for democratic decision in Parliament.[76]

In the context of equal pay and equal treatment issues, and in relation to indirect discrimination,[77] UK judges will have to decide how to establish whether a rule has a disparate effect as between men and women to such a degree as to amount to indirect discrimination for the purposes of Article 141 of the Treaty. This will involve deciding whether the statistics available[78] are valid and can be taken into account, i.e. whether they constitute a respresentative sample, whether they illustrate purely fortuitous or short-term phenomena, and whether, in general, they appear to be significant.[79] They will also have to satisfy themselves whether the statistics available indicate that a considerably smaller percentage of women than men is able to fulfil the requirement imposed by that measure, given that to date the ECJ has yet to elaborate on a guiding principle as to what is to be regarded as considerable. The only guidance from the ECJ is that statistics whereby 77.4 per cent of men and 68.9 per cent of women fulfilled a particular require-

---

74. Case C-169/91 *City of Stoke-on-Trent v B & Q*, which was joined by others: Case 306/88 *Rochdale Borough Council v Anders*; Case 304/90 *Reading Borough Council v Payless DIY* [1993] CMLR 426, para. 905; [1993] 1 All ER 481; and answered in one single judgment at [1992] ECR I-6635.
75. They have on occasions been further extended to domestic-based claims. See Chapter 1.
76. Hoffmann J in *Stoke-on-Trent City Council v B & Q* [1990] 3 CMLR 31.
77. Namely where a criterion other than sex is used to apply differential treatment and the use of this criterion amounts to discrimination on grounds of sex.
78. And what to do if such evidence can be given little weight or is irrelevant.
79. See Case C-127/92 *Enderby* [1993] ECR I-5535, para. 17.

ment did not appear to show that a *considerably* smaller percentage of women than men is able to fulfil the requirement imposed by a disputed rule.[80] UK judges will also have to make value judgments as to what constitutes a legitimate aim of social policy and whether the disputed rule, as a means to its achievement, is capable of advancing that aim. This in turn will mean that judges in the UK will have to be prepared to hear and accept evidence which is commonplace in the ECJ, but still unfamiliar to them. They will have to consider evidence about the parliamentary history of a particular piece of legislation and the intended or actual social and economic impact of the measure.

The case of *Seymour-Smith*[81] provides a recent illustration of the challenges for UK judges. In an application for judicial review of the Unfair Dismissal (Variation of Qualifying Period) Order 1985,[82] the House of Lords had to determine (i) the legal test for establishing whether the Order had a disparate effect as between men and women to such a degree as to amount to indirect discrimination for the purposes of Article 141 EC, and (ii) the legal conditions for establishing whether the Order was objectively justified.[83] In particular they had to ascertain what material is to be adduced in support of the grounds for justification of indirect discrimination.

Community law is part of UK law and British judges have generally been very willing to act as Community judges when enforcing Community law, and to rely on Community techniques and methods of interpretation. Still, there remain instances where it is difficult to ascertain the precise content of Community requirements. Even when those can be ascertained, the UK courts might feel they need additional guidance, or even legitimisation. Fortunately, Article 234 EC provides for a possibility of dialogue between the UK courts and the ECJ as the next chapter will show. However, as will be seen, the preliminary ruling procedure itself has problems.

---

80. Case C-167/97 *R v Secretary of State for Employment, ex parte Seymour-Smith and Perez*. Judgment of the Court of 9 February 1999 (not yet reported), para. 64.
81. Case C-167/97 *op. cit.*
82. S.I. 1985 No. 782 which amended section 54 of the Employment Protection (Consolidation) Act 1978.
83. Unlike direct discrimination, indirect discrimination under Article 141 may be justified.

CHAPTER FOUR

Ascertaining the substance of Community rights

Sitting as a judge in a national court, asked to decide questions of Community law, I am very conscious of the advantages enjoyed by the Court of Justice. It has a panoramic view of the Community and of its institutions, a detailed knowledge of the Treaties and of much subordinate legislation made under them, and an intimate familiarity with the functioning of the Community market which no national judge denied the collective experience of the Court of Justice could hope to achieve . . . where comparison falls to be made between Community texts in different languages, all texts being equally authentic, the multinational court is equipped to carry out the task in a way that no national judge whatever his linguistic skills could rival . . . the choice between alternative submissions may turn not on purely legal considerations, but on a broader view of what the orderly development of the Community may require.[1]

I do not consider that it is appropriate, or indeed possible, for the Court to continue to respond fully to all references which, through the creativity of lawyers and judges, are couched in terms of interpretation, even though the reference might in a particular case be better characterised as concerning the application of the law rather than its interpretation . . . the only appropriate solution is a greater measure of self-restraint on the part of both national courts and this Court.[2]

This chapter discusses the role of Article 234 in the enforcement of Community law. The respective roles of the ECJ and of the referring court, and practice in the UK courts, will also be considered.

[1.] Bingham J in *Customs & Excise Commissioners v Samex* [1983] 3 CMLR 194.
[2.] Jacobs AG's Opinion in Case C-338/95 *Wiener S.I. GmbH v Hauptzollamt Emmerich* [1997] ECR I-6495, paras 17 and 18.

Article 234 provides:

The Court of Justice shall have jurisdiction to give preliminary rulings concerning:

   (a) the interpretation of this Treaty;

   (b) the validity and interpretation of acts of the institutions of the Community;

   (c) the interpretation of the statutes of bodies established by an act of the Council where those statutes so provide.

Where such a question is raised before any court or tribunal of the Member State, the court or tribunal *may*, if it considers that a decision on the question is necessary to enable it to give judgment, request the Court of Justice to give a ruling thereon.

Where any such question is raised in a case pending before a court or tribunal of a Member State, against whose decisions there is no judicial remedy under national law, that court or tribunal *shall* bring the matter before the Court of Justice.[3]

Article 234 serves various functions; for the present purposes the main ones are considered to be as follows. Firstly, Article 234 allows the Community legal order to develop, as the substance of Community provisions is often explained and expanded in the course of enforcement. Secondly, it gives legitimacy and authority to national courts when these are asked to grant specific remedies in order to effectuate Community rights.

What is an Article 234 preliminary ruling?

The reference procedure enables a national court or tribunal, when confronted with questions about the meaning of a provision of Community law or questions about the Community requirements concerning the effective protection of Community rights, to stay its own proceedings and refer these questions to the ECJ in order to obtain an authoritative ruling on the law to be applied or on how to apply it. 'Preliminary' is a bit of a misnomer,[4] as the reference is in fact an intermediate step in proceedings which *begin* and *end* in the national court. Accordingly, the success of the procedure depends primarily on national courts.

Article 234 is based on a distinct separation of functions

---

3. Emphasis added.
4. S. Paisley, *A guide to EEC Law in Northern Ireland* (SLS Belfast, 1986), p. 61.

between national courts on the one hand and the ECJ on the other. Article 234 does not give the ECJ jurisdiction to take cognisance of the facts of the case, or to criticise the reasons for reference;[5] its jurisdiction is limited to the interpretation of the rules of Community law. The facts and the relevant rules of national law must be established by the referring court, which will decide the case by applying, to the extent necessary, the interpretation of the relevant rules of Community law provided by the ECJ. In practice, as will be shown, these clear divisions of roles are difficult to observe.

The different functions

UK courts have shown a willingness to adapt to Community methods of interpretation,[6] yet, like other national courts, they have in applying Community law inevitably encountered problems concerning its interpretation and validity.[7] These difficulties stem from the 'language dimension' and the nature of Community law.[8] Article 234 guarantees the independence and autonomy of Community law in so far as it prevents varying interpretations of the same provisions in the different national courts, leading to different applications of the Treaties in the Member States and thereby defeating the whole Community enterprise. To ensure uniformity in the interpretation and application of Community law, establishing the ECJ as a supreme court of appeal would have been desirable, but this was not politically acceptable as the Member States did not want a court that could overrule their own supreme courts. Accordingly, a solution was found in co-operation between equals, *i.e.* between the national judiciaries and the ECJ.[9] Uniform interpretation and application of Community law are fundamental requirements in the Community, as the preamble to Council Decision 93/350[10] makes clear. The establishment of a Court of First Instance, in respect of actions requiring close examination of com-

---

[5.] Case 13/68 *Salgoil* [1968] ECR 661.

[6.] See further Chapter 8.

[7.] This chapter will only be concerned with questions of interpretation; validity is discussed in Chapter 10.

[8.] See Chapters 2 and 3.

[9.] Brinkhorst and Schermers, *Judicial Remedies in the European Communities*, 2nd ed. (Kluwer, 1977), p. 250.

[10.] OJ 1994 L144/21 amending Decision 88/591; OJ 1988 L319/1 establishing the Court of First Instance.

plex facts, was intended to improve the judicial protection of individual interests. The attachment of this second court to the ECJ was equally meant 'to enable the Court of Justice to concentrate its activities on its fundamental task of ensuring the uniform interpretation of Community law' and thereby 'maintain the quality and effectiveness of judicial review in the Community legal order'.

Besides ensuring a correct and uniform interpretation and application of Community law by national courts, Article 234 has strengthened the mechanisms designed to secure Member States' compliance with their Community obligations:

> The vigilance of individuals to protect their rights amounts to an effective supervision in addition to the supervision entrusted by Articles 169 and 170 to the diligence of the Commission and of the Member States.[11]

However, actions brought by individuals in national courts and those brought by the Commission under Article 226 are not mutually exclusive, and the Court has been dealing at the same time under the two procedures with the same course of action by a Member State.[12] Nevertheless, Article 234 gives the Court no jurisdiction either to apply the Treaty to a specific case or to decide upon the validity of a provision of domestic law in relation to the Treaty, as it would be possible for it to do under Article 226.[13] The ECJ cannot rule on issues of national law,[14] and it cannot rule on the compatibility of national law with Community law.[15] This disclaimer of jurisdiction is at times one of form rather than substance.

The procedure does not merely serve Community interests. Through Article 234, individuals have gained access to direct legal protection of their Community rights, even if such protection is limited by the procedural and material scope of the Article. However, if the wishes of the parties may occasionally play a role in

---

11. Case 26/62 *van Gend en Loos v Nederlandse Administratie der Belastingen* [1963] ECR 1; *Emerald Meats* [1993] ECR I-209, para. 40.
12. Case C-221/89 *R v Secretary of State for Transport, ex parte Factortame* [1991] ECR I-3905, and Case C-246/89 *Commission v United Kingdom* [1991] ECR I-4585; but also Case C-288/89 *Gouda* [1991] ECR I-3905, and Case C-288/89 *Commission v Netherlands* [1991] ECR I-4007; *R v Pharmaceutical Society of Great Britain* [1987] 3 CMLR 951.
13. Case 6/64 *Costa v ENEL* [1964] ECR 585.
14. Case 26/62 *van Gend en Loos v Nederlandse Administratie der Belastingen, op. cit.*
15. Although it did so in Case 261/81 *Walter Rau v De Smedt* [1982] ECR 3961.

persuading the national judge to refer, and if in the UK the parties themselves are encouraged to agree upon the form of the questions and the material to be placed before the ECJ, litigants have *no* Community right to have their case referred to the ECJ: 'Article 177 does not constitute a means of redress available to the parties to a case pending before a national court.'[16]

The procedure allows individuals to control and prevent possible violations of Community law by the Member States. It also allows the Community legal order to develop, as the scope of a Community provision may be expanded upon in the enforcement process.[17] Thus, Directive 76/207 is no longer 'confined simply to discrimination based on sex',[18] as was established on the occasion of a request for a preliminary ruling by the chairman of the industrial tribunal of Truro. The procedure has been instrumental in defining the outer limits of Article 28, as the Sunday trading saga and *Keck and Mithouard*[19] illustrated well. The importance of Article 234 and the role played by national courts for the development of Community law can hardly be overstated. The twin pillars of Community constitutional law, direct effect and primacy, were laid down in Article 234 references in the context of small claims disputes, and so were leading judgments regarding general principles of law.

Article 234 allows some[20] obstacles to the enforcement of the rights to be challenged. In the words of the Court:

> whilst it thus aims to avoid divergences in the interpretation of Community law which national courts have to apply, it likewise tends to ensure this application by making available to the national judge *a means of eliminating difficulties which may be occasioned by the requirement of giving Community law its full effect* within the framework of the judicial systems of the Member States.[21]

The *Factortame* litigation provides an illustration of the different functions served by Article 234. The challenge of the Merchant Shipping Act 1988 gave rise to three separate sets of questions.

---

16. Case 283/81 *CILFIT v Ministero della Sanità* [1982] ECR 3415 at para. 9.
17. Lenaerts, 'Interaction Between Judges and Politicians' (1992) 12 YEL 11.
18. Case C-13/94 *P v S and Cornwall County Council* [1996] ECR I-2143, para. 14.
19. Cases C-267–268/91 [1993] ECR I-6097.
20. See Chapter 3.
21. Cases 146 and 166/73 *Rheinmühlen* [1974] ECR 33. (Emphasis added.)

One involved determining the scope of Article 43,[22] another concerned the extent of the obligations of a national court to protect the interim position of litigants trying to ascertain putative Community rights,[23] while the last concerned the award of a remedy in damages.[24]

What can go wrong

The ECJ still has an open-door policy: it encourages references and reformulates inadequate questions. However, it now takes special care to ensure that the procedure is not employed for purposes not intended by the Treaties. The ECJ may declare a reference inadmissible, either because the referring body lacks power to refer, or because the question cannot be considered as acceptable. Can one identify a type of court from which questions are accepted? Are there particular types of questions which are refused?

Which bodies have jurisdiction to refer?

Article 234 confers jurisdiction on any 'court' or 'tribunal'. The concept does not refer to the internal law of the Member States. The fact that national law does not recognise a body as a 'court' or 'tribunal' within the meaning of Article 234 is irrelevant.[25] Conversely, the fact that national law does so recognise is not conclusive.[26] The ECJ has defined the term 'court' or 'tribunal' for the purpose of Article 234 by specifying the criteria a qualifying forum must satisfy. The body must be established by law, have a permanent jurisdiction, be bound by rules of adversary procedure and be required to give a ruling, in complete independence, in proceedings intended to result in a judicial decision. The requirement of independence seems of particular importance, although it

---

22. Case C-221/89 R v Secretary of State for Transport, ex parte Factortame [1991] ECR I-3905.
23. Case C-213/89 [1990] ECR I-2433.
24. Case C-48/93 [1996] ECR I-1029.
25. Case 61/65 Vaassen-Gobbels [1966] ECR 261; Case 246/80 Broeckmeulen v Huisarts Registratie Commissie [1981] ECR 2311; and see A. Barav, 'Aspects of the Preliminary Ruling Procedure in EC Law' (1977) 2 ELR 3.
26. In Case C-24/92 Corbiau [1993] ECR I-1277, Darmon AG pointed to the domestic recognition of the body in question as a court.

'should be interpreted more rigorously',[27] a comment made apropos the admissibility of preliminary rulings from administrative authorities.[28]

Administrative[29] or disciplinary[30] tribunals, a professional body appeals committee,[31] and a board supervising the procedures for the award of public contracts[32] have all been held to constitute a court or tribunal: but a public prosecutor or a private arbitrator[33] does not qualify, nor does a Director of Direct Taxes and Excise Duties:[34] 'The concept of a Court or tribunal within the meaning of Article 177 of the Treaty is a concept of Community law which, by its very nature can only mean an authority acting as a third party in relation to the authority adopting the decision under appeal.'

In Member States where, in the resolution of taxation matters, an administrative stage precedes the judicial phase, this delays the possibility for taxpayers to have a preliminary question referred to the ECJ.[35] Likewise, the decision not to allow private arbitrators to refer questions to the ECJ[36] creates additional delay for litigants. National courts in their role of supervisors of arbitration proceedings have a duty to ensure the observance of Community law and to refer; in England, the Court of Appeal was prepared to adopt a different approach when dealing with an application for leave to appeal against an arbitration award in *Bulk Oil v Sun*.[37]

---

27. Ruiz-Jarabo Colomer AG in Case 74 and 129/95, *Criminal proceedings against X* [1996] ECR I-6609, point 10 of his Opinion.
28. Ruiz-Jarabo Colomer AG *op. cit.*, citing Cases C-260/91 and C-261/91 *Diversinte and Iberlactan* [1993] ECR I-1885.
29. The Dutch *tariefcommissie* in Case 26/62 *van Gend en Loos*, fn 14 above.
30. Case 61/65 *Vaasen-Goebbels v Bestuur van het Beambtenfonds voor het Mijnbedrijf* [1966] ECR 261.
31. Case 246/80 *Broeckmeulen v Huisarts Registratie Commissie* [1981] ECR 2311.
32. Case C-54/96 *Dorsch Consult Ingenieurgesellschaft mbH v Bundesbaugesellschaft Berlin* [1997] ECR I-1709.
33. Case 102/81 *Nordsee v Reederei Mond* [1982] ECR 1095.
34. Case C-24/92 *Corbiau* [1993] ECR I-1277.
35. J. Woulers, 'The Case Law of the ECJ on Direct Taxation: Variations upon a Theme' (1994) 1 MJECL 208.
36. Case 102/81 *Nordsee v Reederei Mond, op. cit.*; and see J. Murray, 'Arbitrability in the EU' in Campbell and Voyatzi (eds), *Essays in Honour of Lord Mackenzie Stuart* (Trenton, 1996).
37. [1984] 1 All ER 386.

The type of questions which are refused

National courts alone have a direct knowledge of the facts of the case, hence they are in the best position to appreciate, with full knowledge of the matter before them, the necessity for preliminary rulings to enable them to give judgment.[38] So where the referring court has duly translated a Community law point into a question of interpretation, the Court is in principle bound to give a ruling. There are a number of limits to this principle:

- The Court cannot answer questions relating to the validity of national law, although it has often extracted from questions imperfectly formulated those which alone pertain to the interpretation of the Treaty.
- The Court refuses to answer 'hypothetical questions'[39] or entertain 'fictive litigation'.

In addition, the Court has shown a greater willingness to examine the relevance of questions submitted to it,[40] particularly when submitted by inferior national courts.[41] So, whilst in theory the ECJ has no jurisdiction relating to the facts of the case, in practice closer examination of the conditions in which cases are referred to it has, on occasion, appeared necessary in the light of some abuse of the procedure.

The Court's willingness to co-operate with national courts remains the rule, as evidenced by *Enderby*[42] (emphasis added):

> Article 177 provides the framework for close cooperation between national courts and the Court of Justice, based on a division of responsibilities between them. Within that framework, it is *solely for the national court* before which the dispute has been brought, and which must assume the responsibility for the subsequent judicial decision, to determine in the light of the particular circumstances of each case both *the need for a preliminary ruling* in order to enable it to deliver judgment and the *relevance of the question* which it submits to the Court. Accordingly, where the

38. Case 83/78 *Pigs Marketing Board v Redmond* [1978] ECR 2347, and Case C-412/93 *Société d'Importation Edouard, Leclerc-Siplec v TF1 Publicité SA* [1995] ECR I-6609.
39. Case 104/79 *Foglia v Novello* [1980] ECR 745, p. 74.
40. Case C-343/90 *Lourenco Dias* [1992] ECR I-4673; Case C-83/91 *Meilicke* [1992] ECR I-4871.
41. D. Anderson, *References to the European Court* (Sweet & Maxwell, 1996).
42. Case C-127/92 *Enderby v Frenchay Health Authority* [1993] ECR I-5535.

national court's request concerns the interpretation of a provision of Community law, the Court is bound to reply to it, unless it is being asked to rule on a purely hypothetical general problem without having available the information as to fact or law necessary to enable it to give a useful reply to the questions referred. In this case, the Court of Appeal, like the tribunals which heard the case below, decided in accordance with the British legislation and with the agreement of the parties to examine the question of the objective justification of the difference in pay before that of the equivalence of the jobs in issue, which may require more complex investigation. It is for that reason that the preliminary questions were based on the assumption that those jobs were of equal value . . . Where, as here, the Court receives a request for interpretation of Community law which is *not manifestly unrelated to the reality or the subject-matter of the main proceedings*, it must reply to that request and is not required to consider the validity of a hypothesis which it is for the referring court to verify subsequently if that should prove to be necessary.[43]

Leclerc-Siplec[44] also clarifies the Court's jurisdiction and role under Article 234. Since it has no jurisdiction to give an advisory opinion on general or hypothetical questions of law, examination of the conditions in which the case has been referred may in certain circumstances be necessary in order to determine whether the reference is admissible. Requests for preliminary rulings have been declared inadmissible where Article 234 was used as a 'procedural device'[45] or an 'artificial expedient'[46] by parties who engage in contrived litigation in order to obtain a finding that some provisions of national legislation are contrary to Community law.[47] Still, the fact that the parties to the main proceedings are in agreement as to the result to be obtained makes the dispute no less real. The ECJ has also declined jurisdiction to give a preliminary ruling on a question raised before a national court where *the interpretation of Community law has no connection whatever with the circumstances or purpose of* the main proceedings.[48] So the Court has demonstrated a willingness to determine the limits of its jurisdic-

---

43. *Ibid.*, paras 10–12.
44. Case C-412/93 *Société d'importation Edouard Leclerc-Siplec v TF1 Publicité SA & M6 Publicité SA* [1995] ECR I-179.
45. Case 244/80 *Foglia v Novello (No. 2)* [1981] ECR 3045.
46. Case 104/79 *Foglia v Novello (No. 1)* [1980] ECR 745.
47. Jacobs AG in Case C-412/93, point 6 of Opinion.
48. Case C-412/93, para. 13 (emphasis added).

tion. Some control over the many requests for a preliminary ruling submitted is at any rate required to secure the viability of the procedure. The ECJ itself[49] acknowledged the practical problems which beset the present system, namely its increasing workload and the time which can elapse before a ruling is obtained.[50] Other methods need to be devised to limit the Court's jurisdiction.[51] The insignificant percentage of cases where the ECJ declined jurisdiction should be treated as 'small prices to pay for optimising the Court's resources'.[52]

From a UK perspective, the ECJ capacity to limit the use of Article 234 is insignificant. Only one reference from the UK courts has, to date, been declared inadmissible,[53] being a case where the ECJ was invited to construe Community law outside its Community field of application. The applicant bank had started an action in England for the repayment of sums paid to the City of Glasgow pursuant to a contract subsequently rescinded. A statute broadly taking over the solutions adopted in the Brussels Convention governs conflicts of jurisdiction between the courts of England and Scotland. Glasgow City Council considered that the Scottish courts had jurisdiction, and the Court of Appeal sought preliminary rulings on the interpretation of the statute from the ECJ to determine restitution actions in the context of the Brussels Convention. The ECJ declared the reference inadmissible as the Brussels Convention itself was not applicable in the circumstances of the case, even if conflicts of jurisdiction between the English and Scottish courts were governed by rules inspired by it. The House of Lords nevertheless held that full regard should be had to decisions of the ECJ interpreting the Convention.[54]

The ECJ has issued a note for guidance on references by national courts for preliminary rulings[55] containing 'practical information which, in the light of experience in applying the

---

49. Report of the Court of Justice on certain aspects of the application of the TEU, May 1995.
50. 21.4 months.
51. Andenas (ed), *Article 177 References to the European Court, Policy and Practice* (Butterworths, 1994).
52. K. Lenaerts, 'Form and Substance of the Preliminary Ruling Procedure' in D. Curtin and T. Heukels (eds), *Essays in honour of H. Schermers* (Martinus Nijhoff, 1994), p. 357.
53. Case C-346/93 *Kleinwort Benson Ltd v City of Glasgow* [1995] ECR I-615.
54. [1997] 3WLR 923.
55. Proceedings of the Court, No 34/96.

ASCERTAINING THE SUBSTANCE OF COMMUNITY RIGHTS

preliminary ruling procedure, may help prevent the kind of difficulties the Court has sometimes encountered'. The success of the procedure rests principally on the willingness of national courts to co-operate. National courts must make the reference, then accept and apply the judgment of the Court. Even so, the victory can be a Pyrrhic one when interim relief is not forthcoming.[56]

The national courts as main players

National courts too may be tempted to limit recourse to Article 234. One must distinguish between courts with a *power* and those with a *duty* to refer. But before examining how UK courts have exercised their discretion or discharged their obligation, let us briefly examine the distinction.

Reference to the ECJ is mandatory if the court is one 'against whose decisions there is no judicial remedy under national law'. Whilst this appears straightforward, the question of which courts are required to ask for a preliminary ruling and which have the option to do so has in fact been the subject of some controversy. This is rather odd, given that the text of Article 234 is unequivocal. It clearly suggests that not only are the highest courts of each Member State under such an obligation, but also any courts in a case from which no appeal lies. This raises an issue of particular relevance in the UK,[57] where there may be no systematic right of appeal, but rather a system by which an appeal court may be asked for and may grant or refuse 'leave to appeal' against not only interlocutory but also final judgments. Should a court with a power to grant or refuse leave to appeal be treated as a final court? In *Pharmaceutical Society*[58] the Court of Appeal – although it did refer – did not think so, stating that 'a court or tribunal below the House of Lords can only fall within the last paragraph where there is no possibility of any further appeal from it. There is a judicial remedy against a decision of this court by applying for leave to this court and then to the House of Lords itself if necessary'.

56. *R v Secretary of State for the Environment, ex parte Royal Society for the Protection of Birds*, 13 March 1997 (unreported), House of Lords; and see Chapter 3.
57. C. Haguenau, *L'Application effective du Droit Communautaire en Droit Interne* (Bruylant, 1995); L. Collins, *European Community Law in the United Kingdom*, 4th ed. (Butterworths, 1990).
58. *R v Pharmaceutical Society* [1987] 3 CMLR 951 at 969, per Kerr LJ.

In England in criminal matters, there can be no appeal to the House of Lords unless a point of law is certified for consideration by the House of Lords. Further, there is no appeal against the refusal of the Court to certify a point of law. Although in *Magnavision*[59] it was accepted that 'by refusing to certify a point of law we have turned ourselves into a court of final decision', the Divisional Court refused to make a reference. Likewise, in *Hagen v Moretti*,[60] Buckley LJ accepted that the ultimate court of appeal 'is either this court if leave to appeal to the House of Lords is not obtainable, or the House of Lords'. Accordingly,

> parties seeking a reference in these circumstances must ensure that the court be asked during argument to proceed on the basis that if it is minded to refuse leave to appeal to the House of Lords, it must approach the question of a preliminary ruling on the basis that it is already a final court,[61]

or that it should give leave, which in practice would be done.[62]

Discretionary jurisdiction

The attitude of inferior courts is particularly important. They can avoid the costly and cumbersome procedure involved in pursuing an action through to the final court:[63] 'the Court of Justice in Luxembourg is in a far better position to reach a decision which is *communautaire* than this court . . . an immediate reference will obviously save considerable time and costs'.[63] However, inferior courts may be disinclined to make references, or alternatively their decision to refer may be the subject of an appeal to a superior court.

The discretion to refer is a matter for the national courts alone: 'a court has an unfettered discretion to refer if it considers that a decision on the question is necessary in order to enable it to give judgement'.[64] In *Bulmer v Bollinger*[65] Denning LJ set out guidelines. In his view, a reference was only 'necessary' if:

---

59. *Magnavision v General Optical Council* [1987] 2 CMLR 262.
60. [1980] 3 CMLR 253 at 255.
61. D. Anderson, *References to the European Court* (Sweet & Maxwell, 1995), p. 161.
62. L. Collins, *European Community Law in the United Kingdom*, 4th ed. (Butterworths, 1990), p. 154.
63. *R v Pharmaceutical Society*, fn 58 above, at 972.
64. Cases 28–30/62 *Da Costa en Schakke NV v Nederlandse Belastingadministratie* [1963] ECR 31.
65. [1974] 3 WLR 202.

1. the point of reference was conclusive for the outcome of the case;
2. the ECJ had not already given judgment on the question;
3. the matter was not considered to be reasonably clear and free from doubt;
4. the facts had been decided.

Further, the court contemplating a reference was to exercise its discretion only after considering the delay in obtaining a ruling,[66] the need to avoid overloading the ECJ, the wishes of the parties and the expenses of obtaining a ruling. Finally, he reminded English courts that it would be preferable if English judges decided the point themselves, but that if a reference was to be made, they should formulate questions clearly – another reason for ascertaining the facts first. Denning's guidelines seemed to discourage the use of the procedure and had some influence. They were reviewed in *Samex*[67] and from then on a more *communautaire* approach prevailed. The 'aberrant interpretation'[68] of the notion of quantitative restrictions and the ensuing results might also explain the change in the attitude of, at least, the English judiciary. Lord Diplock in *Henn and Darby*[69] observed:

> it serves as a *timely warning* to English judges not to be too ready to hold that because the meaning of the English text (which is one of six of equal authority[70]) seems plain to them no question of interpretation can be involved.

The national court also has complete discretion as to the timing of the reference, and the ECJ has confirmed that the considerations of procedural organisation and efficiency dictating timing have to be weighed by the national courts.[71] Such timing has varied. In England, requests for a preliminary ruling have been made in inter-

---

66. The very delays now involved in references do encourage judges to decide points on their own: see Bingham in Andenas (ed), *op. cit.*, Chapter 5.
67. *Customs & Excise Commissioners v Samex* [1983] 3 CMLR 194.
68. Gormley, 'The Application of Community law in the UK' (1986) 23 CMLRev 287.
69. [1980] 2 CMLR 229 at 234 (emphasis added).
70. Now one of 12 in the case of Treaty provision, and one of 11 for Community legislation.
71. Case 36/80 *Irish Creamery Milk Suppliers Association v Ireland* [1981] ECR 735, para. 8.

locutory proceedings,[72] and on the grant of leave to apply for judicial review.[73]

However, Lord Denning's requirement that the relevant facts be established has generally been observed. In *Lord Bethell v Sabena*[74] it was held that 'until all the facts have been investigated, it is impossible to frame a question which will ensure that the court is provided with real assistance'; and in *Hagen v Moretti*[75] that 'for a court to know which are the right questions to formulate, it is most important that all the relevant facts be established'.

In Scotland, guidelines were given by Lord Cameron:[76]

a reference to the European Court can competently be made when it appears it may be necessary to do so at any appropriate stage of a litigation. Having regard, however, to our Scottish system of pleading, I would not normally be persuaded that such a necessity, with whatever degree of urgency that word may be interpreted, should be held to arise until the pleadings have been adjusted and the real question in dispute focused on the pleadings. I am fortified in this view of the matter by reference to the judgment of Lord Denning in the case of *Bulmer v Bollinger*. In particular, I should find it difficult to make such a reference where preliminary issues of title, competency and relevancy remain unresolved.

The advice that the facts should always be decided first before any question of a preliminary ruling arises has not always been found entirely sound, on the ground that a national court may not be able to evaluate the relevance of a particular fact until the point of Community law has been resolved.[77] Besides, in practice, when the referring national court had not determined all the relevant findings in fact, the Court tended to offer a very general interpretation, leaving the national court to deal with further procedure.[78] Further, where the interpretation required depended upon the determination of facts as well as law, and although the fact-finding powers lie principally with the national courts making the refer-

---

72. Case 107/76 *Hoffmann la Roche v Centrafarm* [1977] ECR 957.
73. *R v Minister of Agriculture, Fisheries and Foods, ex parte FEDESA* [1988] 3 CMLR 207.
74. [1983] 3 CMLR 9, per Parker J.
75. [1980] 3 CMLR 253.
76. *Prince v Secretary of State for Scotland* [1985] SLT 74 at 78.
77. J.W. Bridge, 'Community Law and English Courts and Tribunals: General Principles and Preliminary Rulings' (1975–6) 1 ELR 20.
78. Case 222/84 *Johnston v Chief Constable of the RUC* [1986] ECR 1651; Case C-127/92 *Enderby v Frenchay Health Authority* [1993] ECR I-5535.

ence, the ECJ has on occasion shown itself willing to admit or call for evidence[79] to explain the background or complete the facts as stated in the order for reference so as to enable it to understand the question better. However, given the Court's emphasis on its need to have a clear understanding of the factual and legal context[80] of the proceedings, ascertainment of the facts seems advisable. It also seems prudent, given that the Court has, albeit on recent and rare occasions, declared the reference inadmissible when the description of the legal and factual background of the case has been found inadequate.[81] Finally, one must be aware that Article 234 is ill-suited to the process of fact-finding.[82]

Appeal against a decision to refer

As a matter of Community law, the national court's discretion to refer cannot be fettered by decisions of superior courts.[83] *Rheinmühlen* also establishes that inferior courts in a Member State cannot be bound on a question of Community law by any decision of their superior courts, unless the higher court has itself obtained a ruling from the ECJ on this very issue. A UK court therefore must remain free to refer notwithstanding the existence of what would ordinarily be the binding authority of a superior UK court on the point.

Rheinmühlen also demonstrates how Article 234 can alter the powers and rules of procedure of national courts.[84] It has been observed that

> there can be no doubt that any court or tribunal has the right at all times to refer a question of interpretation to the Court of Justice under Article 177. But it is much more difficult to decide whether a national court which, by virtue of its national law, is no longer able to give a ruling on a question, is given back the right to do so by Article 177 of the EEC Treaty.[85]

---

79. See *Webb v EMO Air Cargo* [1994] QBD 718 at 728–36.
80. See *Notes for Guidance for Preliminary Rulings* [1997] 1 CMLR 78.
81. Cases C-320–322/90 *Telemarsicabruzzo* [1993] ECR I-393.
82. Anderson, *op. cit.*, fn 61, at pp. 75–6.
83. Cases 146 and 166/73 *Rheinmühlen* [1974] ECR 33.
84. See above Chapter 2.
85. F. Dumon, *The Case Law of the Court of Justice – A Critical Examination on the Methods of Interpretation* (Judicial and Academic Conference, 27–28 September 1976; Court of Justice of the European Communities, Luxembourg, 1976) at III-160.

This comment overlooks the fact that, when giving effect to Community law, national judges act as Community judges; accordingly national judicial procedures, conventions, codes or practices may have to be set aside, an area which nowadays ought to be free from difficulty,[86] but is not.[87]

So from a Community perspective the discretion of national courts should not be interfered with. In some Member States, steps have been taken to prevent appeals against decisions by lower courts to refer.[88] In others, decisions to refer have been questioned.[89] In the UK this has been rare. In England, the Court of Appeal has set aside an order of the Divisional Court making a reference.[90]

> I understand the correct approach in principle of a national court (other than a final court of appeal) to be quite clear, if the facts have been found and the Community law issue is critical to the court's final decision, the appropriate course is to refer unless the national court can with complete confidence resolve the issue itself. In considering whether it can with complete confidence resolve the issue itself, the national court must be mindful of the differences between national and Community legislation, of the pitfalls which face a national court venturing into what may be an unfamiliar field, of the need for uniform interpretation throughout the Community and of the great advantages enjoyed by the Court of Justice in construing Community instruments.[91]

This decision has been criticised, but it has also been interpreted as a strong encouragement to refer; national judges have been invited and encouraged for years to become and behave like Community judges. It is therefore hardly surprising that their familiarity with

---

86. Case C-213/89 *R v Secretary of State for Transport, ex parte Factortame* [1990] ECR I-2433.
87. See further Chapter 6, and Case C-312/93 *Peterbroeck* [1995] ECR I-4599.
88. In France, the Cour de Cassation has prohibited appeals against reference in interlocutory judgments: see (1988) vol. 108 *GazPal*, pp. 7–8. In Ireland, the possibility of an appeal from the exercise of lower courts' discretion to refer is not recognised: *Campus Oil* [1983] IR 82 (Irish SC) and *SPUC Grogan* [1990] ILRM 350.
89. D. O'Keeffe, 'Appeals against an Order to Refer under Article 177' (1984) 9 ELR 87.
90. *R v International Stock Exchange of the United Kingdom and the Republic of Ireland, ex parte Else* [1993] 2 CMLR 677, [1993] 1 All ER 420; D. Wash, 'The Appeal of an Article 177 Referral' (1993) 56 MLR 881.
91. *Else, op. cit.*, p. 426.

Community matters should grow and that, as a result, their confidence should increase.[92]

In Scotland, the High Court[93] was satisfied it had jurisdiction[94] to hear an appeal against a decision of a judge of first instance to seek a preliminary ruling, but decided it would not be justified in interfering with the exercise of the Sheriff's discretion to refer unless it were thought that the decision of the Sheriff was plainly wrong.

Where an Article 234 reference may be pending in another case, the outcome of which may be relevant to other domestic proceedings, it may then be possible to obtain a stay of the proceedings until it has been heard.[95]

Courts with an obligation to refer

The particular objective of the obligation to refer for courts against whose decisions there is no judicial remedy under national law, is to prevent a body of national case law not in accordance with the rules of Community law from coming into existence in any Member State.[96] The obligation laid down in Article 234(3) is not absolute. The authority of an interpretation under Article 234 already given by the ECJ, especially on a materially identical question, may relieve a national court against whose decisions there is no judicial remedy from its obligation to make a reference.[97] Further, as indicated in *CILFIT*,[98] there is no obligation to refer

> where previous decisions of the Court have already dealt with the point of law in question, irrespective of the nature of the proceedings which led to those decisions, even though the question at issue are not strictly identical . . . or where the correct application of Community law may be so obvious as to leave no scope for any reasonable doubt as to the manner in which the question raised is to be resolved.

92. Anderson, *op. cit.*
93. *Wither v Cowie* 1991 SLT 401.
94. The Lord Justice-Clerk (Ross) referred to the Act of Adjournal (Consolidation) 1988 which permits an appeal to the High Court against a decision of a single judge to seek a preliminary ruling from the ECJ: 1991 SLT 401 at 405.
95. *Brown v Rentokil* [1998] ECR I-4185.
96. Case 107/76 *Hoffmann la Roche v Centrafarm*, fn 72 above, para. 5.
97. Cases 28-30/62 *Da Costa en Schaake NV and others v Nederlandse Belastingadministratie* [1963] ECR 31.
98. Case 283/81 *CILFIT* [1982] ECR 3415.

However, national courts should consider *carefully* before deciding points of Community law on their own, given 'the specific characteristics of Community law, the particular difficulties to which its interpretation gives rise and the risk of divergences in judicial decisions within the Community'. So *CILFIT* appears a rather ambiguous limitation of the obligation to refer. Rasmussen[99] noted that 'the real strategy of *CILFIT* was not to incorporate an *acte clair* concept into Community law. It is to call the national judiciaries to circumspection when they are faced with problems of interpretation and application of Community law.'

Be that as it may, the strict requirements laid down in *CILFIT* need to be reconsidered. As Jacobs AG remarked in *Weiner*,[100] they were designed at a time where national supreme courts were defiant of the authority of the ECJ, a situation which has changed. If today, occasionally, final courts still fail to refer, and even adopt a wrong interpretation of Community law, this reality is insufficient to warrant a strict interpretation of the obligation to refer.

> It seems to me, however, disproportionate to base a general theory of Article 177 on isolated instances of what might amount to its improper application. Such a theory will in any event not resolve the problem if the national court is deliberately taking a different view. That theory would require the application of a sledgehammer without cracking the nut.

In the UK, a deliberate refusal by a court of final appeal to comply with its obligation to refer is potentially challengeable. When the European Convention on Human Rights and Fundamental Freedoms is incorporated into UK law, it will be open to a party to argue that a refusal to refer violates the right to effective judicial protection and that accordingly a remedy should be provided under national law. An analogy could be drawn with the German experience, where a refusal to comply with an obligation to refer has been treated as arbitrary and as constituting a violation of a fundamental right. The German Constitutional Court has tried to provide a remedy under national law when a German court unreasonably refuses to refer a case to the ECJ, by holding that no one should be removed from the jurisdiction of their lawful judge,[101] which in matters of Community law is the ECJ.

---

99. (1984) 9 ELR 242.
100. Case C-338/95, cited fn 2, para. 63 of Opinion.
101. [1987] 3 CMLR 32, and Article 101 of the Basic Law of Germany.

In the UK, in spite of some refusals to refer, there has never been an established pattern of defiance of the authority of the ECJ, unlike the situation with the French *Conseil d'Etat*.[102] The UK courts sought no interpretation as none was required. Thus, in *Finnegan*,[103] the House of Lords found that since UK law governed the case, the court best placed to provide an interpretation was a UK court and not the ECJ. In *R v London Boroughs Transport Council, ex parte Freight Transport Associations Ltd*,[104] it held that 'no plausible grounds were advanced for a reference to the ECJ'. In a criminal matter the High Court found that it was not under any obligation to refer, because it did not require an interpretation[105] and that, final judgment having already been given, the court was *functus officio* and the case was no longer 'pending' within the meaning of Article 234(4).[106] Finally, no question of interpretation can arise where the meaning of a Community provision is clear. In spite of isolated resort to the doctrine of *acte clair* in Scotland[107] and in England, overall[108] the UK courts seem to be aware that they should hesitate before reaching the conclusion that the matter is clear.[109]

Interpreting and applying the Court's ruling

The ruling of the ECJ is binding on the referring court,[110] and the operative part of the judgment should always be interpreted in the light of the reasoning that precedes it.[111] If interpretation and ap-

---

102. Haguenau, *L'Application effective du Droit Communautaire en Droit Interne* (Bruylant, 1995), p. 149.
103. [1990] 2 CMLR 859.
104. [1992] 1 CMLR 5 at 21.
105. *Magnavision v General Optical Council* [1987] 2 CMLR 262, para. 15.
106. *Ibid.* para. 16.
107. For example, *Westwater v Thomson* 1993 SLT 703 in Scotland; in England *R v London Boroughs Transport Committee, ex parte Freight Transport Associations Ltd* [1992] 1 CMLR 5 *op. cit.*, and comments by Weatherill in (1992) 17 ELR 299–322; *R v Secretary of State for Social Services, ex parte Bomore* [1986] 1 CMLR 228.
108. But see A. Arnull, 'The Use and Abuse of Article 177' (1989) 52 MLR 622.
109. Bingham J in *Customs & Excise Commissioners v Samex* [1983] 3 CMLR 194, or *R v HM Treasury, ex parte Daily Mail and General Trust plc* [1987] 2 CMLR 1 para. 23, or *R v Pharmaceutical Society* [1987] 3 CMLR 951, para. 34.
110. And has wider implications: see Chapter 1.
111. Opinion of Warner AG in Case 135/77 *Bosch GmbH v Hauptzollamt Hildesheim* [1978] ECR 855 at 861.

plication can theoretically be distinguished, and if the ECJ has been careful to redraft questions relating to the validity of national law, national courts often have little choice in applying the Court's ruling. As both the major and minor premises are already fixed, national courts have only to pull the trigger, for the aim has already been taken.[112]

Occasionally, the temporal effect of preliminary rulings has given rise to difficulties. The basic rule[113] is that the interpretation which the ECJ gives to a rule of Community law clarifies and defines where necessary the meaning and scope of that rule

> as it must be or ought to have been understood and applied from the time of its coming into force. It follows that the rule as thus interpreted may, and must, be applied by the courts even to legal relationships arising and established before the judgment ruling on the request for interpretation, provided that in other respects the conditions enabling an action relating to the application of that rule to be brought before the courts having jurisdiction, are satisfied.

Exceptionally,[114] the ECJ may

> in application of the general principle of legal certainty inherent in the Community legal order and in taking account of the serious effects which its judgment might have, as regards the past, on legal relationships established in good faith, be moved to restrict for any person concerned the opportunity of relying upon the provision as thus interpreted with a view to calling in question those legal relationships.

Therefore the ECJ *only* has the power to limit the temporal effect of a ruling,[115] although it may be – and has been – asked to reconsider the question of a temporal effect. Illustration of such issues is provided by the reception of the *Barber* ruling.[116] In *Barber*,[117]

---

112. Caranta, 'Judicial Protection against Member States: the Indirect Effects of Articles 173, 175 and 177' in Micklitz & Reich (eds), *Public Interest Litigation before European Courts* (Nomos, 1996), p. 102.
113. Case 61/79 *Amministrazione delle Finanze dello Stato v Denkavit Italiana* [1980] ECR 1205, para 16.
114. As in Case 43/75 *Defrenne v Sabena* [1976] ECR 455.
115. For an attempt by the Member States to do so, see Protocol to the Maastricht Treaty.
116. For a detailed account, see Steiner and Woods, *EC Law*, 5th ed. (Blackstone, 1996).
117. Case C-262/88, *Barber v Guardian Royal Exchange Assurance Group* [1990] ECR I-1889, para. 44.

given 'overriding considerations of legal certainty' and the need not to 'upset retroactively the financial balance of many contracted-out pension schemes', the ECJ decided that the direct effect of Article 141

> may not be relied upon in order to claim entitlement to a pension with effect from a date prior to that of this judgment, except in the case of workers or those claiming under them who have before that date initiated legal proceedings or raised an equivalent claim under the applicable national law.

The ways in which national rules governing time limits for lodging a claim may also limit the temporal effect of a preliminary ruling will be explored later.[118]

Practice: some figures

Annexes to the Annual Reports on *Monitoring the Application of Community Law* contain comments on the application of Community law by national courts.[119] The following figures are extracted from the 14th Annual Report.

Number of references per the UK for 1990–97

1990	1991	1992	1993	1994	1995	1996	1997
12	13	15	12	24	20	21	18

In 1996 UK courts made 21 references, 3 of which originated in the House of Lords, a pattern consistent with that observed in other Member States and with practice in recent years as evidenced by the breakdown of all UK references by year and type of court.[120] Research carried out by the Research and Documentation Department of the ECJ did not show any cases in the UK where decisions against which there was no appeal were taken without a reference for a preliminary ruling even though they turned on a point of Community law whose interpretation was less than per-

---

[118]. Chapter 6.
[119]. COM (98) 317 final Annex VI pp. 291–315.
[120]. Andenas (ed), *Article 177 References to the European Court, Policy and Practice* (Butterworths, 1994) pp. 34–6.

fectly obvious.[121] No indication was given as to whether these statistics took account of the leave of appeal issue.

The breakdown by jurisdiction is as follows. In England towards the end of 1995, the Court of Appeal had referred an aggregate of 30 cases, whilst the House of Lords had only made 17 referrals. Of referrals from the UK, 34 per cent emanate from the High Court of Justice (79 referrals).[122] Scotland has one of the lowest number of references *per capita* of any jurisdiction in the Union, and made no references in the first ten years of UK membership.

The subject matter of cases referred by UK courts break down as follows: questions concerning labour law come first (36 cases), mainly from the area of equal pay and equal treatment, then agriculture and fisheries (31 cases), Article 28 (28 cases) and social security (21 cases).[123]

In the Article 234 procedure, both Member States – including third party Member States – and Community institutions have the option of intervening and making observations to the ECJ. The UK Government intervened in nearly 80 per cent of cases coming from UK courts, a figure which no other government matches, an indication that 'not only the courts of the UK but also its government takes a strong interest in European Law'.[124] The extra-judicial view from Luxembourg[125] is that courts in the UK have been very willing to make references and have loyally complied with preliminary judgments; that references from UK courts make good reading and are nearly always well-reasoned; that the case law of the ECJ appears ascertained and the problems clearly identified, and that they nearly always raise substantial points of interpretation.

'We see Community law through a glass, darkly'

This view is to be contrasted with that of a counsel to the Equal Opportunities Commission who, after 12 years of UK membership, wrote that the experience of the parties – especially applicant employees – at first sight a success story,[126] as all but one of the

---

121. Although such cases were reported in the Netherlands, Germany, France, Italy and Sweden.
122. Figures from Lenz and Grill, 'The Preliminary Ruling and the UK' (1996) Fordham Int. LJ pp. 844–65.
123. Lenz and Grill, *loc. cit.*   124. *Ibid.*   125. *Ibid.,* at 856–7.
126. A. Lester (see Chapter 3, fn 29), pp. 176 and 194.

applicants had succeeded in their claims, could upon closer analysis give cause for concern. Substantial legal costs had been incurred without establishing clear and coherent principles of Community law; interpreting and applying the Court's decisions had been difficult; there had been very long delays in obtaining a reference or a decision under Article 234; and parties and national courts had become more reluctant to seek or to order references.

A few years later the conclusion to be drawn is that if English courts have referred many important cases[127] for the development of Community constitutional law, *inter alia Van Duyn*,[128] *Johnston*,[129] *Marshall I* and *II*,[130] the litigant's perspective is rather more disappointing. Typically, an important case[131] such as *Johnston* was also a Pyrrhic victory for Mrs Johnston, for 'her continuing loss and damage had, by the date of the reference, exceeded the maximum amount of compensation which was – then[132] – recoverable under national law'. Without the assistance of the Equal Opportunities Commission, the *Marshall* saga could not have been financed.

Conclusion

In a number of circumstances, Article 234 provides the only possibility of a remedy for victims of breaches of Community law. However, the procedure has obvious weaknesses, some identifiable at the ECJ level,[133] others being the responsibility of national courts and others, like delays in obtaining a reference, attributable

---

127. All of these are discussed further in Chapters 5, 6, and 8.
128. Case 41/74 *Van Duyn v Home Office* [1974] ECR 1337.
129. Case 222/84 *Johnston v Chief Constable of the RUC* [1986] ECR 1651.
130. Case 152/84 *Marshall v Southampton and South West Hampshire Area Health Authority (Marshall I)*[1986] ECR 723, and Case C-271/91 *Marshall II* [1993] ECR I-4367.
131. See further Chapter 6.
132. This indeed was changed following *Marshall II*.
133. Some solutions must be found for the ever-increasing case load of the Court; the question of how to tackle it is outwith the remit of this book. For some useful reflections on this issue and more generally the reform of the Community judicial system, see Kennedy, 'First Step Towards a European Certiorari' in (1993) 18 ELR 121; Jacobs AG's Opinion in Case C-338/95, cited fn 2; Mancini and Keeling, 'From CILFIT to ERT: the Constitutional Challenges facing the European Court' (1991) 10 YEL 1.

to both sides. The ECJ is the victim of its own success.[134] In the UK, the significant delays in making references have been caused by a variety of contributory factors. These have included the refusal of an inferior court to refer, the time needed by the parties to agree the relevant facts or questions of interpretation, and the delays involved where leave to appeal was sought against a decision to refer.

The most serious weakness seems to be the 'dilution' of the procedure. The procedure might work better if the ECJ was 'able to decide questions referred under Article 234 in a manner which enables Community law to develop on the basis of intelligible and rational principles'.[135] Redrafting of the questions by the ECJ has sometimes led the Court to apply Community law to the facts of the case, and even in some instances to facts treated as peripheral by all parties involved.[136] Since the main function of Article 234 is the uniform interpretation and application of Community law, the main task of the ECJ is 'not so much the administration of justice in individual cases, but the function of overseeing the development of Community law in important principled cases'.[137] These remarks are echoed by the call for a reappraisal of the current division of tasks between the ECJ and national courts. Jacobs AG pointed out in *Wiener*[138] that it is necessary to address the question whether it is appropriate for the Court to be asked to rule in every case where a question of interpretation of Community law arises. The appropriateness of a reference can be assessed in the light of the objective of Article 234, namely to ensure that the law is the same in all the Member States. Certainly the Court's function under Article 234 is not merely to give the national court the correct answer in a given case, but to give rulings of general significance.[139] Accordingly Article 234, like other provisions of

---

134. Weiler, 'The European Court, National Courts and References for Preliminary Rulings – The Paradox of Success: A Revisionist View of Article 177' in *Article 177: Experiences and Problems* (TMC Asser Instituut, 1987), pp. 366–78.

135. A. Lester, *op. cit.*, p. 29, and his discussion of Case 69/80 *Worringham & Humphreys v Lloyds Bank Ltd* [1981] ECR 767 and other references in the field of occupational pension schemes, or that of *Macarthys Ltd v Smith* [1979] 3 CMLR 44.

136. *Ibid.*

137. Weiler, 'The White Paper and the Application of Community Law' in Bieber and others (eds) *One European Market?* (Nomos, 1988), p. 368.

138. By Jacobs AG in Case C-338/95, cited fn 2.

139. Case C-338/95 (see fn 2), para. 50.

Community law, should be interpreted in an evolutionary way. Excessive resort to preliminary rulings seems increasingly likely to prejudice the quality, coherence and even accessibility,[140] of the case law, and may therefore be counterproductive to the ultimate aim of ensuring the uniform application of the law throughout the Community.[141] In many fields, a body of case law developed by the ECJ exists to which national courts can resort in resolving new questions of Community law, and in a number of technical matters national courts are able to extrapolate from the principles developed in this case law. If only cases raising a point of general importance are referred, a more principled case law and a more balanced development of case law is likely to result. At the same time the Court of Justice's workload may be alleviated.

The function of Article 234 is not to see that justice is done between the parties, but to ensure that Community law is uniformly interpreted and applied throughout the Community. If this view is accepted by national courts as well as the ECJ, it is a strong argument for a principled rather than a case by case approach. This ultimately will ensure a better protection of litigants.

---

140. See also Opinion of Ruiz Jarabo Colomer AG in Case C-394/96 *Brown v Rentokil* [1998] ECR I-4185.
141. *Ibid.*, para. 60.

CHAPTER FIVE

Giving effect to
Community law

The doctrine of direct effect seeks to ensure that rights accruing from Community law are available to the individual, whilst the doctrine of primacy ensures that such rights will take precedence over any national rule or practice.[1]

Enforcement of Community law is driven by individuals with a direct interest in the vindication of their rights or interests. This chapter discusses, from a Community perspective, the different techniques available to give effect to Community law in national courts.

First, Community law must be available, and to this end, the ECJ has ensured that Community law can be invoked before national courts. But to say that Community law can be invoked before national courts inevitably leads to problems. The ECJ thereupon had to devise mechanisms for the resolution of substantive conflicts between national law and Community law. The precedence of Community law over national law renders automatically inapplicable any conflicting provisions of national law; national judges must set aside any provisions of national law which conflict with the Community rule, whether prior or subsequent to the Community rule.[2] In certain circumstances, Community law can be applied directly. In other instances, Community law is used as an aid to the interpretation of national law. When a Community right cannot be effectuated through either of these techniques, it can give rise to an action for damages against the defaulting Member State.

---

1. D. Edward and R. Lane, *European Community Law – An Introduction*, 2nd ed. (Butterworths/Law Society of Scotland, 1995) para. 135.
2. Case 6/64 *Costa v ENEL* [1964] ECR 585; Case 106/77 *Amministrazione delle Finanze dello Stato v Simmenthal* [1978] ECR 629.

Direct effect

Direct effect has a dual meaning. On the one hand, it refers to the fact that, on accession, Community law becomes an integral part of the legal system of the Member State which its courts are bound to apply, irrespective of the national constitutional arrangements governing the relationship between international agreements and domestic law. In other words, Community law can be invoked. On the other hand, direct effect is sometimes used to refer to the capacity of a specific Community provision to be applied as it stands, to be applied directly. Community law in *certain circumstances* confers rights on and/or creates duties for individuals which must be recognised by the national legal systems, and which must be enforced in the national courts against or for the benefit of individuals or companies.

Today, it is no longer disputed that Community law may be invoked before national courts. Throughout the Community, Community law is invoked and applied by national courts in a wide range of situations. What remains a matter of some contention and difficulty however, is *what* litigants are entitled to expect from national courts. Given that the literature often contains references to concepts such as *horizontal* or *vertical direct effect*, terms which have not been approved by the ECJ, these terms will be touched upon. Nevertheless, it is contended that this nomenclature can often detract from an understanding of this area of Community law which, put simply, involves consideration of the different duties imposed on national judges.

National judges as Community judges

This is known variously as 'decentralised enforcement', 'enforcement in national courts', or 'private policing' of Community law. A few remarks must be made at the outset. Since direct effect is a judicial invention, the criteria used in its application are sometimes subject to differing interpretations by the ECJ and national courts. Furthermore, the usefulness of direct effect varies and is dependent upon the particular field of Community policy under consideration. The role of individuals in enforcing Community law varies from one policy area to another. The principle has so far been of limited use in the field of

Community environmental protection.[3] Direct effect is not a uniform concept. It involves a wide range of tasks and duties for national judges. Finally, the capacity to apply Community law directly varies with the type of provisions in which the Community right is embodied. This refers to the concepts of *horizontal* and *vertical direct effect*.

The direct effect of Treaty provisions

When is a Treaty provision capable of having direct effect, and which Treaty provisions fall into the category? A Treaty provision must fulfil certain requirements in order to have direct effect, but the question of whether this is so should be a matter for the ECJ rather than one for national courts, as the latter may take differing views on the matter. Still, such decisions have been taken by UK courts, for example in relation to Article 14[4] and Article 17[5] EC.

First, the provision must be clear and sufficiently precise. The Community's vision of what can be considered clear and sufficiently precise might not necessarily match the UK courts' understanding of these notions. For the ECJ, what matters is that Community law be effective. A striking illustration is provided by the interpretation of 'principle' in Article 141: in *Defrenne*,[6] the ECJ found that rather than indicating a lack of precision or referring to a policy objective, the term actually stressed the fundamental nature of the provision. Often rules acquire the clarity and precision required during the enforcement process itself.

> The interpretation which, in the exercise of the jurisdiction conferred upon it by Article 177, the Court of Justice gives to a rule of Community law clarifies and defines where necessary the meaning and scope of that rule as it must be or ought to have been understood and applied from the time of its coming into force.[7]

Secondly, the provision must be unconditional, *i.e.* it must not

---

3. Joined Cases 372 to 374/85 *Traen* [1987] ECR 2141, Case C-236/92 *Comitato di Coordinamento per la Difesa della Cava and others v Regione Lombardia* [1994] ECR I-483.
4. *R v Secretary of State for the Home Department, ex parte Flynn* [1995] 3 CMLR 397, [1997] 3 CMLR 888, but see Case C-378/97 currently pending.
5. *Phull v Secretary of State for the Home Department* [1996] Imm AR 72.
6. Case 43/75 *Defrenne v SABENA* [1976] ECR 455, para. 28.
7. Case 61/79 *Amministrazione delle Finanze dello Stato v Denkavit Italiana* [1980] ECR 1205, at para. 16; and see also Chapter 3.

be dependent, in its implementation or effects, on further action being taken by Community or national authorities. As with clarity and precision, these requirements bear their own meaning in the Community legal order. So reference in the Treaty to implementing measures is no bar to the recognition of a certain degree of direct effect, as the case law on the direct effect of Articles 43, 49, 141 EC exemplifies.[8] Equally – and consistent with the approach in national administrative law – existence of a discretionary power does not *per se* preclude the possibility of judicial control. Still, it is difficult to ascertain the frontier between conditions that prevent and those that do not prevent direct effect, because this is dependent on the willingness of the ECJ to set out the parameters for the operation of the conditions giving rise to judicial control.[9] In addition, Community law provisions may develop from being clearly not directly effective into provisions which can have direct effect.[10] In sum, 'direct effect appears to be in a way *l'art du possible*, as from the point of view of Community law, it is to be expected that national courts are willing to carry the operation of the rules of Community law up to the limits of what appears to be feasible, considering the nature of their judicial function'.[11]

Practically, for national judges direct effect involves anything from the straightforward application of a clearly defined obligation to an investigation of sophisticated economic evidence. An illustration of the latter is provided by Article 86(2), which translates as 'the duty of the national court to investigate whether an undertaking which invokes the provisions of Article 86(2), for the purpose of claiming a derogation from the rules of the Treaty has in fact been entrusted with the operation of a service of general economic interest, and if so, whether its conduct is necessary to enable it to perform its task'.[12]

Some Treaty provisions can have direct effect in any type of litigation, whatever the nature and identity of the parties to the

---

8. See C. Boch, 'Rules to enforce the rules: Subsidiarity v Uniformity in the implementation of the Single European Market Policy' in D. Mayes (ed), *The Evolution of Rules for a Single European Market, Part II: Rules, Democracy and the Environment* (Office for Official Publications of the European Communities, Luxembourg, 1995) p. 1.

9. Weatherill and Beaumont, *EC Law*, 2nd ed. (Penguin, 1995), at p. 340.

10. See evolution of the case law on Article 86(2): *ibid.*, 341.

11. Pescatore, 'The Doctrine of Direct Effect: An Infant Disease of Community Law' (1983) 8 ELR 155.

12. Cases C-114/95 and C-115/95 *Texaco* [1997] ECR I-4263 para. 46.

dispute. Article 141, although addressed to Member States, is capable of being applied directly in all types of disputes, irrespective of the identity of the defendants:

> Since Article 119 is mandatory in nature, the prohibition on discrimination between men and women applies not only to the action of public authorities, but also extends *to all agreements which are intended to regulate paid labour collectively, as well as to contracts between individuals.*[13]

Equally, the rules on the free movement of workers impose obligations on individuals, private employers, trade associations and interested professional bodies, as the Treaty does not distinguish between the sources of discrimination or restriction to be abolished:

> Article 48 not only applies to the action of public authorities, but extends also *to rules of any other nature* aimed at regulating gainful employment in a collective manner.[14]

Articles 25, 28, 29, 31, 43, 49, 81, 82, 86 and 88 EC also have direct effect, although not every provision in these Articles can be enforced by national courts. So for example, in relation to the application of the competition rules, whilst Articles 81(1) and (2) can be applied by national courts, Article 81(3) cannot: only the Commission has power to grant an exemption. With regard to the State aids rules,[15] the role of national courts is limited. A failure to comply with the procedural obligation laid down in Article 88(3) is justiciable in the national courts, and the latter also have an active role to play in relation to repayment of unlawful aids and aids which have not been notified. Accordingly, national courts may have cause to interpret and apply the concept of aid.[16] However, national courts have no competence to decide on the compatibility

13. Case 43/75 *Defrenne v SABENA* [1976] ECR 455, para. 25 (emphasis supplied).
14. Case C-415/93 *URBSFA v Bosman* [1995] ECR I-5050, para. 82 (emphasis supplied) for Article 39, and for Article 43 earlier Case 36/74 *Walrave and Koch v Association Union Cycliste Internationale* [1974] ECR 1405.
15. Articles 92–94 EC.
16. Case C-39/94 *Syndicat Français de l'Express International and others v la Poste* [1996] ECR I-3547; see also G.B. Abbamonte, 'Competitors' Rights to challenge illegally granted aid and the problem of conflicting decisions in the field of competition law' (1997) ECLR 87.

of a State aid with the Common Market: only the Commission possesses such a power, subject to review by the ECJ.[17]

The direct effect of Regulations and Decisions

The language of Article 249 envisages that regulations will immediately become part of the domestic law of the Member States. The Court has confirmed that they are capable of being relied upon by individuals and against individuals and can be subject to direct enforcement in national courts.[18] Decisions can also be invoked before national courts,[19] as it would be incompatible with the binding effect attributed to them by Article 249 to exclude in principle the possibility that persons affected may invoke the obligation imposed thereby.

The Community legislative instruments which have given rise to most controversy are directives.

Direct effect of directives

Whilst directives lay down a binding obligation of result, they leave Member States a margin of discretion as to the means of implementation of this obligation, although such discretion is strictly supervised by the Court.[20] Implementation is required within a defined period of time, usually two to three years. Although addressed to Member States, directives do not seek merely to regulate relationships between individuals; in fact, they regulate more and more legal relationships between natural or legal persons – to quote but a few, the Product Liability Directive, the Equal Pay and Equal Treatment Directives, the Directive on Unfair Terms of Contract, and the Directive on Misleading Advertising. Yet the nature of a directive as a legal instrument remains unchanged in the Treaty. Directives therefore seem by definition unable to qualify for direct effect. Still, the ECJ found otherwise,[21] on the ground of effectiveness. The first UK reference to the ECJ provided this opportunity.

17. For the respective roles of the Commission and the national courts see the Notice on *Cooperation between national courts and the Commission in the State aids field*, OJ 1995 C312/7.
18. Case 43/71 *Politi* [1974] ECR 1039.
19. Case 9/70 *Grad v Finanzamt Traunstein* [1970] ECR 825.
20. See Chapter 1 and Case C-59/89 *Commission v Germany* [1991] ECR I-2607, para. 24.
21. Case 33/70 *SACE* [1970] ECR 1214, but the directive was relied upon alongside Treaty provisions.

The UK, relying on public policy grounds, refused entry to a Dutch national, Ms van Duyn. The High Court referred several questions, in particular whether Article 3(1) of Directive 64/221, which provides 'that measures taken on grounds of public policy or public security shall be based exclusively on the personal conduct of the individual concerned', conferred on individuals rights enforceable by them in national courts. The ECJ found that this provision did not require the intervention of any other measures either of Community institutions or of Member States, that it was intended to limit the discretionary power generally conferred on national authorities responsible for the entry and expulsion of foreign nationals, and that legal certainty for the persons concerned required that they should be able to rely on this provision. Accordingly it held that:

> it would be incompatible with the *binding effect* attributed to a directive by Article 189 to exclude in principle the possibility that the obligation which it imposes may be invoked by those concerned. In particular, where the Communities' authorities have, by directive, imposed on Member States the obligation to pursue a particular course of conduct, the *useful effect* of such an act would be weakened if individuals were prevented from relying on it before their national courts and if the latter were prevented from taking it into consideration as an element of Community law.[22]

This ruling was confirmed in subsequent cases.[23] However, in *Ratti*,[24] the ECJ reasoning shifted from binding effect to personal bar: Member States cannot take advantage of their own failure to comply with their Community obligations to deprive individuals of the rights contained in a directive.

As for Treaty provisions, so the provisions of a directive must fulfil certain requirements in order to be relied upon directly. Such requirements have had to be relaxed since, as they stand, they would never appear capable of being satisfied. Given that, by definition, directives require Member States' intervention, they are not unconditional; they also lack clarity and precision in so far as Member States have, again by definition, discretion as to the forms

22. Case 41/74 *Van Duyn v Home Office* [1974] ECR 1337 (emphasis added).
23. Case 51/76 *Verbond van Nederlandse Ondernemingen v Inspecteur der Invoerrechten en Accijnzen* [1977] ECR 113; Case 38/77 *Enka v Inspecteur der Invoerrechten en Accijnzen* [1977] ECR 2203.
24. Case 148/78 *Ratti* [1979] ECR 1629.

and methods used to reach the specific objective fixed. As with Treaty Articles, the requirements for direct effect have a Community and not a domestic meaning. Clarity and precision are evolving concepts: certain provisions of a directive may acquire clarity and precision over time, as the ECJ clarifies principles of Community law, as was the case for Article 6 of the Equal Treatment Directive.[25]

Do directives need to create individual rights in order to have direct effect? It is important to note that on occasion direct effect and the granting of rights seem related, while in other instances no such linkage exists. The language of rights, however, requires clarification. Indeed, the 'rights' which directives may confer vary from one directive to another. The question of justiciability of directives could sometimes be approached as a question of judicial control of discretionary power. Individuals are given the right to invoke directives before national courts, in order for these courts to check whether the competent national authority, in exercising the choice left to it as to the form and methods for implementing the directive, has kept within the limits of its discretion as set out in the directive.[26] So a private company may rely upon the provisions of a directive to challenge the validity of the authorisation issued by a national authority, on the basis of that directive, to one of its competitors.[27] Directives imposing the introduction of particular procedures would also fall within this category. In such circumstances, the national judge can verify *only* whether or not such procedure exists, whether it is open in all required circumstances and whether or not it offers the guarantees it ought to afford. Where no procedure has been introduced, the directive is incapable of giving individuals a right to which the judge could give effect, as national judges have no power to make a positive order providing for a procedural machinery. Nevertheless, the individual has the right to invoke the directive for the purpose of seeking a public remedy such as a remedy for a failure to respect procedural obligations. The consequences to be attached by national judges to the

---

[25]. Case C-271/91 *Marshall v Southampton and South West Hampshire Area Health Authority (Marshall II)*, in contrast with earlier case law.
[26]. Case C-72/95 *Kraaijeveld BV and others v Gedeputeerde Staten van Zuid-Holland* [1996] ECR I-5403.
[27]. Case C-201/94 *R v The Medicines Control Agency, ex parte Smith & Nephew Pharmaceuticals Ltd* and *Primecrown Ltd v The Medicine Control Agency* [1996] ECR I-5819.

non-observance of procedural obligations vary. Other directives still may involve the creation of a private law right to equal pay or a right to equal treatment and can be relied upon for the purpose of asking the national court to substitute the directive for conflicting national legislation, or to interpret the national legislation in the light of the directive.

Enforcing directives against the State or an emanation thereof

The most important limitation on the direct effect of directives is that a directive can only be applied directly against the State or an emanation thereof – the so-called 'vertical effect'. The ECJ must have the last word on what is an emanation of the State, otherwise the uniform application of Community law would be jeopardised. It is on a reference from a UK court that this question was first addressed. In *Marshall*,[28] the ECJ decided:

> With regard to the argument that a Directive may not be relied upon against an individual, it must be emphasised that according to Article 189 of the EEC Treaty the binding nature of a directive, which constitutes the basis for the possibility of relying on the directive before a national court, exists only in relation to 'each Member State to which it is addressed'. It follows that a directive may not of itself impose obligations on an individual and that a provision of a directive may not be relied upon as such against such a person . . . In that respect it must be pointed out that where a person involved in legal proceedings is able to rely on a directive as against the State he may do so *regardless of the capacity in which the latter is acting, whether employer or public authority*. In either case it is necessary to prevent the State from taking advantage of its own failure to comply with Community law.

The decision to limit the direct effect of directives, a decision perhaps prompted by some hostile reactions from the French Conseil d'Etat and the German Bundesfinanzhof, has been the source of intense academic controversy,[29] and, without a doubt, a source of

---

28. Case 152/84 *Marshall v Southampton & South West Hampshire Health Authority (Marshall I)* [1986] ECR 723.
29. For an overview, see S. Prechal, *Directives in European Community Law: A Study on EC Directives and their Enforcement by National Courts* (OUP), 1995).

serious obstacles to the enforcement of Community rights in litigation between private parties.[30] Moreover, the idea that in a Community governed by the rule of law, the outcome of a litigation may be determined by the identity of the defendant, is disturbing. There is no room in a work of this size to elaborate on the different arguments in favour of, or against the full direct effect of directives. Suffice it to say that if the justification for direct effect is to ensure that Member States are prevented from taking advantage of their own failure, the nature of the legal relationships involved should play no role at all. Neither the many anomalies created by this decision, or the repeated calls[31] made to the ECJ, including those of three of its Advocates General,[32] had any success. The decision that the provision of a directive may not, as such, be relied upon against an individual has been maintained, most forcefully in *Dori*.[33] In that case an individual sought to withdraw from a contract for a language correspondence course under the conditions laid down in Directive 85/577 on doorstep selling, namely the right of cancellation of the contract during the 'cooling-off' period. The ECJ held that 'consumers cannot derive from the directive itself a right of cancellation as against traders with whom they have concluded a contract or enforce such a right in a national court.' Given the justification provided, it seems unlikely that this issue can ever be reconsidered: 'the effect of extending that case law[34] to the sphere of relations between individuals would be to recognise a power in the Community to enact obligations for individuals with immediate effect, whereas it has competence to do so *only when it is empowered to adopt regulations*.' The consequences of this ruling will be explored fully below. However one aspect must be stressed. A rather strange paradox results, that the more a directive is concerned with relationships between individuals, the more it appears to lay down obligations between and for individuals, the less likely it is going to be legally capable of doing so directly.

---

30. Jacobs AG at para. 33 of his Opinion in C-316/93 *Vaneetveld v SA le Foyer* [1994] ECR I-763; Tridimas, 'Horizontal Effect of Directives: A Missed Opportunity?' (1994) 19 ELR 621, pp. 633–5.
31. Case C-192/94 *El Cortes Inglés SA v C. Blázquez Rivero* [1996] ECR I-1281.
32. Point 12 of Van Gerven AG's opinion in Case C-271/91 *Marshall II*, para. 12 [1993] ECR I-4367, Jacob AG's Opinion in C-316/93 *Vaneetveld v SA le Foyer* [1994] ECR I-763, paras 15ff, Lenz AG's Opinion in Case C-91/92 *Dori v Recreb srl* [1994] ECR I-3325, paras 47ff.
33. Case C-91/92 *Faccini Dori v Recreb srl* [1994] ECR I-3325.
34. The ECJ here refers to *Marshall I*.

Broadening the concept of the State or an emanation thereof

Having introduced a limitation on the scope of the direct effect of directives, the ECJ proceeded to broaden the notion of the State. The State, in any of its manifestations, is bound by Community obligations and should not, in any of its forms, benefit from its own wrong and deprive individuals of the rights which directives may confer. This view is consistent with the general approach of Community and public international law, which refuses to differentiate among the various constitutional organs of the State, and the same line has been adopted in the context of Article 226 proceedings and in relation to State liability for breach of Community law. The definition of an 'emanation of the State' is under strict supervision by the ECJ as the Community legal order cannot be bound by domestic definitions, variable between Member States. A wide range of bodies, entities and authorities fell within the category, including those so far removed from responsibility for the implementation of the directives, that it may be asked how the rationale that the State may not benefit from its own wrong, still validly applies.

UK courts have made three references on this issue. Various bodies have been held as bound to apply the provisions of directives. In *Marshall I*,[35] the ECJ held that the provisions of a directive could be relied on against a health authority irrespective of the capacity in which the latter is acting, whether as public authority or employer. Directives can also be relied upon in litigation against constitutionally independent authorities responsible for the maintenance of public order and security, namely a Chief Constable,[36] and against nationalised companies.[37]

Directives can also be used by individuals against a city council.[38] So Member States cannot rely on local government reorganisation as a way to escape their Community obligations – 'all organs of the administration, including *decentralised authorities* regional or local such as municipalities, are obliged to apply those provisions'.[39] 'Emanation of the State' is such a flexible concept that, at

---

35. *Op. cit.*, fn 28.
36. Case 222/84 *Johnston v Chief Constable of RUC* [1986] ECR 1651.
37. Case C-188/89 *Foster v British Gas* [1990] ECR I-3313; a ruling applied to privatised utilities, see Chapter 8.
38. Case 103/88 *Fratelli Costanzo SpA v Commune di Milano* [1989] ECR 1839.
39. *Ibid.*, para. 31.

least on one occasion, in *Carpaneto*, a local authority has been assimilated to an individual and held entitled to rely on the provisions of a directive for the purpose of opposing the application of a national provision making it subject to VAT payments.[40] An indication that the concept is interpreted in the way which best achieves the objectives of the directive at issue, even if it leads to further confusion, as in *Carpaneto*, a distinction was drawn between the different activities in which a public body may engage, a distinction specifically ruled out in *Marshall I*.

Alternative therapies

However flexible, the notion cannot stretch indefinitely. Are individuals limited in their capacity to remedy defective implementation? What happens to directives in litigation between private parties, in cases of wrongful or non-implementation? Do their provisions remain without effect? Even where the provisions of a directive cannot be applied directly, they are still of *considerable use* in litigation between private parties. The ECJ has given effect to directives by resorting to various mechanisms. Where the provisions of a directive are meant to, or are capable of creating enforceable rights, but a Member State fails to implement the directive within the given time period or does so incorrectly, other routes are available to secure the judicial protection of the rights created.

So direct effect is merely one of the techniques to give effect to rights which might be conferred by a directive, but a directive can confer rights which cannot be effectuated directly. A directive can confer rights without being capable of having direct effect.[41] The rights conferred in a directive may be protected by means other than direct effect, namely through the interpretative duty or State liability for breach of Community law. Directives cannot of themselves impose obligations on individuals, but this does not mean that the rights they are capable of creating cannot be protected. From recent cases, it appears that the direct effect of directives has become one of several judicial techniques available to ensure the

---

40. Cases 231/87 and 129/88 *Commune di Carpaneto* [1989] ECR 3233, paras 31 and 33.
41. Cases C-6/90 and C-9/90 *Francovich and others v Italy* [1991] ECR I-5357.

protection of rights contained in a directive. The ECJ has now shifted the focus from enforceable rights of individuals to both the obligation of national courts to interpret the terms of their national law in the light of the requirements of Community Law and to State liability. The link between direct effect, uniform interpretation and damages was also made clear in *Dori*.[42] Still, the standard of protection of the rights conferred by a given directive is not necessarily the same.[43]

Interpretation?

The first of these alternative techniques, known as the 'uniform interpretation duty' (*interprétation conforme*) – or duty of 'sympathetic interpretation' or 'indirect effect of directives' or 'substantive effectiveness of directives' – is simply an interpretative duty imposed on national courts. Community law is to be applied indirectly as domestic law by way of interpretation. National courts are not asked to enforce the provisions of the Directive, rather they are asked to *interpret national law in such a way as to ensure that the objectives of the Directive are achieved*. Through this device, what is at issue is not the effect of the directive, rather the emphasis is on the *effect of national law* as interpreted by the national courts, in accordance with Community law. Community law is invoked, but it is not applied; it only comes into play indirectly. National judges are not asked to apply the provisions of the directive, rather they are required to use the directive as an aid to the interpretation of national legislation.

This duty of the national courts to interpret national law in accordance with the terms and objectives of a directive, extends to all national legislation existing in the field which the directive purports to regulate, whether adopted prior to or following the adoption of the directive. The duty does not only relate to the specific implementing provisions, it concerns all relevant national law; indeed it is most useful when it operates in cases of non-implemented directives. Further, the duty applies regardless of the identities of the parties to the litigation. Interpreting legislation purporting to implement a directive in conformity with it does not

---

[42.] *Op. cit.*, fn 33, paras 26 and 27, and in C-334/92 W. *Miret v Fondo de Garantia Salarial* [1993] ECR I-6911.
[43.] See Tridimas, *op. cit.* at fn 30.

pose major problems for national courts. They would simply apply some doctrine akin to the British principle according to which Parliament must be presumed to be willing to conform with its international obligations. Yet difficulties arise when the legislation pre-dates the directive and can hardly benefit from such a presumption. At times, uniform interpretation requires national judges to set aside classic canons of statutory interpretation.

Limits to interpretation

Although the uniform interpretation duty has considerable breadth, it is not without limit. The first obvious limit is that for national judges to be able to interpret national legislation in the light of the directive, there must be some national legislation existing in the field which can be considered as covering roughly the same field as the directive. If there is no implementing legislation or no legislation coming within the scope regulated by the directive, then simply there is nothing to interpret and therefore no uniform interpretation duty to discharge.[44] The second limit is that national courts are not under such a duty when such interpretation would have the effect, on the basis of the directive, and independently of national law, of determining or aggravating the liability in criminal law of persons acting in contravention of its provisions.[45] In practice, primacy is set aside since 'there is no method of procedure in Community law allowing the national court to eliminate national provisions contrary to the provisions of a directive not transposed where that directive cannot be relied upon before the national court'.[46]

As has been suggested, a directive should never be construed as imposing obligations on individuals where that would confer rights on the defaulting State.[47] The idea that a Member State, having failed to discharge its obligations to implement the directive, could then be allowed to rely on it against an individual, short of national implementing measures, seems in breach of natural justice.

44. As in Cases C-6/90 and C-9/90 *Francovich and others v Italy* [1991] ECR I-5357.
45. Case 80/86 *Kolpinghuis Nijmegen* [1987] ECR 3969, para. 13; C-168/95 *Arcaro* [1996] ECR I-4705, para. 42.
46. *Arcaro, op. cit.* para. 43.
47. Jacobs AG at point 33 of his Opinion in C-316/93 *Vaneetveld v SA le Foyer* [1994] ECR I-763.

There is another limit to the interpretative duty, the parameters of which are difficult to determine with precision, as the ECJ uses such formulae as 'the national court called upon to interpret it (its domestic law) is required to do so, *as far as possible* in the light of the wording and purpose of the directive in order to achieve the result pursued by the latter',[48] or 'it is for the national court to interpret and apply the legislation . . . in conformity with the requirements of Community law *in so far as it is given discretion to do so under national law'*.[49] Since it is for judges – through interpretation – to ensure that directives are properly incorporated into national law, different views will arise as to the proper role of the judiciary, the proper extent of judicial powers. Moreover, given that judicial protection of the rights contained in the directive proceeds on a case by case basis, it is subject to inconsistencies. The interpretative duty also generates a great deal of uncertainty as to the exact scope of national law and conflicts with legal certainty – a general principle of Community law – particularly when obligations are imposed on private parties. This is evidently so when one considers that, on many occasions, the objectives pursued by a directive – objectives which may well involve imposing obligations upon individuals – will only be revealed through interpretation by the ECJ. Individuals may expect that national law would be construed in accordance with national canons of interpretation. The difficulties encountered by the UK courts in relation to the uniform interpretation duty will be discussed later.[50]

Legal basis

The foundation for the national courts' duty to ensure the protection of Community rights is Article 10 EC:

> Member States shall take all appropriate measures, whether general or particular, to ensure fulfilment of the obligations arising out of this Treaty or resulting from action taken by the institutions of the Community. They shall facilitate the achievement of the Community's tasks, they shall abstain from any measure which could jeopardize the attainment of the Community's tasks.

48. C-106/89 *Marleasing v La Comercial Internacional de Alimentacion* [1990] ECR I-4135 (emphasis supplied).
49. Case 14/83 *Von Colson and Kamann v Land Nordrhein-Westphalen* [1984] ECR 1891, para. 28 (emphasis supplied).
50. See Chapter 8.

The uniform interpretation duty was developed by the ECJ in accordance with the following reasoning. The obligation imposed on Member States by Article 10 EC to achieve the result laid down in a directive applies to all national authorities, including judicial authorities. The duty of national courts to interpret national law in conformity with the provisions of a directive facilitates the achievement of the Community's objectives, and Article 10 EC also serves as the legal basis for the granting of an effective remedy.[51] This interpretation technique has to be used in order to maximise the effect of Community rules, thus it is not limited to giving effect to directly effective provisions of Community law. This is confirmed by the very case,[52] in which the duty was developed.

Objections

The uniform interpretation duty raises a number of objections. As noted earlier, it charges national courts with tasks normally discharged by the other branches of government. Further directives may have a decisive impact on the outcome of a dispute between two private parties through an interpretation of a domestic provision.[53] Such interpretation, although in conformity with Community requirements, could not really be expected by the parties on which obligations are thus imposed.

The main objection, however, is that the ECJ seems to imply that directives may never, of themselves, impose obligations on individuals; directives are constitutionally unable to impose obligations upon individuals directly. But interpretation often results in obligations being placed on private parties,[54] albeit indirectly, an issue which has given rise to particular problems in the UK.[55] Greater rights for individuals following a particular 'construction'

51. See further Chapter 6.
52. Case 14/83 *Von Colson and Kamann v Land Nordrhein-Westphalen* [1984] ECR 1895.
53. Case C-472/93 *Luigi Spano and Others v Fiat Geotech SpA & Fiat Hitachi Excavators SpA* [1995] ECR I-4321.
54. Case C-106/89 *Marleasing v La Comercial Internacional de Alimentación* [1990] ECR I-4135; Case C-32/93 *Webb v EMO Air Cargo Ltd* [1994] ECR I-3567; Case C-129/94 *Criminal proceedings against Rafael Ruiz Bernaldez* [1996] ECR I-1829. See Tesauro AG's Opinion in C-46/93 and 48/93, *op. cit.* at fn 35, 'so much so that in the ultimate analysis, one is not so far removed from the practical effects which would be achieved by the horizontal effect, pure and simple, of precise and unconditional directives.'
55. See Chapter 8.

of national law often translates into greater obligations for another party, and sometimes that party happens to be a private one. In *Ruiz Bernaldez*,[56] the compatibility with Directive 72/166 of an exclusion of cover from a compulsory insurance contract was considered. The ECJ held that a compulsory insurance contract may not provide that in certain cases, in particular where the driver of the vehicle was intoxicated, the insurer is not obliged to pay compensation for the damage to property and personal injuries caused to third parties by the insured vehicle. The practical result is that third parties have a right against private insurance companies to be compensated for the damage to property and personal injuries caused by the insured vehicle, and insurance companies have the corresponding obligation to provide compensation. In *Pafitis*,[57] the Second Company Directive came into play between, on the one hand a private bank and its new shareholders, and on the other, the old shareholders who objected to the increase in the capital of TKE Bank by decision of the Governor of the Bank of Greece. The ECJ found that the Directive precludes national legislation under which the capital of a bank constituted in the form of a plc may be increased by an administrative measure, without a resolution of the general meeting.

So although directives only have limited – vertical – direct effect, they come into play in litigation between private parties as an aid to construction of national law, and they may impose obligations on private parties, albeit indirectly. Directives may also be relied upon to render national law inapplicable. In the UK, however, the 'distinction between using a directive as a source of rights and as a means of disapplying a restriction on rights which would otherwise be available in domestic law' has not found much sympathy in the House of Lords.[58]

---

56. Case C-129/94 *Criminal proceedings against Rafael Ruiz Bernaldez* [1996] ECR I-1829. Spanish legislation provided that cover of damage to property caused when the driver is intoxicated is excluded from the compulsory car insurance.
57. Case C-441/93 *Pafitis v Trapeza Kentrikis Ellados AE* [1996] ECR I-1347.
58. *R v Secretary of State for Employment, ex parte Seymour Smith* [1997] 2 CMLR 904.

Additional roles

In *CIA Security*,[59] a declaration of inapplicability of an obligation of national law, an obligation contrary to Community law, was sought and secured. Accordingly, national provisions adopted in violation of requirements laid down in Directive 83/189[60] could not be applied nor enforced. CIA, a private company, brought an action for unfair trade practices against trade competitors advertising that the alarm systems manufactured and distributed by CIA were not in compliance with Belgian technical specifications. As a defence, the competitors argued that CIA should be barred from marketing non-approved security systems. CIA relied on Directive 83/189, arguing that the technical standards laid down in Belgian law were inapplicable since the notification procedure had not been observed. The case was referred to the ECJ. The central issue concerned the consequences flowing from non-compliance with procedural obligations and the nature and extent of the rights individuals can derive from the non-observance of procedural provisions.

What effects must a national court attach to breach of a notification procedure? The consequences of failure to comply with a notification procedure depends on the nature and intended effect of a notification procedure, both of which are matters for the ECJ. In *Enichem*,[61] a municipal council, *i.e.* a decentralised authority bound by the Directive,[62] had introduced a prohibition on the sale and use of plastic bags and non-biodegradable containers, without notifiying this measure.[63] The ECJ held that the notification procedure was only intended to inform the Commission, which might then decide to take steps for harmonisation, and did not make the entry into force of the envisaged rules subject to the Commission's approval. The procedure did not grant individuals any right capable of being infringed by a failure to notify. Individuals had no

---

59. Case C-194/94, *CIA Security International v Signalson and Securitel* [1996] ECR I-2201; see also Case C-201/94 *R v The Medicines Control Agency, ex parte Smith & Nephew Pharmaceuticals Ltd* and *Primecrown Ltd v The Medicine Control Agency, op. cit.* at fn 27.
60. OJ 1983 L109/8, providing for a notification procedure before the introduction of new technical standards (as amended by Directive 94/10, OJ 1994 L100/30).
61. Case 380/87 *Enichem Base v Commune di Cinisello Balsamo* [1989] ECR 2491, paras 19–24.
62. Case 103/88 *Fratelli Costanzo SpA v Commune di Milano* [1989] ECR 1839.
63. In breach of Directive 75/442: OJ 1975 L194/39, on the disposal of waste.

Community right which they may enforce before national courts in order to obtain annulment or suspension of national rules adopted in breach of this notification procedure. The practical result for traders was that they could sell only products complying with the un-notified measures. It is certainly noteworthy that the measures challenged in *Enichem* were in fact in conformity with the purpose of the directive, namely protection of the environment.[64] In *CIA Security* the ECJ distinguished *Enichem*: the nature of the notification procedure in Directive 83/189 was not merely informing the Commission, it had the more general aim of eliminating or restricting obstacles to trade. The *effectiveness* of this Community control would be enhanced if breach of the obligation to notify was treated as a substantial procedural defect, thereby rendering the technical regulations inapplicable between individuals.[65] The practical result for traders was that they can sell products which do not comply with national technical specifications.

By contrast with the notification procedure under consideration in *Enichem*, the procedure in *CIA Security* was found capable of giving rights to individuals with the result that rules adopted in breach thereof were inapplicable. Another way of differentiating between the two cases is to highlight the consequences of absence of notification, in breach of the Community regime: in *Enichem* it serves the purpose of the Directive, in *CIA Security* it defeats the purpose of the Community procedure. Breach by a Member State of its obligation to notify technical specifications may render them inapplicable. Directive 83/189 served as a basis to invalidate technical regulations, in litigation between private parties. The distinction between *Dori* and *CIA Security* has been found unconvincing.[66] It appears on the contrary that the two cases can be very easily differentiated. Indeed, in *CIA Security*, the provisions of the Directive do not come into play whereas in *Dori* what is sought is the application of the provisions of the directive in preference to national provisions. Litigants may use a directive to protect themselves against national law,[67] even in a litigation against private parties, but the provisions of the directive as such are not applied directly by the national court.

In *CIA Security*, the ECJ 'makes a very useful contribution to

---

64. Para. 7 of the judgment.
65. Case C-194/94 *CIA Security International v Signalson, op. cit.* para. 48.
66. J. Coppel in (1997) 26 ILJ 69 at 71–2.
67. A right against State interference: see J. Stuyck (1996) CMLRev 1261 at 1272.

the completion of the internal market'.[68] To this extent, the case demonstrates how Community law acquires flesh in the enforcement process. The notification procedure does not merely concern relationships between, on the one hand, the Member State wishing to introduce new technical standard and, on the other, the Commission and the rest of the Member States. Since the Directive impacts directly on the main actors in the Single Market, namely undertakings, they must be able to prevent the emergence of new obstacles to trade. So, alongside Articles 226 and 227 EC, individuals must be empowered to take action. As a result of private litigation, the validity of the un-notified specifications is affected. Private enforcement of the Community regime ensures a better level of compliance on the part of Member States. This position is consistent with the view the ECJ took from the outset;[69] supervision and application of Community law by Member States should not be a matter for the Commission and the Member States alone, individuals too have a role to play in ensuring Member States discharge their Community obligations.

Directives may also be relied upon for the purpose of founding a claim in damages. In *Francovich*,[70] the ECJ established the principle that Member States may be liable for loss caused by the failure to implement a directive, even where the directive does not give rise to directly effective rights. The principle of State liability has since been extended to breach of Treaty provisions and will be considered alongside other remedies for breach of Community law.[71]

Conclusion

It will have become apparent that the role of directives in litigation has become increasingly complex, and clarification of the case law is needed in the interests of judicial protection of *all* parties, and of those in charge of applying Community law. It is also in the interests of the Community that Community law should not become a jungle. Direct effect and primacy ensure that Community law can

68. Slot (1996) 33 CMLRev 1035 at 1043.
69. Case 26/62 *Van Gend en Loos v Nederlandse Administratie der Belastingen* [1963] ECR 1.
70. *Op. cit.* at fn 41. 71. Chapter 9.

be invoked in the UK courts, and prevail over inconsistent UK law, yet these doctrines do not categorise the rights Community law may confer, or indicate which remedies are available to sanction violation of Community law. This chapter started with the suggestion that 'the doctrine of direct effect seeks to ensure that rights accruing from Community law are available to the individual, whilst the doctrine of primacy ensures that such rights will take precedence over *any* national rule or practice.'[72] There is real force in the proposition that, if the primacy of Community law requires, as a general rule, that in case of conflict between a substantive provision of national law and a substantive provision of Community law, the Community provision should prevail, then, *a fortiori*, primacy requires that rules governing procedures or remedies be overridden. However, in practice, the full requirements of primacy are still a matter of contention, and the next chapter will explain why.

[72.] Edward and Lane, *European Community Law – An Introduction, op. cit.* at fn 1, para. 135.

CHAPTER SIX

National remedies for breach of EC law

The Court supplemented the classic public international law scheme of judicial supervision of Member-State compliance with Community law, with one that essentially relies on the initiative of private parties and the authority of national judicial systems. As a consequence, the Community must trust these systems, particularly the efficiency of their rules of procedure.[1]

The rules of the internal market must have equivalent effect throughout the Community.[2]

It is for the national legal system of each Member State to determine which court has jurisdiction to hear disputes involving individual rights derived from Community law, but at the same time the Member States are responsible for ensuring that those rights are *effectively* protected in each case; *subject to that reservation* it is not for the Court to intervene in order to resolve any questions of jurisdiction which may arise, within the national judicial system, as regards the definition of certain legal situations based on Community law.[3]

This chapter investigates the extent to which Community law influences the working of national judicial systems. The Community requirements will be studied through a selection of cases where national procedural rules or substantive rules governing the remedy were challenged as falling below the standard of protection which Community law requires. As will be shown, Community law has

---

1. K. Lenaerts, 'Interaction between judges and politicians' (1992) 12 YEL 1 at 6.
2. Sutherland Report: *The Internal Market after 1992: Meeting the Challenge*, Report to the EEC Commission by the High Level Group on the operation of the internal market (1993).
3. Case 179/84 *Bozetti* [1985] ECR 2301, para. 17 (emphasis supplied).

had a real impact at all stages of the judicial process, from access to the domestic courts to the final outcome of the litigation. The question as to whether or not, in the absence of specific Community provisions, Community law grants a right to a specific remedy which national courts should provide, will be addressed.

National courts are responsible for the enforcement and the *full and effective protection* of Community rights. However, in the present stage of development of Community law, there are few Community rules[4] governing the granting of remedies. Respect for Community law is principally organised through and should be guaranteed through national rules. It falls upon national rules to provide the competent authorities, the competent jurisdictions and the procedural and substantive rules. This is known as the principle of institutional autonomy. This two-tier system, whereby the Community enacts rules which the national authorities have to implement and the national courts protect and enforce, has given rise to much litigation. There is now an extensive body of case law for breach of Community rights relating to challenges of national rules governing remedies, on the grounds that these national rules are incompatible with the requirements of Community law. Some of the factors which can impair protection of Community rights at national level have already been discussed.[5] The various guidelines, both general and specific, issued by the ECJ will now be discussed.

The interests at stake: effectiveness v national institutional autonomy

Where the Community system relies on the laws and authorities of the Member States to supply the procedures and remedies for the enforcement of Community law, their availability and effectiveness to enforce Community rights are dependent upon national solutions. From the Community perspective, as well as that of litigants, this dependence presents obvious risks: the Member States have in effect, and not necessarily consciously or through ill-will, the opportunity to *dilute* or *vary* the impact of Community law through inadequate domestic law definitions. As a result, a principle of paramount importance in the Community, the uniform application of the Community obligations, is jeopardised. For this reason the

4. See Chapter 11.   5. See Chapter 3.

ECJ intervened. However, the Court can only ensure an adequate standard of judicial protection on a case by case basis. Such an approach is evidently haphazard and dependent on the financial resources and tenacity of the litigants, and on the willingness of national courts to co-operate. It seems therefore an over-statement to refer to this process as the ECJ embarking upon the harmonisation of national procedural rules, or the development of a new common law.[6] The case law should be understood in the context of the Court's striking a balance between, on the one hand, the need for national courts to provide proper protection for Community rights and, on the other, the importance of respecting – within appropriate limits – the procedural and indeed organisational autonomy of the Member States' legal systems.[7]

If uniform rules and uniformity in the implementation, application and enforcement of the rules might be desirable from an efficiency perspective, the adoption of such rules by the Community legislature has consistently proven politically difficult. This in turn begs the question as to whether it is appropriate for the ECJ to fill this lacunae.[8] The fact that the principle of national institutional autonomy carries with it undesirable limitations, such as a *varying* degree of protection to the *same* Community rights, does not suffice to give the ECJ a mandate to establish such rules. If the decentralised system of implementation, application and enforcement of Community rules carries with it inherent drawbacks, divergence and possibly non-operation, it protects the integrity and diversity of national legal systems. National sanctions, for example, differ in their severity or modes of application, because they are often historically conceived for other purposes by a

---

6. But for such a view see *inter alia* Van Gerven, 'Bridging the gap between Community and National Laws: towards a principle of homogeneity in the field of legal remedies?' (1995) 32 CMLRev 679; R. Caranta, 'Judicial Protection against Member States: a new *ius commune* is taking shape' (1995) 32 CMLRev 703.

7. See AG Jacobs Opinion in Case C-62/93 *BP* v *Supergas* [1995] ECR I-1883 para. 53, Case C-312/93 *Peterbroeck, van Campenhout & Cie* v *Belgium*, [1995] ECR I-4599, and J. Lonbay and A. Biondi (eds), *Remedies for Breach of EC Law* (Wiley, 1997), pp. 26–8.

8. C. Boch, 'Rules to enforce the rules: Subsidiarity v Uniformity in the implementation of the Single European Market Policy' in D. Mayes (ed): *The Evolution of Rules for a Single European Market Part II: Rules, Democracy and the Environment* (Office for Official Publications of the European Communities, Luxembourg, 1995).

defined social group and reflect that group's values and priorities. National institutional autonomy constitutes an application of the principle of subsidiarity,[9] and the ECJ has had to take on board the trend towards greater scrutiny of the extent of Community competences. Finally, the interest in full and uniform application has to be balanced against considerations such as legal certainty, sound administration and the orderly conduct of proceedings by the courts. All legal systems commonly impose various restrictions which, in the absence of a reasonable degree of diligence on the part of the plaintiffs, will lead to a full or partial denial of their claims and therefore denial of their rights[10] irrespective of the merits of their claims. The Community system itself follows such an approach. Such restrictions have been adopted to limit the time within which challenges to the legality of Community acts may be mounted. To justify the very strict time-limits imposed to challenges to the validity of Community legislation under Article 230 EC, the ECJ held that:

> the limitation period for bringing an action fulfils a generally recognised need, namely the need to prevent the legality of administrative decisions from being called into question indefinitely, and this means that there is a prohibition on reopening a question after the limitation period has expired.[11]

Balancing effectiveness with national procedural autonomy

In the absence of specific Community provisions, is the national court hearing a Community-based claim bound by domestic rules of procedure? This question has been addressed by the ECJ. Initially, it recognised that the manner in which national courts protected Community rights was left essentially untouched, however as national courts have been seeking increasingly precise guidance, the ECJ has had to become significantly bolder.

The general principles are that in the (regrettable) absence of any relevant Community rules, it is for the domestic legal system of each Member State to designate the competent courts and to lay

---

9. Boch *op. cit.*   10. Jacobs AG, *op. cit.*, at fn 7.
11. Case 156/67 *Commission v Belgium* [1978] ECR 1881.

down the procedural rules for proceedings designed to ensure the protection of rights which individuals acquire from Community law, provided that such rules are not less favourable than those governing the same right of action on an internal matter[12] nor framed so as to render the application of Community law impossible or excessively difficult. These two principles are cumulative. Accordingly, where these conditions are not met the national rule will have to be set aside, even if this has the result that the pursuer of the Community right will have an advantage over the litigant pursuing a national law right.[13] Equally, even where there is *no* judicial protection for the purely internal claim, protection will have to be provided for the Community-based claim.

The requirement that the conditions laid down by national provisions governing remedies should not make it impossible, or excessively difficult in practice to exercise the Community rights, has been qualified by *the principle of effectiveness*.[14] Furthermore, the duty of national courts to give effective protection to Community rights is no longer limited to those rights which can be construed as directly effective.[15]

These principles, although easy to state, are not simple to apply in practice, as will now be shown.

Finding an equivalent comparator

The non-discrimination principle in effect requires national courts to enforce an EC law-based claim in the same way they would enforce similar claims in national law. But what is a similar action or sanction of a domestic nature? The ECJ is repeatedly confronted with the issue, and gives vague or rather inconsistent indications. In *Draehmpaehl*,[16] the ECJ had regard to *other provisions of*

---

12. Case 45/76 *Comet v Produktschap voor Siergewassen* [1976] ECR 2043.
13. Case 33/76 *Rewe v Landwirtschaftskammer für das Saarland* [1976] ECR 1989; Case 199/82 *Amministrazione delle Finanze dello Stato v San Georgio* [1983] ECR 3595.
14. Case C-87/90 *A. Verholen e.a. v Sociale Verzekeringsbank* [1991] ECR I-3757.
15. Joined Cases C-6/90 & C-9/90 *Francovich* [1991] ECR I-5357, para. 42, Case C-312/93 *Peterbroeck v Belgium* [1995] ECR I-4599, para. 12; Joined Cases C-430/93 & C-431/93 *Van Schijndel and Van Veen v SPF* [1995] ECR I-4705, para. 17.
16. Case C-180/95 *Draehmpaehl v Urania Immobilienservice OHG* [1997] ECR I-2195.

domestic civil law and labour law when assessing whether a given sanction met the comparability test. By contrast, in *EDIS*,[17] it indicated that the principle of equivalence requires that the rule at issue be applied without distinction, whether the infringement alleged is of Community law or national law, where the purpose and cause of action are *similar*, but that it does not require extending the most favourable rules governing recovery under national law to all actions for repayment of charges or dues levied in breach of Community law. This was confirmed in *B.S. Levez v T.H. Jennings (Harlow Pools) Ltd*;[18] the principle of equivalence is not to be interpreted as requiring Member States to extend their most favourable rules to all actions brought in the field of employment law. In order to determine whether the principle of equivalence has been complied with, national courts – which alone have a direct knowledge of the procedural rules governing actions in a particular field – must consider both the *purpose and the essential characteristics* of allegedly similar domestic actions.

In *BP* v *Supergas*[19] Advocate General Jacobs stated in his Opinion:

> It follows from the principle that claims based on Community law must not be treated less favourably than claims based on national law that, wherever taxable persons are entitled to a refund of tax in respect of a particular tax year on grounds recognised by national law, that possibility must extend to claims based on Community law; that is so regardless of the nature of the grounds recognised by national law. It is not, in my view, necessary to engage in the difficult and somewhat artificial exercise of seeking a comparable claim under national law. Indeed such an approach does not follow from the Court's case-law on this matter . . . it is for the Member States, in the absence of harmonised rules, to decide upon the appropriate balance between the requirements of legal certainty and sound administration and the need to ensure the correct application of the tax in a particular tax year. Where a Member State allows a tax year to be re-opened at the instance of the taxable person within a certain period on any ground, it accepts by implication that for the period for which the claim is permitted it is the need to ensure correct application of the tax which takes precedence. The Member State cannot therefore object

---

17. Case C-231/96 *Edilizia Industriale Siderurgica Srl (EDIS)* v *Ministero delle Finanze* [1998] ECR I-5025, para. 36.
18. Case C-326/96 [1998] (not yet reported).
19. Case C-62/93 *BP* v *Supergas* [1995] ECR I-1883.

that a claim based on the Community law must be refused on grounds of legal certainty or sound administration.

In this case, a remedy existed, and had to be made available for the Community-based claims even where the Community claim was not strictly identical to the domestic one. Accordingly, it would appear that the relevant test hinges on the *existence* of a remedy giving the required redress and not on the *availability* of a particular remedy under national law. However, in the light of recent case law[20] where the ECJ seems prepared to leave national courts a broader discretion in their approach to the principle of equivalence, it may be asked whether the general test proposed by Advocate General Jacobs should still be used.

The matching of a domestic form of process with the enforcement of a Community-law right has also proved challenging[21] given that EC law does not lend itself to classifications with which UK courts may be familiar. It confers rights and obligations in private and public law, irrespective of how national law chooses to classify them, thus cutting across traditional legal boundaries. National courts must find ways in which to accommodate this reality, and in so far as national habits of characterisation might impede effective enforcement of Community law, they may have to be set aside,[22] and new causes of action or forms of process may have to be developed. Certainly in the context of claims for damages for breach of duty under the 1977 Banking Directive, it has been held that 'a claim for damages should be regarded as a claim of a different type not known to the common law, namely a claim for damages for breach of a duty imposed by Community law or for the infringement of a right conferred by Community law.'[23]

Not each and every judge may happen to be so *communautaire*. Identifying the competent form of process can be laborious for the many Community-based claims which do not conform to traditional domestic pigeonholes.[24]

---

20. Case C-231/96 *Edilizia Industriale Siderurgica Srl (EDIS) v Ministero delle Finanze* [1998] ECR I-5025, para. 36; Case C-326/96 *B.S. Levez v T.H. Jennings (Harlow Pools) Ltd* [1998] ECR (not yet reported).
21. J. Steiner, *Enforcing EC Law* (Blackstone, 1995) pp. 66, 67, 98; Jacobs AG in Case 312/93 *Peterbroeck v Belgium* [1995] ECR I-4599, paras 20–7.
22. J. Convery, 'State Liability in the UK after *Brasserie du Pêcheur*' (1997) 34 CMLRev 603 at 625.
23. *Three Rivers DC v Bank of England* [1997] 3 CMLR 429, per Clarke J at 470.
24. See Chapters 3 and 8.

The range of remedies available

National rules must not make the application of Community law or the exercise of Community rights impossible or excessively difficult. This formulation has invited litigation. Whilst it might be straightforward to establish that it is impossible to exercise a Community right, 'excessively difficult' is an ambiguous formulation, and presumably one which will vary from Member State to Member State. Yet across the Community individuals are supposed to be granted the same Community rights, which ought to be available with the same ease. Litigants from a Member State with a long-standing tradition of public interest litigation might regard limitations on the *locus standi* of associations in another Member State where they might happen to have to pursue their claim, as making it excessively difficult for them to pursue the exercise of what remains the same Community right. The difficult question for the Community is how to ensure that judicial protection of the same Community right is consistent throughout the Community and does not vary from Member State to Member State, thereby altering the substance of that right.

Uncertainties remain with regard to the *right* level of protection. The ECJ has recognised that the *choice* of an *appropriate remedy*[25] or *sanction*[26] falls to the national courts. But often the chosen remedy is challenged as failing to attain the right level of protection. Does Community law require the granting of a specific relief; for example, could a party insist on specific performance, where compensatory damages would be available?[27]

Another dimension to this question concerns situations where Community law arises as a public law issue.[28] In such cases, no identifiable economic loss either exists or no loss is suffered by the parties bringing the action. Where recompense is not available, or is irrelevant, does 'effectiveness' require that domestic courts exer-

---

25. Case 34/67 *Firma Gebrüder Lück v Hauptzollamt Köln Rheinau* [1968] ECR 359.
26. Case 50/76 *Amsterdam Bulb Bv v Produktschap voor Siergewassen* [1977] ECR 137.
27. Compare *Co-operative Insurance Society Ltd v Argyll Stores (Holdings) Ltd* [1997] 2 WLR 898; *Retail Parks Investments Ltd v The Royal Bank of Scotland plc* 1996 SLT 669.
28. *Equal Opportunities Commission v Secretary of State for Employment (the EOC case)* [1994] 2 WLR 409; *R v Secretary of State for the Environment, ex parte Royal Society for the protection of Birds* (1995) 7 Admin LR 434.

cise the power to compel action in accordance with Community law? In such circumstances, a power vested in national courts to make an order to amend the legislation might be the most appropriate remedy,[29] yet it is not always clear-cut whether and in which circumstances Community law requires it.

Certainly, many cases[30] indicate that the jurisdiction of a national court, when deployed for the purpose of enforcing Community law, must be exercised in a specific way.[31] In *Simmenthal*[32] one of the issues was whether an ordinary Italian court could ignore that the Constitutional Court alone has jurisdiction to set aside national legislation. Protection of Community rights must be immediate and not dependent on the Italian Constitutional court ruling. Accordingly, the allocation of jurisdiction had to be set aside by an inferior court. *Simmenthal* did not merely contain a restatement of primacy: national rules contrary to Community law must necessarily be disapplied. Beyond issues of substantive incompatibility between national law and Community law, *Simmenthal* concerned the right to a specific remedy, as a remedy was available, albeit not an immediate one, and not from the court hearing the case. *Simmenthal* charges national courts with the duty to give immediate full force and effect to Community rights even if it is beyond their jurisdiction as a matter of national law to do so. In *Factortame*,[33] the ECJ merely followed these principles when it had to consider a gap in the availability of administrative law remedies which affected protection of Community-law based claims.

More on effectiveness

Effectiveness, a rather ambiguous notion, does not lend itself easily to objective assessment. It can either be measured from the individ-

---

29. In the *EOC* case, the House of Lords expressly recognised that an association acting in the public interest may seek a declaration that a particular Act of Parliament is in breach of Community law, but did not make an order compelling Parliament to amend it.

30. S. Prechal, 'EC requirements for an effective remedy' in J. Lonbay and A. Biondi (eds), *Remedies for Breach of EC Law* (Wiley, 1997), p. 7; Boch and Lane, 'European Community Law in National Courts' (1992) 5 LJIL p. 173.

31. Case C-177/88 *Dekker v Stichting Vormingscentrum voor Jong Volwassenen Plus* [1990] ECR I-3941.

32. Case 106/77, [1978] ECR 629.

33. Case C-213/89 *R v Secretary of State for Transport, ex parte Factortame Ltd (No 2)* [1990] ECR I-2433.

ual litigant's perspective or from a public interest perspective, *i.e.* ensuring that a public interest behind a particular rule is upheld by securing enforcement of the rule.

As more specific questions have been referred by national courts, the ECJ had to become more precise in confirming the duties of national courts. Thus, with regard to sanctions[34] it held:

> Whilst the choice of penalties remains within the Member States' discretion, they must ensure in particular that infringements of Community law are penalised under conditions, both procedural and substantive, which are *analogous* to those applicable to *infringements of national law* of a *similar nature* and *importance*, and which, in any event, make the *penalty effective, proportionate* and *dissuasive.*[35]

The notion of 'effectiveness of legal control at a distance' has been the subject of some academic debate.[36] If the doctrine of primacy is relatively well known, the obligation of loyalty derived from Article 10 EC remains rather vague and at any rate is an obligation of result rather than method. The criteria laid down by the ECJ[37] still lack specificity. Many questions remain unanswered, such as to the existence of any imperative requirement for the use of particular means of enforcement in a juridical sense, *e.g.* criminal as opposed to administrative proceedings, or such as what must be taken into account when granting an effective remedy. Does effectiveness depend on the context of enforcement, or on the nature of the rule or principle infringed? Should the gravity of the infringement, or that of the damage caused, or both, be taken into account? Should the need to guarantee future respect of the rule be considered? To what extent is the current discretion to choose any particular sanction limited?

Some of these issues were addressed in *Hansen*[38] where criminal proceedings were initiated against a driver's employer, on the

---

34. Case 68/88 *Commission v Greece* [1989] ECR 2965, paras 23–4, and Case C-7/90 *Vandevenne* [1991] ECR I-4371, para. 11.
35. Case C-326/88 *Anklagemyndigheden v Hansen* [1990] ECR I-2911, para 17 (emphasis added).
36. C. Harding, 'Member State Enforcement of European Community Measures: The Chimera of Effective Enforcement' in (1997) 4 MJECL pp. 5–24; S. Prechal in Lonbay and Biondi (eds) *op. cit.*; Curtin and Mortelmans in Curtin and Heukels (eds), *The Institutional Dynamics of European Integration* (Kluwer, 1994).
37. See *supra*.   38. *Op. cit.*, fn 35.

ground that his driver had infringed certain provisions of the tachograph regulation. The use of a particular penalty – a system of criminal liability under which the employer of the offending driver was liable to a fine without proof of any intentional act or negligence on the part of that employer – was challenged as contrary to Community law. The ECJ noted[39] that the introduction of strict criminal liability corresponded to the system generally applicable in Denmark for the protection of the working environment, and was therefore in conformity with the assimilation principle. The Court then remarked that such sanction may prompt the employer to organise the work of his employee in such a way as to ensure compliance with the regulation, thereby satisfying the effectiveness test. The choice of such a sanction was justified by the fact that road safety, one objective of the regulation, was a public interest matter. Finally, the sanction was found to satisfy the proportionality test – proportionality measured in relation to the objective pursued; the proportionality of the amount of the fine was not challenged in this case.[40]

The need to take account of the particular context of enforcement, of the rule breached and interests violated was also considered by the Advocate General in the case:

> The promotion of road safety and the improvement of working conditions of employees and environmental protection are interests of a general nature, in the sense that infringement of the rule is not necessarily detrimental to specific individuals – which in fact greatly reduces the risk of prosecution and punishment but instead can be economically advantageous to the employer. In those circumstances, a Member State's interest in protecting such interests (values) by recourse to criminal law – without any recourse to fault or culpability – can take precedence over the right of employees or undertakings as a matter of principle to be penalised only in respect of facts which can be imputed to them personally.[41']

Assessing proportionality and dissuasion

Proportionality can simply be assessed having regard to alternative methods of enforcement; a less invasive method, if it exists, must

---

[39]. Paras 18 and 19.   [40]. See further Chapter 10 for challenge of level of fines.
[41]. Van Gerven AG's Opinion, para. 15.

be preferred. Proportionality may also require employing a level of resources and exercising of powers appropriate to the nature of the interest to be protected. The nature of the interest to be protected determines the appropriate level of resources to be allocated and/or the exercise of a particular power. If proportionality must be defined by reference to the nature of the interest to be protected, this involves careful consideration of the nature of the interest to be protected. If assessing proportionality does not simply require analysing whether or not other methods are available, then any determination of a proportionate response presupposes a ranking of both method and sanction in relation to the nature of the interest to be guaranteed. Such ranking is a matter of policy and moral evaluation greatly influenced by national perceptions, and likely to remain so, if any of the calls for subsidiarity are meant to deliver anything. How does the interest in fisheries conservation compare with that of health and safety of workers within a single Member State, and then from Member State to Member State? In the same way, the ambivalence between the desire to reduce costs of transport operators, ensure road safety and maintain good air quality is unlikely to call for the same response in the different Member States. Determination of a proportionate response is also determined by the costs issue. The nature of the interest at stake determines not just the power to be exercised, but the appropriate level of resources to be used. Again this calls for a ranking of interests and a balancing exercise between the nature of the interest to be enforced and what is regarded as the appropriate investment of resources. National courts are ill-equipped to make such decisions.

Striking the right balance

The ECJ has given further indications as to how national courts should approach the question of whether a national procedural provision prevents effective protection of a Community right:[42]

> The national procedural provision must be analysed by reference to the *role of that provision in the procedure; its progress* and its *special features,* viewed *as a whole,* before the various national

---

42. Joined Cases C-430/93 and 431/93 *Van Schijndel* [1995] ECR I-4705, para. 19 (emphasis added).

instances. In the light of that analysis, the basic principles of the domestic judicial system, such as *protection of the rights of the defence, legal certainty* and *proper conduct of the procedure*, must, where appropriate, be taken into consideration.

But one must bear in mind that national systems engage in such a balancing exercise all the time, and that such an exercise is, in the main, not altogether that far removed from the test proposed by the ECJ. Ultimately, therefore, national rules should remain untouched, even if it might lead to denial of Community-based claims. In addition, given the ECJ insistence on the need to assess national rules by reference to the national legal system as a whole, it is arguable that hardly any national rule could be changed because of the consequent domino effect for the entire legal system. A different reading of this case law has been proposed, according to which once it is established that the national provision hinders the application of Community law, the national court must examine whether the limitation at issue can be justified by some fundamental principles of the domestic legal system. The national court must balance the interests served by the national rules at issue and the effectiveness of Community law.[43]

Some specific remedies will now be discussed. The right to a specific remedy, *i.e.* State liability for breach of Community law will be studied separately.

Existence of a judicial remedy

The principle of effective judicial protection is included in a number of specific legislative provisions; however, it has become a general principle of Community law, a principle with far-ranging practical applications.

Community law confers rights, and the existence of a remedy of a judicial nature against any decision of a national authority refusing the benefit of that right is essential in order to secure for the individual effective protection of that right. Therefore an individual must be able to challenge in the courts the legality of a decision by a public body refusing to accept that he has a Community law right. The right to effective judicial protection, first enunciated in

---

43. S. Prechal (1998) 35 CMLRev 681.

Johnston,[44] encompasses a right to a judicial remedy, the possibility for the judge hearing the proceedings to seek from the competent authorities disclosure of the grounds on which the contested measures were based, and a duty on the judge to impose a sanction which has a real deterrent effect. In this way, Community law brought about basic minimum standards with regard to judicial review.

The principle of effective judicial protection, initially affirmed in relation to a directive was extended in *Heylens*[45] to the exercise of a fundamental Treaty freedom. Its scope is even wider, since it applies to any national decision taken in application of Community law or which is part of a Community procedure.[46] Its reach is further broadened by another aspect of the case law of the ECJ. The Court has shown a willingness readily to identify rights where mere legal interests are at stake,[47] 'whenever non-compliance with the measures required by the directives in question might endanger the health of persons, those concerned should be able to rely on mandatory rules in order to enforce their rights.'

The right to have decisions judicially reviewed has in practice also meant that the category of reviewable acts under national law has to be widened for the purpose of Community-law based claims. First, an 'ouster clause' excluding the jurisdiction of the courts had to be set aside, and a certificate issued by a national authority stating that the conditions for derogating from the principle of equal treatment – normally to be treated as conclusive evidence so as to exclude the exercise of any power of review by the courts[48] – had to be subject to judicial review. As the ECJ explained, while the principle of legality does not exclude consideration of the demands of public order, this concept cannot be used as justification to exclude all possibility of judicial review of government action. Secondly, preparatory acts which normally are not subject to judicial review may have to be reviewed.[49] In this way, the scope of the jurisdiction of administrative courts may, on occasion, be altered.

44. Case 222/84 *Johnston v Chief Constable of the RUC* [1986] ECR 1651.
45. Case 222/86 *UNECTEF v Heylens* [1987] ECR 4097, paras 14 and 15.
46. Case C-97/91 *Oleificio Borelli spa v Commission* [1992] ECR I-6313.
47. Case C-58/89 *Commission v Germany* [1991] ECR I-4983.
48. Case 222/84 *Johnston v Chief Constable of the RUC* [1986] ECR 1651, para. 21.
49. Case C-97/91 *Oleificio Borelli spa v Commission* [1992] ECR I-6313.

The right to effective judicial protection has also influenced the pre-litigation stage in so far as it requires that national administrations take a reasoned opinion, and national judges are empowered to ask public bodies to provide a proper statement of reasons. 'Any decision must be justiciable and its legality under Community law can be reviewed; and in any event, the person concerned must be given proper notice, in due time, of the grounds on which it is based'.[50] Effective judicial review must be able to cover the legality of the reasons for the contested decision. It therefore presupposes that the court to which the matter is referred may require the competent authority to notify its reasons.[51] Such a statement of reasons, in turn, enables the judge to exercise judicial control over the reasoning of the decision-maker. Hence, in the context of claims based on a breach of the principle of proportionality, the statement of reasons plays a central role.

Title and interest

The principle of effective judicial protection has also influenced national rules governing an individual's standing and legal interest in bringing proceedings. 'While it is, in principle, for national law to determine an individual's standing and legal interest in bringing proceedings, Community law nevertheless requires that the national legislation does not undermine the right to effective judicial protection'.[52]

In *Verholen*, an individual was allowed to rely on Directive 79/7 before a national court because he bore the effects of a discriminatory national provision regarding his spouse, who came within the scope of the Directive although she was not herself a party to the proceedings. The ECJ held that the right to rely on the provisions of Directive 79/7 was not confined to individuals coming within the scope *rationae personae* of the Directive; other persons may have a direct interest in ensuring that the principle of non-discrimination is respected, as regards persons who are protected.[53] So the category of persons concerned includes not only those who are directly protected by or named in a particular Community instrument, but also those who have an interest in the

[50] Case C-340/89 *Vlassopoulou* [1991] ECR I-2357.
[51] Case 222/86 *UNECTEF v Heylens* [1987] ECR 4097, para. 16.
[52] Case C-87/90 *A. Verholen e.a. v Sociale Verzekeringsbank* [1991] ECR I-3757.
[53] *Ibid.*, at para. 25.

application of the rule. The boundaries of this latter category, however, are vague.[54] The judgment therefore raises the question of who has an interest in securing compliance with Community obligations. This is an important issue for many Community instruments, either because their scope *rationae personae* cannot easily be deduced from the wording of their provisions, or because breach of them does not affect a particular interest. Thus, many environmental directives aim at protecting the environment as such, rather than being concerned with securing advantages to individual members of a given class. Identifying who might be recognised as having an interest in securing compliance with Community obligations raises other issues,[55] and Advocate General Capotorti has expressed himself strongly against such an *actio popularis* being allowed, pointing notably to the fact that too many people would have an interest in the Member States complying with their Community obligations.[56]

In the *Butter Buying Cruises* case,[57] an action was brought by traders against German customs authorities asking the German court to order proper application of Community law. The plaintiffs were requesting the court to order the customs authorities to comply with the Common Customs Tariffs, *i.e.* to discontinue the exemptions from customs duties – exemptions in breach of Community law – to other traders in competition with themselves, rather than claiming damages for the loss incurred by them as a result of these unlawful exemptions. The ECJ therefore had to consider whether Community law gave the right to a trader to request a national court to require the authorities of a Member State to observe Community law in a given situation in which that trader was not involved, but was economically adversely affected by the failure to observe Community law. The ECJ observed that if the economic interests of a person to whom Community law applies are adversely affected by the non-application of a Community provision to a third party – either through the action of a Member State or that of the Community authorities – that person may in-

---

54. Prechal, *Directives in European Community Law: A Study on EC Directives and their Enforcement by National Courts* (OUP, 1995), p. 167.
55. Micklitz: 'The interest in Public Interest Litigation' in Micklitz and Reich (eds), *Public Interest Litigation in European Courts*' (Baden-Baden: Nomos Verl. 1996).
56. Para. 6 of his Opinion in Case 158/80 *Rewe Handelsgesellschaft Nord v Hauptzollamt Kiel (Butter-Buying Cruises)* [1981] ECR 1805.
57. Case 158/80 *Op. cit.*; and see note by Usher (1981) 6 ELR 451.

stitute proceedings before national courts in order to compel national authorities to apply the provisions in question or to refrain from infringing them.[58] But the ECJ insisted on the fact that the remedy sought was in fact available under German law, so that it merely had to be extended to the Community-law based claim. Accordingly, an unconditional Community law right to a private action to compel public authorities to act to enforce the law does not seem to exist at present. The failure by a Member State to apply a particular provision of Community law to another person, can only be remedied by a private person through an action in the national courts under the conditions set by national law. So, a national rule which makes the right of an individual to compel public authorities to act to enforce the law conditional upon that individual's ability to show a special interest beyond that of the public at large, might not breach Community law. Lastly, the right to effective judicial protection may impact on the right of the parties to raise new issues at a late stage in proceedings. This point is closely connected with the extent to which national courts are permitted or obliged to raise new issues of their own motion and will be explored below.

Community law and national evidential rules

On occasion, the principle of effective judicial protection has shifted the onus of proof and has changed evidential requirements.

The ECJ has recognised that it is normally for the person alleging facts in support of a claim to adduce proof of such facts. However, the onus may shift. It may be necessary to avoid depriving workers who appear to be the victims of discrimination of any effective means of enforcing the principle of equal pay. Thus, where an undertaking applies a system of pay which is wholly lacking in transparency, it is for the employer to prove that its practice in terms of wages is not discriminatory.[59] Directive 76/207 precludes the application of provisions of national law which

---

58. Para. 40.
59. Case 109/88 *Danfoss* [1989] ECR 3199, paras 13 and 14; Case C-127/92 *Enderby* [1993] ECR I-5535, paras 13, 14 and 164; and now Directive 97/80 on the burden of proof in cases of discrimination based on sex (OJ 1998 L14/6).

make reparation of damage suffered as a result of sex discrimination, subject to the requirement of fault.[60] Whenever a national authority relies on a derogation to the rules on free movement, it is for that authority to adduce evidence to the effect that reliance on the derogation is justified. Hence, if a national administration may require an importer to submit all the information in his possession to enable it to adduce such evidence, it cannot make the authorisation to market vitamins subject to proof by the importer that these vitamins are not harmful to health.[61]

In matters of reimbursement of tax unduly paid, Member States may require proof that the burden of the tax has not been passed on to other persons. However, special limitations concerning the form of the evidence to be adduced, such as the exclusion of any kind of evidence other than documentary evidence, make the exercise of the Community right virtually impossible and will have to be set aside.[62]

Procedural rules

Rules on time limits

Apart from certain specific legislative provisions fixing time limits,[63] procedural autonomy is the norm. The ECJ has recognised that the interests of legal certainty require limitation periods for bringing proceedings, even though the expiry of such limitation periods entails by definition the rejection, wholly or in part, of the action brought.[64] Accordingly, the *length* of limitation period has never been questioned. So a time limit of 30 days has been held reasonable in relation to both Dutch tax law[65] and German administrative law.[66] The only limitations to the autonomy of the

60. Case C-180/95 *Draehmpaehl v Urania Immobilienservice OHG* [1997] ECR I-2195.
61. Case 174/82 *Sandoz* [1983] ECR 2445, para. 22.
62. Case 199/82 *Amministrazione delle Finanze dello Stato v San Giorgio* [1983] ECR 3595.
63. *E.g.* article 236(2) of Regulation 2913/92, OJ 1992 L302/1, or article 10(1), Directive 85/37 on the approximation of the laws, regulations and administrative provisions of the Member States concerning liability for defective products, OJ 1985 L210/29.
64. Case C-188/95 *Fantask and Others* [1997] ECR I-6783, para. 48.
65. Case 45/76 *Comet* [1976] ECR 2043.
66. Case 33/76 *Rewe-Zentralfinanz and Rewe-Zentral v Landwirschaftskammer für das Saarland* [1976] ECR 1989.

Member States concerns exceptional circumstances which will now be discussed.

First, the ECJ has denied a Member State the possibility to change a time limit in order to evade claims for repayment of national taxes levied in breach of Community law:

> A national legislature may not, subsequent to a judgment of the Court from which it follows that certain legislation is incompatible with the Treaty, adopt a procedural rule which specifically reduces the possibility of bringing proceedings for recovery of taxes which were wrongly levied under that legislation.[67]

Secondly, in *Emmot*,[68] the ECJ held that so long as a directive had not been properly implemented into national law, the period laid down in national law within which proceedings must be brought *cannot begin to run*. Indeed, individuals are unable to ascertain the full extent of their rights until such time as a directive has been properly transposed. In *Steenhorst-Neerings*[69] and *Johnson*,[70] the Court held that the *Emmott* ruling was to be regarded 'as confined to the particular circumstances of that case, in which a time-bar had the result of depriving the applicant of *any* opportunity whatever to rely on her right to equal treatment under the directive.'

In sum, a time limit on bringing a claim is contrary to Community law if it makes it impossible to assert a Community right. So limitation periods under national law regarding initiation of proceedings cannot begin to run until such time as a directive has been properly transposed. In other words, national rules on time limit governing the *access to a remedy* cannot start running before the right for which the remedy is sought is available in the legal system. However, Community law does not preclude the application of a generally applicable rule limiting claims in arrears.

Thirdly, when the Court gives a ruling under Article 234 as to the interpretation and scope of Community law, the Court's judgment governs all national measures and individual transactions subject to that rule, whether taking place before or after the date of the judgment. Exceptionally, the ECJ may limit the temporal effect of its ruling so that it should only apply for the future. Such restrictions may be allowed only in the judgment ruling upon the

---

67. Case 240/87 *Deville* [1988] ECR 3513.
68. Case C-208/90 *Emmot v Minister of Social Welfare* [1991] ECR I-4269.
69. Case C-338/91 *Steenhorst-Neerings* [1993] ECR I-5475.
70. Case C-410/92 *E.R. Johnson II* [1994] ECR I-5438.

interpretation sought. Therefore, a legislative provision which limited reimbursement of supplementary enrolment fees solely to students who had brought an action for reimbursement prior to the delivery of the judgment from which it followed that these fees infringed Community law, cannot be applied by national courts.[71]

Interim measures

Without interim protection judicial protection of Community law may be inadequate or even illusory. In *Factortame*[72] the ECJ was, in substance, asked whether the English courts had, as a matter of Community law, a duty to grant interim injunctive relief against the Crown, when as a matter of English law they had no such power. Having reformulated the question, the Court repeated the wide-sweeping statement made in *Simmenthal*:[73]

> Any provision of a national legal system and any legislative, administrative or judicial practice which might impair the effectiveness of Community law by withholding from the national court having jurisdiction to apply such law the power to do everything necessary at the moment of its application to set aside national legislative provisions which might prevent, *even temporarily*, Community rules from having full force and effect are incompatible with those requirements.

Factortame established that a rule against granting an interim injunction against the Crown cannot prevent a national court granting a remedy to ensure the effective protection of a Community right. Further, although the ECJ took care to reformulate the questions referred, it is suggested that *Factortame* is authority for the proposition that a court or tribunal which has no jurisdiction at all to grant interim protection would have such a jurisdiction by virtue of Community law.[74] Finally, the criteria for determining whether to grant interim relief are not solely a matter of national law.[75]

---

71. Case 309/85 *Barra* [1988] ECR 355, para. 19.
72. Case C-221/89 *R v Secretary of State for Transport, ex parte Factortame* [1991] ECR I-3905.
73. Case 106/77 *Amministrazione delle Finanze dello Stato v Simmenthal* [1978] ECR 629.
74. See *contra* C. Lewis, *Remedies in Community Law* (Sweet & Maxwell, 1997) p. 72.
75. *Infra*, Chapter 9.

Recovery of sums unduly paid

One must distinguish between the situations where the State has levied sums in violation of Community law, and where the State has allocated sums in violation of Community law. The latter will be examined first by reference to recovery of aids illegally granted.

Whilst national courts have no power to decide on the compatibility of a State aid with Community law, they must enforce the procedural obligation to notify a State aid and they may be confronted with a claim by a trader wanting to prevent a national authority from granting a State aid in breach of the State aid rules to a competitor. In addition, national courts must provide assistance to recover unlawful State aids. On occasions, this requires setting aside rules of national administrative law on time limits, and legitimate expectations.

> Although the Community legal order cannot preclude national legislation which provides that the principle of legitimate expectations and legal certainty are to be observed with regard to recovery, it must be noted that, in view of the mandatory nature of the supervision of State aids by the Commission under Article 93 of the Treaty, undertakings to which aid has been granted may not, in principle, entertain a legitimate expectation that the aid is lawful unlesss it has been granted in compliance with the procedure laid down in that Article. A *diligent businessman* should normally be able to determine whether that procedure has been followed.[76]

Restitution of charges and duties levied by the public administration in breach of Community law

The following developments only concern charges which do not fall within the scope of the Community Customs Code.[77]

Whether and under which conditions individuals have a right to reimbursement of charges levied in breach of Community law has given rise to an extensive body of case law.[78] The right to obtain a

---

76. Case C-24/95 *Land Rheinland Pfalz v Alcan Deutschland* [1997] ECR I-1591, para. 25 (emphasis added).
77. Regulation 2913/92, OJ 1992 L 302/1. See further Chapter 11.
78. *Inter alia*, Case 33/76 *Rewe-Zentralfinanz and Rewe-Zentral v Landwirtschafts-kammer für das Saarland* [1976] ECR 1989; Case 68/79 *Hans Just I/Sl v Danish Ministry for Fiscal Affairs* [1980] ECR 501; Case 61/79 *Amministrazione delle Finanze dello Stato v Denkavit Italiana* [1980] ECR 1205; Case 199/82 *San*

refund of amounts charged by a Member State in breach of Community law is the consequence and complement of the rights conferred on individuals by the Community provisions as interpreted by the ECJ. Still, such a refund has to be sought in the framework of the substantive and procedural conditions laid down by the various relevant national laws,[79] subject to the equivalence and effectiveness tests. The main obstacle in the way of recovery of sums unduly paid stems from the possibility of Member States taking into account the fact that such charges had been incorporated into the price of goods. Provisions which prevent the reimbursement of taxes, charges and duties levied in breach of Community law are not contrary to Community law where it is established that the person required to pay those charges has in fact passed them on to other persons. The ECJ has recognised that Member States are entitled to refuse repayment when it would result in the unjust enrichment of the recipients, but has laid down strict limits. A Member State may resist repayment to the trader of a charge levied in breach of Community law *only* where it is established that the charge has been borne *in its entirety* by another person and that reimbursement of the trader would constitute unjust enrichment. Where the burden of the charge has been passed on only in part, the trader must be reimbursed the amount not passed on. Even where traders have a legal obligation to incorporate the charge in the cost price, and even where failure to comply with that obligation carries a penalty, this legal obligation does not entail a presumption that the entire charge has been passed on. Finally, the ECJ indicated that even where the charge has been passed on to another person, traders should be able to claim that the illegal levying of the charge has caused them damage. As the ECJ noted, such damage could be caused by, *inter alia*, the fact that the unlawful charge by increasing the price of the imported goods has reduced sales and thus profits. So traders may not be prevented from applying to the competent national courts for rep-

---

Giorgio v Amministrazione delle Finanze dello Stato [1983] ECR 3595; Case 177/78 Pigs & Bacon Commission v McCarren & Co. Ltd [1979] ECR 2161; Case 378/85 Bianco and Girard v Directeur Général des Douanes et Droits Indirects [1988] ECR 1099; Case C-62/93 BP v Supergas [1995] ECR I-1883. For a summary of the case law in the area see Joined cases C-192/95 to C-218/95 Société Comateb v Directeur Général des Douanes et Droits Indirects [1997] ECR I-165.

79. For time limits, see above.

aration of the loss caused by the levying of illegal charges irrespective of whether those charges have been passed on.[80] Such an action would be subject to the conditions laid down by the ECJ in its case law on State liability for breach of Community law.[81]

Whether it follows from the case law that a client would be better advised to bring an action for damages rather than an action for reimbursement of charges unduly paid is still unclear.

Finally, given that the illegality of a charge under Community law is a defence to an action for unpaid charge,[82] the best course of action might be to resist payment of the charge.

Raising Community law points *ex proprio motu*

For Community law to be applied, it must be invoked. But in adversarial systems where the ambit of the dispute is defined by the parties, who may knowingly or in ignorance not have raised a Community law point, the application of Community law is jeopardised. To what extent can a national/Community judge, raise a Community law point of his own motion? To what extent can Community law be regarded as a public policy issue – *moyen d'ordre public* – which the judge should raise *ex officio*? Further, which Community law rules are public policy matters? Some of these issues have been addressed by the ECJ.

The question was first raised in *Rheinmühlen*.[83] In *Verholen*,[84] the ECJ held that Community law does not preclude a national court from examining of its own motion whether national rules are in conformity with the precise and unconditional provisions of a directive where the individual had not relied on the directive before it. In *Peterbroeck*[85] the ECJ held that 'Community law precludes the application of a domestic procedural rule whose effect, is to prevent a national court from considering of its own motion whether a measure of domestic law is compatible with a

---

80. C-192/95 to C-218/95 *Société Comateb v Directeur Général des Douanes et Droits Indirects* [1997] ECR I-165.
81. See Chapter 7.
82. Case 222/82 *Apple and Pear Development Council v K.J. Lewis Ltd and others* [1983] ECR 4083, para. 39.
83. Cases 146 and 166/73 *Rheinmühlen* [1974] ECR 33, para. 3.
84. Case C-87/90 *Verholen* [1991] ECR I-3757.
85. C-312/93 *Peterbroeck van Campenhout 2 Cie CSC v Belgium* [1995] ECR I-4599.

provision of Community law when the latter provision has not been invoked by the litigant within a certain period.' By contrast, in *Van Schijndel*[86] the ECJ held

> Community law *does not require* national courts to raise of their own motion an issue concerning the breach of provisions of Community law where examination of that issue would oblige them to abandon *the passive role assigned to them by going beyond the ambit of the dispute defined by the parties themselves* and relying on facts and circumstances other than those on which the party with an interest in application of those provisions bases his claim.

But if the rationale for judges raising Community law points is that Community rules are public policy matters, then why should the wishes of the parties be a relevant consideration?

In *Kraaijeveld*[87] the ECJ considered again whether a national court should of its own motion raise the question of whether the national authorities had exceeded their discretion under a directive. It confirmed that a national court has such a power, 'where under *national law* a court must or may raise of its own motion pleas in law based on *binding domestic rules* which have not been raised by the parties'.[88] In practice, 'given the age and background of the judges in the field of Community law, it is a subject which none of them, so to speak, grew up with academically, and therefore it is not particularly likely that at any rate the older judges would spot European problems that the parties had not spotted'.[89]

Miscellaneous influences

Community law has influenced the workings of national systems in other ways. National contract law can be affected by the requirements of Community law. Thus in *Haberman Beltermann*,[90] the application of national rules regarding misrepresentation and

---

86. C-430–431/93 *Van Schijndel* [1995] ECR I-4705 (emphasis added).
87. Case C-72/95 *Kraaijeveld BV and others v Gedeputeerde Staten van Zuid-Holland* [1996] ECR I-5403; and see C. Boch, 'The enforcement of the EIA Directive: A breach in the Dyke?' (1997) 9 JEL 129.
88. Para. 83.
89. Bingham, 'The National Judge's View' in Andenas (ed), *Article 177 References to the European Court, Policy and Practice* (Butterworths, 1994), p. 45.
90. Case C-421/92 [1994] ECR I-1657.

nullity of contracts was blocked by Directive 76/207. In *Dekker* general provisions governing civil liability were held to be affected in so far as the grounds of exemption provided under national law may not be invoked in certain circumstances.

> Although Directive 76/207 leaves the Member States, as regards sanctions for breach of the prohibition of discrimination, freedom to choose one of the various methods suitable for achieving this objective, it nevertheless requires that where a Member State chooses a sanction which forms part of the rules on civil liability, any breach of the prohibition of discrimination must in itself be sufficient to impose full liability without it being possible to take account of grounds of exemption provided for by national law.[91]

Marshall II[92] shows how the rules on compensation may be affected, as statutory limits on quantum of damages had to be set aside. Equally, the availability of interest appears no longer to be strictly a matter for national law. In *Marshall II* the ECJ held that:

> reparation of the loss and damage sustained by a person injured as a result of a discriminatory dismissal may not be limited by excluding an award of interest to compensate for the loss sustained by the recipient of the compensation as a result of the effluxion of time until the capital sum awarded is actually paid.

The ECJ might be called upon to adjudicate on the question of the rate of interest or the date from which it is to be paid. Whether the principles developed in *Marshall* in the context of a claim for compensation for breach of a Community right can be extended to claims for restitution is still undecided.

The next chapter discusses a Community remedy, State liability for breach of Community law, and its application by the UK courts.

---

91. Case C-177/88 *Dekker v Stichting Vormingscentrum voor Jong Volwassenen Plus* [1990] ECR I-3941.
92. Case C-271/91 *Marshall v Southampton and South West Area Health Authority (Marshall II)* [1993] ECR I-4367.

CHAPTER SEVEN

A right to a specific remedy: State liability for breach of Community law

I cannot but remind myself that it was the Member States which completely freely agreed the contractual rules underlying the system as a whole, and that the Member States are still the decisive protagonists in the process for the formulation of Community measures. Consequently to hold that liability exists for failure to fulfil obligations is tantamount simply to increasing the effectiveness of the system and does not involve any activity supplementing, let alone supplanting the legislature.[1]

A Member State's obligation to make reparation for the loss and damage so caused is subject to three conditions: the rule of law infringed must be intended to confer rights on individuals; the breach must be sufficiently serious; and there must be a direct causal link between the breach of the obligation resting on the State and the damage sustained by the injured parties . . . While the right to reparation is founded directly on Community law where the three conditions set out above are fulfilled, the national law on liability provides the framework within which the State must make reparation for the consequences of the loss and damage caused, provided always that the conditions laid down by national law relating to reparation of loss and damage must not be less favourable than those relating to similar domestic claims and must not be so framed as to make it virtually impossible or excessively difficult to obtain reparation.[2]

Community law requires a remedy in damages to be made available in the national courts to those parties who sustain loss as a

---

1. Tesauro AG's Opinion in Cases C-46/93 and 48/93 *Brasserie du Pêcheur SA v Germany*; and *R v Secretary of State for Transport, ex parte Factortame* [1996] ECR I-1029, hereafter *Brasserie du Pêcheur*, at para. 26.
2. Case C-66/95 *R v Secretary of State for Social Security, ex parte E. Sutton* [1997] ECR I-2163, paras 32–3.

result of breaches of Community rules by public authorities. This chapter will trace the evolution of this new remedy in the case law of the ECJ and examine its relationship with other national remedies. Further, it will analyse the existing case law and its application in the UK courts.[3]

The recognition of the principle of State liability

The question was first addressed in *Francovich*.[4] A 1980 directive[5] required Member States to create a guarantee fund designed to protect employees' wages in the event of their employers' insolvency. Italy failed to take any steps to implement the directive, a failure formally established in enforcement proceedings brought by the Commission.[6] Mr Francovich and Mrs Bonifaci were employed by firms, both of which had become insolvent. They brought proceedings in the Italian courts against the Italian State for payments in respect of unpaid salaries and wages or, in the alternative, damages. Their claims were based on the unimplemented directive. Both Italian courts referred questions to the ECJ. The Court held that the directive was clear and precise as to the beneficiary of the guarantee, but not clear and precise as to the identity of the person liable under the guarantee, and that the Italian State could not be regarded as the guarantee institution merely because it had failed timeously to implement the directive.[7] In other words, an interested individual could *not* rely upon the directive to ask a national court to effectuate directly a right to payment against the State. However, the Court went on to hold that the Italian State was liable to pay damages.

The Court recalled that it had long been settled through its own case law, dealing with the nature and effect of Community law, that national courts responsible for the application of provisions of Community law are under a duty, in cases within their jurisdiction, to ensure that those provisions are given full and effective protection. Such protection would be called into question if individuals had no opportunity to obtain compensation where their

---

3. For a useful web site on State liability see http://www.unimaas.nl/~egmilieu/dossier/francovi.htm.
4. Cases C-6 and 9/90 *Francovich and others v Italy* [1991] ECR I-5357.
5. Directive 80/987, OJ 1980 L283/23.
6. Case 22/87 *Commission v Italy* [1989] ECR 143.
7. *Francovich, op. cit.*, para. 26.

rights were infringed owing to a breach by a Member State of its Community obligations. Community law, therefore, imposed an obligation on Member States to recompense individuals for loss caused by such a breach. 'The principle . . . is inherent in the system of the Treaty'.[8] The Court also invoked Article 10, but made no reference to the general principles common to the laws of the Member States, thereby indicating that this new remedy was a consequence of the unique nature of Community law and a requirement of primacy.[9]

If Community law required a Member State to make good a loss incurred by individuals as a result of infringements of its Community obligations, the principle was not without qualifications. In *Francovich* the provisions of Community law infringed were contained in a directive. Hence it was held that 'the result laid down in the directive involves the *granting of rights for the benefit of individuals* and the *substance of those rights must be identifiable on the basis of the provisions of the directive.*'[10] *Francovich* was decided in a particular factual context: a total failure to transpose a directive, failure definitively established by the ECJ itself in a previous judgment. So Member States could be held liable for this type of infringement, yet many questions were not addressed because of this particular factual context. The Court was not called upon to establish whether a right in damages would lie also where transposition was incomplete, incorrect or belated. Nor did it have the opportunity to pronounce upon whether bad faith was an essential component of the violation. Given that the breach had been established previously by the ECJ in an Article 226 judgment, issues such as how and by whom should the breach be identified or constituted were not raised either. The difficult questions as to whether national courts themselves would also be competent to establish the existence of a breach, and following which criteria, were not addressed. At least one thing could be deduced from *Francovich* – that the principle was not limited to directives, but could be extended to infringement of any Community right for the benefit of individuals. *Francovich* inaugurated a series of decisions which have helped to clarify the different conditions under which Member States' actions can give rise to a right to reparation.

---

8. *Ibid.* para. 35.
9. See C. Haguenau, *L'Application effective du Droit Communautaire en Droit Interne* (Bruylant, 1995).
10. *Op. cit.*, para. 40.

What is the fuss about?

Francovich did not come as a complete surprise. The idea that the Community legislature itself ought to establish a system of liability on the part of the Member States for failure to comply with Community law was proposed by the ECJ as early as 1975 in suggestions submitted for the Tindemans Report.[11] There had also been some case law anticipating *Francovich*. The Court had indicated the *possibility* of national courts hearing such claims and that State liability would draw the full consequences of an Article 226 action.[12] Compliance by a Member State with its Community obligations after the date set in the reasoned opinion will not prevent a finding that the Member State was in breach of these obligations as the judgment 'may be of substantive interest as establishing the basis of a responsibility that a Member State can incur as a result of its default, as regards other Member States, the Community *or private parties*'.[13] There were further oblique references in *Russo*[14] to the effect that 'whenever damage has been caused through an infringement of Community law, the State is liable to the injured party of the consequences in the context of national law on the liability of the State.'

However, these cases alluded only to the *possibility* of such actions: *Francovich*, went a stage further and removed any ambiguity. The ECJ imposed a *duty* on the Member States to provide a remedy in damages and to make available a procedure by which individuals may claim damages in case of breach of Community law, where no such remedy and procedure was provided for under existing national rules. However, if, following *Francovich*, national courts, as organs of the State, are put under the obligation to provide a remedy in damages against the State, or even create it where it does not exist, for some national courts this new remedy simply means evolving further their own domestic law on public tort lia-

---

11. *Bull.* EC 9/75 p. 19.
12. See also Mischo AG's suggestion in *Francovich, op. cit.*, points 62–66 of his Opinion.
13. Case 39/72 *Commission v Italy* [1973] ECR 101 (emphasis added); Case 309/84 *Commission v Italy* [1986] ECR 599; Case 154/85 *Commission v Italy* [1987] ECR 2717; Case C-249/88 *Commission v Belgium* [1991] ECR-I 1275; for Article 86 ECSC Treaty see Case 6/60 *Humblet v Belgium* [1960] ECR 559.
14. Case 69/75 *Russo v Aima* [1976] ECR 45, para. 9; and see Case 6/60 *Humblet v Belgium* [1960] ECR 559; Cases 106 to 120/87 *Asteris* [1988] ECR 5515.

bility. Typically, the House of Lords, had already been dealing with this issue.[15]

Part of the doctrine saw *Francovich* as the logical product of the ECJ case law: 'seen from the perspective of the Community, one must inevitably wonder why it took more than 30 years for the Court to come to a conclusion which seems to be so inherent to the whole legal system'.[16] Others argued that *Francovich* continues to improve the protection afforded by the national legal systems,[17] and in this respect, *Francovich* involves no more difficulties for national courts than other requirements of the ECJ. The profound effect Community law has had on the exercise of judicial powers in the Member States, has been explored above.[18] Community law is generally accepted as the superior norm in the various national legal systems, even when such recognition entails assault on constitutional fundamentals. Moreover, following *Francovich*, the party ultimately made liable is the party actually responsible for the mismatch between Community law and national law, whereas in other instances[19] national courts have had to interpret national legislation in the light of Community law, thereby placing burdens on private parties who could not, on any view, be regarded as responsible for the failure to comply with Community obligations. So from the perspective of the debate relating to 'shifting the means of enforcement of Community law',[20] *Francovich* unquestionably introduces a fairness element.

It is tempting to argue that Member States have nothing to fear from the principle of State liability, provided they comply faithfully with the Community obligations they willingly undertook. Such a vision, however, overlooks the fact that not all Community obligations are regarded by the Member States as *willingly undertaken.*

15. N. Green and A. Barav, 'National Damages in the National Courts for Breach of Community Law' (1986) 6 YEL 55.
16. M. Waelbroeck, 'Treaty violations and liability of Member States and the EC: Convergence or Divergence' in D. Curtin and T. Heukels (eds), *The Institutional Dynamics of European Integration* (Kluwer, 1994), p. 468.
17. Tesauro AG, para. 32 in *Brasserie du Pêcheur, op. cit.* at fn 1. See also J. Coppel, 'Rights, Duties, and the end of *Marshall*' (1994) 57 MLR 859.
18. See Chapters 2 and 6.
19. E.g. Case C-32/93 *Webb v EMO Air Cargo Ltd* [1994] ECR I-3567.
20. J. Steiner, 'From direct effect to *Francovich*' (1993) 18 ELR 3.

Securing compliance with obligations willingly undertaken?

Member States are denied competence to decide on the actual competences they have transferred. The reasons for this are evident: if each Member State were to decide upon the competence issue according to its own criteria a Europe of 'banana republic à la carte'[21] will ensue. In the Community, the ECJ alone has competence authoritatively to state not only the effect, but also the scope of Community law. By accepting the jurisdiction of the ECJ, the Member States (should) have accepted that the ECJ alone would have competence to categorise the Treaty, and competence to ascertain the nature and extent of Community obligations.

Still, these fundamentals are now contested by some national supreme courts; and some national governments, as the revived disputes regarding the exercise of Community powers illustrate. National courts have recently reasserted their willingness to determine what is permissible interpretation and what is unacceptable amendment.[22] Supreme courts in particular insist they have retained jurisdiction to examine the exercise of Community powers to ensure that the Community has not exceeded the limits of the competence granted under the Treaties, in accordance with the various national constitutional requirements.[23] The White Paper on *Partnership of Nations*, whilst restating the UK Government's commitment to a strong and independent Court without which it would be impossible to ensure even application of Community law, proposed to revise the Treaty so as to give the Council the power to curtail what is perceived as an expansionist approach to competence.

In a number of situations, Member States are faced with an increasing number of substantive Community obligations the scope of which has been judicially widened. The true extent of Community obligations is sometimes difficult to embrace, as their

---

21. N. Reich, 'Judge-made "Europe à la carte": Some Remarks on Recent Conflicts between European and German Constitutional law provoked by the Bananas Litigation' (1996) 7 EJIL p. 111.
22. *Brunner v The European Union Treaty (Maastricht-Urteil)* [1994] 1 CMLR 57, paras 49, 55 and 99; also Case 92/308 DC 9 April 1992, [1993] 3 CMLR 345; S. Weatherill, *Law and Integration in the European Union* (OUP, 1995).
23. Boch, 'Home Thoughts from Abroad' in *In Search of New Constitutions*, Hume Papers on Public Policy (EUP, 1994) pp. 28–52.

substance is defined and refined as the process of integration unfolds.[24] A number of non-compliance situations can be traced back to breaches of Community obligations *in the making of which the Member States have not participated*:

> In treating the substantive obligations contained in the Treaty, the Court has frequently been motivated by a particular vision of the evolution of the Common Market, the purity of which, although perhaps traceable to the Treaty, has not been shared by the Member States years later. Thus the Member States have found themselves faced with an increasing number of substantive Treaty obligations whose scope has been judicially widened by interpretatively assigning them direct effect: derogation measures by contrast have been subjected to a very restrictive interpretation. . . . Member States' understanding of the nature of the obligations imposed by the Treaty may have been different from the *constantly evolving conceptions of the Court*.[25]

Community legislation is not always consensual either, in fact it is less and less consensual. This results from a combination of the extension of qualified majority voting, and package-dealing. In sum, not every Community obligation can be regarded as willingly undertaken. Accordingly, violations of Community law should not all be treated in the same way – 'non-compliance is not a phenomenon which always arises out of bad faith and can be tackled in every circumstances by judicial action'.[26] The different Community obligations should not be subject to the same standard of Community discipline. State liability might revive the debate on the competence issues, as Member States may be tempted to argue that the obligations allegedly breached are considered as falling outside the Community sphere of competence.

Clarifying or extending the principle?

Whereas *Francovich* established the principle that individuals were entitled to claim damages against the State, a lot of uncertainty re-

---

24. See Chapter 4.
25. See Weiler, 'The White Paper and the Application of Community Law' in Bieber and others (eds) *1992: One European Market?* (Nomos, 1988) p. 347.
26. P.P. Craig, '*Francovich*, Remedies and the Scope of Damages Liability' (1993) 109 LQR 595.

mained in relation to the exact scope of this principle of State liability. German and British courts referred questions concerning the conditions under which Member States may incur liability for damage caused to individuals by breaches of Community law attributable to the legislature. In *Brasserie du Pêcheur*,[27] an action was brought by a company, Brasserie du Pêcheur, against Germany for reparation of the loss suffered as a result of import restrictions faced by Brasserie du Pêcheur *between 1981 and 1987*. The breach of Community law in that case was attributable to the legislature, which had failed to adapt national law to Article 28 of the Treaty. The illegality of the prohibition on marketing beers imported from other Member States which did not comply with the Rheinheitsgebot, and that on the prohibition of additives, was made clear on 12 March 1987.[28]

In *Factortame*, a claim for damages had been made by individuals and companies covering expenses and losses incurred *between 1 April and 2 November 1989* – the period during which under the Merchant Shipping Act 1988 they were deprived of their fishing rights.[29] A claim was also made for exemplary damages for unconstitutional behaviour on the part of the public authorities.

In both cases, the national legislature was responsible for the infringement in question, the remedy sought was not readily available in the national legal system, and the relevant losses were all purely economic. The ECJ answered the questions raised in the two separate sets of proceedings in a single judgment.[30]

Constitutional objections

Francovich did not come as a complete surprise, nor did it create a revolution for each and every national court, but it was not welcomed with open arms. A number of constitutional objections were raised. The UK Government observed that no basis existed in Community law for the proposition that an individual has the

---

27. *Op. cit.* at fn 1.
28. Case 178/84 *Commission v Germany (Reinheitsgebot)* [1987] ECR 1227.
29. Although the provisions of the Merchant Shipping Act were only declared incompatible with Community law in Case C-221/89 [1991] ECR I-3905 on 25 July 1991, they were amended earlier following the Order of the Court to suspend the application of the statute after the Commission's application for interim measures requiring such suspension.
30. C-46 and 48/93, see fn 1.

right to obtain damages in the domestic court from a Member State for losses sustained as a result of failure to comply with Community obligations. It further contended that the case law of the Court showed that the Treaty was not intended to create new remedies in the national courts to ensure observance of Community law.[31] All of these objections, were raised again in *Factortame III*,[32] but were dismissed by the ECJ relying on the need to answer the questions referred to it by national courts.[33]

> Since the *Treaty* contains *no provision* expressly and specifically governing the consequences of breaches of Community law by Member States, it is for the Court, in pursuance of the task conferred on it by Article 164 of the Treaty, to ensure that in the *interpretation* and *application* of the *Treaty* the law is observed, to rule on such a question in accordance with generally accepted methods of interpretation, in particular by reference to the fundamental principles of the Community legal system and where necessary general principles common to the legal systems of the Member States.[34]

So, the existence and extent of State liability for damage arising from violations of Community law are questions of Treaty interpretation which fall within the jurisdiction of the ECJ.

The other (German) constitutional objection, according to which no compensation is available for a breach attributable to the legislature, was also dismissed. The ECJ relied on its traditional[35] approach – consistent with well-established public international law principles – which refuses to distinguish between the different organs of the State. It held:

---

31. *Francovich op. cit.*, at p. 5368, quoting Case 158/80 *Rewe v Hauptzollamt Kiel* [1981] ECR 1805.
32. Where the German Government argued that a general right to reparation for individuals could only be created by legislation.
33. As in Case 26/62 *Van Gend en Loos v Nederlandse Administratie der Belastingen* [1963] ECR 1, Article 234 EC provides the legal basis to justify and legitimise the European Court's intervention.
34. Para. 27 (emphasis added).
35. An approach consistently applied in relation to Article 226 EC, that a Member State may not plead provisions, practices or circumstances existing in its internal legal system in order to justify a failure to comply with its Community obligations. The overall responsibility of each State for any failure to comply with Community law has always precluded the argument that the breach was brought about by another organ or institution of the State which is independent of the government.

The obligation to make good damage caused to individuals by breaches of Community law *cannot be dependent on domestic rules* as to the division of powers between constitutional authorities[36] . . . , all State authorities are bound in performing their tasks to comply with the rules laid down by Community law directly governing the situation of individuals.[37]

The question whether liability could be incurred in relation to the legislative activity may have been asked because the referring national courts sought legitimacy before granting the remedy sought. Indeed, *Francovich* had already established a principle of State liability for acts of the legislature, in that case not a positive act, but an omission by the legislature.[38] In addition, national – and in particular German – courts are aware that the Court has consistently regarded *all State authorities as bound* by Community obligations. No defence based on national constitutional difficulties,[39] no national interests exceptions have ever been accepted by the ECJ.[40] Finally, even if the legislature is a vital part of the system of government, it is simply an organ of the State. Classification of the powers of an organ as 'legislative' or otherwise is merely a matter of internal organisation and local custom. The real difficulty specific to liability for acts of the legislature is to determine *when* the breach of duty entails an actionable wrong.

The legal basis

The basis for State liability are the principles, inherent in the Community legal order,[41] of the full effectiveness of Community rules, the effective protection of the rights which they confer[42] and the obligation to co-operate imposed on the Member States by Article 10 which, from *Humblet*[43] onwards, included the obligation, for national courts, to nullify the unlawful consequences of a breach of Community law. In *Brasserie du Pêcheur* reference was further made to the general principles common to the legal systems of the Member States.

---

[36]. Para. 33.   [37]. Para. 34.

[38]. The Community institutions' omission to legislate falls within the concept of 'legislative activity': Case 14/78 *Denkavit* [1978] ECR 2497.

[39]. Case 77/69 *Commission v Belgium* [1970] ECR 237.

[40]. *E.g.* Case 128/78 *Commission v United Kingdom* [1979] ECR 419.

[41]. *Brasserie du Pêcheur*, para. 39.

[42]. *Brasserie du Pêcheur*, para 52.

[43]. Case 6/60 *Humblet v Belgium* [1960] ECR 559.

State liability and other available remedies

The relationship between this new remedy and existing ones was another issue the Court was asked to clarify. It held that the principle of State liability also applied to breaches of Community provisions which are directly effective.[44]

> The rights of individuals to rely on the directly effective provisions of the Treaty before national courts is only a minimum guarantee and is not sufficient in itself to ensure the full and complete implementation of the Treaty[45] . . . The purpose of that right is to ensure that provisions of Community law prevail over national provisions. It cannot in every case secure for individuals the benefit of the rights conferred on them by Community law and in particular, avoid their sustaining damage. The full effectiveness of Community law would be impaired if individuals were unable to obtain redress when their rights were infringed by a breach of Community law . . . the right to reparation is the necessary corollary of the direct effect of the Community provision whose breach caused the damage sustained.[46]

In this way, the ECJ confirmed that direct effect can be regarded simply as one of the mechanisms available to ensure the effective operation of Community rules and the effective protection of individual's Community rights.

From a practical perspective this raises the question as to whether individuals would be best advised to pursue an action for damages against the State for breach of Community law in preference to an alternative remedy available under national law. As was seen earlier,[47] national rules of procedure can limit the protection of Community rights. For example, where traders seek reimbursement of sums levied in breach of Community law, they may need to adduce evidence that the burden of the charge illegally levied has not been passed on to another person;[48] an action for payment of benefits due retrospectively under Community law, but denied under defective

---

44. Although there had been no doubt in many writers' minds; see, *e.g.* J Steiner, p. 218 *op. cit.* at fn 20, for whom the breakthrough in *Francovich* lay not so much in the fact that individuals were entitled to claim damages against the State, but that their claim to compensation was independent of the principle of direct effect.
45. *Humblet, op. cit.*, para. 20.   46. *Op. cit.*, para. 22.   47. Chapter 6.
48. C-192/95 to C-218/95 *Société Comateb v Directeur Général des Douanes et Droits Indirects* [1997] ECR I-165.

national legislation, is barred by a national rule restricting the retroactive effect of a claim for benefit. Can individuals be advised that an action for damages against the State should be sought in preference to any other remedy? Such advice may be given only if there is evidence that the limits which can be placed by national law on such an action for damages are less restrictive than the limits which can be placed by national law on other remedies.

This issue was considered in *Sutton*[49] in relation to amounts due by way of social security benefits – interest on arrears of a social security benefit. Under English law, no interest is payable on arrears of social security benefits in respect of a period prior to the decision of the competent body in favour of the claimant. In this case, the ECJ held that neither Article 6 of Directive 79/7 nor Directive 76/207 required that an individual be able to obtain interest on arrears of a social security benefit such as invalid care allowance, even when the delay in payment of the benefit was the result of prohibited discrimination,[50] since payment of interest on arrears of benefits cannot be regarded as compensatory in nature. But the ECJ went on to consider whether the right to payment of interest on arrears of social security benefits flows from the principle of State liability for breach of Community law.

State liability has been referred to as an alternative remedy, yet whether it constitutes a more desirable option remains unclear, given that national law may impose limits on its exercise. If Community law itself imposes a principle of State liability, this remedy has to be applied, nationally. Accordingly, the significance of this remedy,[51] is, in practice, dependent on national courts: mitigation of loss, causation, limitation periods, etc. will be assessed in accordance with domestic rules, and the ECJ will be called upon to elaborate further on what is or is not an acceptable national limitation. Ultimately the lack of uniformity resulting from reliance on divergent national law should prompt the adoption of common rules in this area, a neat illustration of the tension between the need for effective and uniform protection of Community rights and respect of national diversity.[52]

---

49. Case C-66/95 *R v Secretary of State for Social Security, ex parte E. Sutton* [1997] ECR I-2163.
50. *Op. cit.,* para. 27.
51. So far C. Harlow's prediction of 'an illusion of remedy' in '*Francovich* and the Problem of the Disobedient State' (1996) 2 ELJ 199 at 222 seems accurate, and certainly was for Andrea Francovich.
52. See further Chapter 11.

Conditions

The claim for reparation is founded on Community law. Accordingly, it falls to national courts to verify whether or not the Community conditions governing State liability for a breach of Community law are fulfilled. However, the claim in reparation must be pursued in accordance with national rules and procedures, provided that these satisfy the principles of non-discrimination;[53] and effectiveness.[54]

There are three Community conditions: (i) the rule of law infringed must have been intended to confer rights on individuals, (ii) the breach must be sufficiently serious, and (iii) there must be a direct causal link between the breach of the obligation resting on the State and the damage sustained by the injured parties.

Individual rights

In *Brasserie du Pêcheur*, the ECJ held that this condition was 'manifestly satisfied' in the case of Article 28 and Article 43 EC, implying that directly effective provisions of Community law grant correlative rights to individuals. However, *Francovich* establishes that provisions which do not have direct effect may yet be capable of granting rights to individuals. This confirms that direct effect has ceased to be a determinant of the existence of individual rights to become a method of enforcement of Community rights.[55] Still this condition seems to be most problematic, as it is dependent on the approach to the concept of individual rights.[56] Not all Community obligations undertaken by the Member States involve the creation of individual rights, unless the view is taken that Community law grants individuals a right to secure Member States' compliance with each and every Community obligation – such a view could find support in the fact that the legal basis for State liability is Article 10 EC.

In the UK on at least two occasions the courts found that this

---

53. Thus, exemplary damages will have to be awarded only if awarded pursuant to a similar claim or action founded on domestic law (*Brasserie du Pêcheur*, para. 89).
54. *Brasserie du Pêcheur*, para. 84.
55. See Chapter 5, and also J. Coppel, 'Rights, Duties and the end of *Marshall*', (1994) 57 MLR 859.
56. See J. Jans, *European Environmental Law* (Kluwer, 1995) pp. 187–9.

condition was not met. In *Bowden*,[57] in respect of a claim based on EC law the judge found against the plaintiff because he was quite satisfied that none of the three environmental directives involved conferred on him any personal right. In *Three Rivers*,[58] damages were claimed against the Bank of England based on breach of a directive on banking supervision. It was held that although the directive did impose a supervisory duty on the regulator, it did not confer on individuals a right to effective supervision.

A sufficiently serious breach

In *Francovich*, the Court had affirmed that 'the conditions under which State liability give rise to a right to compensation depended on the *nature of the breach* of Community law giving rise to the harm'.[59] In *Brasserie du Pêcheur*, the ECJ affirmed the need for liability for legislative measures of the Member States and of the Community institutions to be assessed according to the same standard, since the protection of the rights which individuals derive from Community law cannot vary depending on whether a national authority or a Community authority is responsible for the damage.[60] Accordingly it held:

> Where Member States act in a field where there is a *wide discretion*, Community law confers a right to reparation where three conditions are met: the rule of law infringed must be *intended to confer rights on individuals*; the *breach* must be *sufficiently serious*; and there must be a direct *causal link* between the breach of the obligation resting on the State and the damage sustained by the injured parties.[61] [Emphasis added.]

The Court explained that the decisive test for finding that a breach of Community law is sufficiently serious is whether the Member States, just like the Community institutions, have *manifestly and gravely* disregarded the limits on their discretionary powers.[62] A breach of Community law which has *persisted* despite a judgment finding the infringement in question to be established, or a preliminary ruling or settled case law of the Court on the matter from

---

57. *Bowden v South West Water Services Ltd* [1998] 3 CMLR 330.
58. *Three Rivers DC v Bank of England* [1997] 3 CMLR 429. See also the Court of Appeal judgment (1998), *The Times*, 10 December, on appeal to the House of Lords.
59. *Francovich, op. cit.*, para. 48.   60. *Brasserie du Pêcheur*, para. 52.
61. *Ibid.*, para. 51.   62. *Ibid.*, para. 42.

which it is clear that the conduct in question constituted an infringement would constitute a sufficiently serious breach.[63]

The Court also elaborated on the factors which can be taken into account by national courts in assessing whether or not a breach would be a sufficiently serious one. These include *inter alia*, the *clarity* and *precision* of the rule breached, the measure of *discretion* left by that rule to the national or Community authorities; whether the infringement and the damage caused was *intentional or involuntary*, whether any *error of law* was excusable or inexcusable, the fact that the *Community institutions* may have *contributed* towards the omission or retention of national measures or practices contrary to Community law.[64] The Court held that these factors were similar to those developed when it constructed a system of rules with regard to Article 288 of the Treaty. In that context the ECJ took into account *inter alia* the *complexity* of the situations to be regulated, the *difficulties* in *interpretation* and *application* of the texts, and the *margin of discretion* available to the author of the act in question.[65]

All these considerations led to the rather strict approach taken towards the liability of the Community in the exercise of its legislative activities.[66] In the sectors coming within the economic policy of the Community, individuals have been required to accept, within reasonable limits, certain harmful effects on their economic interests as a result of a legislative measure without being able to obtain compensation from public funds, even where that measure had been declared null and void,[67] a restrictive approach the legitimacy of which derives from the fact that 'the exercise of the legislative function must not be hindered by the prospect of actions for damages whenever the general interest of the Community requires legislative measures to be adopted which may adversely affect individual interests'.[68]

These considerations echo those previously raised in the English courts:

> The undesirability, in areas in which choices of action depend on judgment, that Member States should be hindered in taking

63. *Ibid.*, para. 57.   64. Para. 56.   65. Para. 43.
66. Case 5/71 *Zuckerfabrik Schoeppenstedt v Council* [1971] ECR 975.
67. Joined Cases 83 and 94/76, 4, 15 and 40/77 *Bayereische HNL Vermehrungsbetriebe GmbH and others v Council and Commission* [1978] ECR 1209, para. 6.
68. *Brasserie du Pêcheur*, para. 45.

legislative action by the prospect of actions for damages if their judgment should ultimately be held to be wrong, unless the action taken constitutes a grave and manifest disregard of the limits on the exercise of its powers, *i.e.* is an abuse of such powers.[69]

In *Factortame* the ECJ case law on liability of the Community institutions was extensively considered by the Divisional court.[70]

The coherence of legal protection of individuals requires that the award of damages by a national court for breach of Community law by a Member State be subject to the same conditions as an award of damages by the ECJ for infringement of Community law by a Community institution. Certainly, such coherence would avoid situations where Member States may incur liability for breach of Community law by one of its authorities, in circumstances where the non-contractual liability of the Community would not arise. Further, it appears desirable, given that the Community liability regime is, by virtue of Article 288 EC, meant to flow from the general principles common to the laws of the Member States. Finally, such coherence appears necessary in the light of cases like *Asteris*[71] where the Court held that a judgment of the Court holding that the Community is not liable in damages in respect of the illegality of an act of its institutions 'precludes a national authority which merely implemented the Community legislative measure and was not responsible for its unlawfulness from being held liable on the same grounds.'

The ECJ's restrictive approach to breach, causation and loss[72] in relation to liability of the Community institutions has meant that few such claims have been successful, and it has been remarked that individual protection is not a central concern at Community level.[73] Unless coherence means a relaxation of the Community institutions regime, State liability will be incurred only exceptionally. This, in turn, begs the question how this new remedy could improve the effective protection of individuals' rights.

---

69. *Bourgoin* [1986] 1 CMLR 267.   70. [1997] 1 CMLR 971, paras 101–20.
71. Cases 106 to 120/87 *Asteris* [1988] ECR 5515, para. 18.
72. Steiner and Woods, 5th ed. (Blackstone, 1996) pp. 460–76.
73. Wathelet and Rapenbuch, 'La Responsabilité des Etats Membres en cas de violation du droit Communautaire: Vers un Alignement de la Responsabilité de l'Etat sur celle de la Communauté ou l'inverse?' (1997) *Cahiers de Droit Européen* 13.

The requirement of breach remains uncertain

In many areas, the Member States do not have a wide discretion when acting in fields governed by Community law, therefore these strict conditions need not apply. In such circumstances, a serious breach may be constituted even in the absence of a 'grave and manifest disregard for the limits of powers.'

In *Lomas*,[74] MAFF refused to grant export licences for live sheep destined for slaughter in Spain on the ground that treatment in Spanish slaughterhouses was contrary to Directive 74/577. This refusal was challenged as contrary to Article 29 EC, and a claim for damages was also made. On a reference from the High Court, the ECJ considered that the ban could not be justified under Article 30 EC. According to well-established case law, recourse to Article 30 EC is no longer possible where a directive provides for harmonisation measures. The ECJ refused to accept that this principle of pre-emption of a Member State's action in the presence of a Community measure could be affected by the fact that the Directive did not lay down any Community procedure for monitoring compliance with its provisions. Given the absence of any discretion, the mere infringement of Community law was sufficient to establish the existence of a sufficiently serious breach.

Implementing directives

In *Dillenkofer*[75] purchasers of package travel who never left for their destination or had to return from their destination at their own expense following the insolvency of tour operators, could not secure reimbursement of their holiday price or of the expenses incurred. They brought actions for compensation based on Article 7 of the Package Travel Directive,[76] arguing that because of the belated transposition of the Directive they were not protected against the insolvency of tour operators in accordance with the Directive. The ECJ found that failure to fully transpose a directive within the prescribed period qualifies as a serious breach of Community law. Within the prescribed period for implementation the national legislature had done no more than adopt the necessary legal framework

---

74. Case C-5/94 *R v MAFF, ex parte H. Lomas* [1996] ECR I- 2553.
75. Cases C-178/94, C-179/94, C-188/94, C-189/94 and C-190/94 [1996] ECR I-4845.
76. Council Directive 90/314, OJ 1990 L158/59.

for requiring organisers by law to provide sufficient evidence of security, when full implementation entailed the guarantee to purchasers of package travel of a refund of the moneys paid and for repatriation in the event of the tour operator's insolvency; having failed to transpose the Directive in time, the Member State thus incurred liability.

By contrast, in *BT*,[77] although Article 8(1) of Directive 90/531 on the procurement procedures of entities operating in the water, energy, transport and telecommunications sectors had been incorrectly transposed, the ECJ found that there had not been a sufficiently serious breach of Community law. It was for the contracting entities themselves, and not for the UK, to determine which telecommunications services were to be excluded from the scope of the Directive in implementation of Article 8(1). However, the provision was found to be imprecisely worded and the interpretation given to it in good faith by the Member State in question, albeit erroneous, was not manifestly contrary to the wording of the Directive or to the objective pursued by it. Accordingly the UK was not obliged to pay BT compensation for damage suffered by it as a result of the error thus committed.

The nature of the rule breached

Although no reference was made to it in *Brasserie du Pêcheur*, the nature of the rule infringed can play an important role in assessing the gravity of the breach. Thus, the Divisional Court in *Factortame* held that it was 'common ground that the prohibition of discrimination on grounds of nationality is one of the fundamental principles of the Treaty',[78] and the Court of Appeal also found that a direct breach of a fundamental principle such as non-discrimination on grounds of nationality 'will almost inevitably create a liability for damages'.[79]

A direct causal link

As the ECJ held in *Brasserie du Pêcheur*,[80] 'it is for the national courts to determine whether there is a direct causal link between

---

[77.] C-392/93 *R v HMT, ex parte BT* [1996] ECR I-1631.
[78.] [1998] 1 CMLR 1353.   [79.] [1998] 3 CMLR 192 at 215.
[80.] *Op. cit.*, at fn 1, para. 65.

the breach of the obligation borne by the State and the damage sustained by the injured parties.' National courts are entitled to use their national approach to causation, and causation can be used as a way of exonerating the Member States. In *Brasserie du Pêcheur*, the Bundesgerichtshof[81] relied on the distinction drawn by the ECJ between the maintenance in force of German legislation prohibiting the marketing under the designation 'Bier' of beers imported from other Member States, which was found to constitute a sufficiently serious breach, and the prohibition on the use of additives, which was not. It then found that the import restrictions had been imposed solely to deal with the prohibition on using unlawful additives, therefore the requirement of a direct causal connection between the infringing act and the damage was not satisfied as regards the breach of the Treaty relating to the use of the designation 'Bier'.

Gallagher[82] provides an illustration of the way in which the English courts approach causation. The case involved a claim for damages for wrongful exclusion resulting from an incorrect transposition of the requirements of Directive 64/221 by the Prevention of Terrorism (Temporary Provisions) Act 1989.[83] It was held that causation is an issue to be decided on the balance of probabilities. The plaintiff must show on the balance of probabilities that the injury for which he seeks compensation was caused by the unlawful conduct of which he complains. The Court of Appeal was satisfied that Mr Gallagher had established a breach of Community law, but found that he had failed to show that such breach probably caused him to be excluded from the UK when he would not otherwise have been excluded. So failure to implement a directive, a failure which deprives an individual of fundamental procedural safeguards, cannot give rise to an action for damages if, on the balance of probabilities, exclusion would have taken place irrespective of whether or not these procedural requirements had been complied with. State liability is of little use in relation to breaches of Community procedural obligations. However, such limits should stem from the fact that all too often violations of procedural obligations cannot give rise to an easily quantifiable damage, which is quite a different thing from saying that the requirements

81. [1997] 1 CMLR 971.
82. *R v Secretary of State for the Home Department, ex parte Gallagher* [1996] 2 CMLR 951.
83. Previously established by the ECJ in Case C-175/94, [1995] ECR 4253.

of causation are not met. The right to ensure that a procedure is adhered to is quite separate from the fact that deportation would have taken place irrespective of whether or not the proper procedure had been followed.

Extent of the reparation

Damages are governed by national law, and the ECJ made no reference to the case law developed under Articles 235 and 308 EC whereby losses are only recoverable if they are certain, specific, proven and quantifiable. Still, the award of damages is influenced by Community law in a number of ways. First, the assimilation and effectiveness principles apply.[84] Secondly, the Court held that compensation must be commensurate with the loss or damage sustained. Given that many Community rights are essentially economic rights, the loss or damage sustained is often going to be, by its nature, purely economic; therefore, any national rule 'not including loss of profit is not compatible with Community law'.[85] National rules governing the extent of reparation will have to be adapted so as to ensure that loss of profit is compensated.[86] The ways in which national rules governing the recovery of pure economic loss may require adaptation has been analysed.[87]

The award of exemplary damages

Such damages are based on domestic law. In *Brasserie du Pêcheur* the ECJ relied on the Divisional Court findings that the public authorities acted oppressively, arbitrarily or unconstitutionally, and held that:

> in so far as such conduct may constitute or aggravate a breach of Community law, an award of exemplary damages pursuant to a claim or an action founded on Community law cannot be ruled out if such damages could be awarded pursuant to a similar claim or action founded on domestic law.[88]

[84.] Cases C-46/93 and 48/93, *Brasserie du Pêcheur, op. cit.*, para. 67.
[85.] *Ibid.*, para. 90.   [86.] *Ibid.*, para. 87.
[87.] Van Gerven, 'Bridging the unbridgeable: Community and national tort laws' (1996) ICLQ 507 examines compensation for pure economic loss under the general rules on negligence in the Dutch, English, French and German systems.
[88.] *Op. cit.*, para. 89.

The High Court when applying this ruling did not award exemplary damages, as the assimilation principle did not require it. It held that it did not have to award punitive damages as it would not do so in a similar case under English law. In English law the correct nature of State liability for a breach of Community law is best understood as a breach of statutory duty. As regards breaches of statutory duty, the English law is that unless the statute expressly provides it, punitive damages cannot be awarded. It was further observed that:

> [f]or English law to give the remedy of penal damages for breaches of Community law would decrease the move towards uniformity, it would involve distinctions between the practice of national courts and the liabilities of different Member States and between the Community, the UK and the Community institutions, and would accordingly in itself be potentially discriminatory since litigants in England would be treated differently from those elsewhere. . . . it would risk introducing into the law of Community obligations, anomalies and conflicts which do not at present exist and would not serve a useful purpose.[89]

Mitigation

National courts may inquire whether the injured person showed reasonable care so as to avoid the loss or damage or to mitigate it.[90] A package traveller who has paid the whole travel price cannot be regarded as acting negligently simply because he has not taken advantage of the possibility of not paying more than 10 per cent of the total travel price before obtaining the travel documents.[91]

State liability for breach of Community law in the UK courts:[92] finding the right cause of action

Prior to *Francovich*, state liability in the UK had been influenced by: (i) the way in which Community law was introduced into the legal systems of the UK and (ii) the procedural differences between public and private law remedies.[93]

---

89. [1998] 1 CMLR 1353.   90. *Brasserie du Pêcheur*, para. 84.
91. *Dillenkoffer, op. cit.*, at fn 76, para. 73.
92. J. Convery, 'State Liability in the UK after *Brasserie du Pêcheur*' (1997) 34 CMLRev 603.
93. J. Usher, 'La sanction des Infractions au droit communautaire', FIDE (1992) p 389 at 391.

Suggestions that breaches of specific provisions of Community law might constitute new heads of tort in English law were made on several occasions.[94] These suggestions were based on the fact that under the European Communities Act 1972 rights arising under Community law were referred to as *'enforceable Community rights'* and not as rights arising under UK law. Still, a breach of Community law was classified under existing causes of action as either a remedy in damages for the tort of breach of statutory duty or the tort of misfeasance in public office. Breach of statutory duty is available where it is apparent that the obligation or prohibition is imposed by a statute for the benefit or protection of a particular class or individuals or where the statute creates a public law right and a particular member of the public suffers in a different way. The second issue related to whether the rights conferred by Community law should be classified as public law rights, a breach of which could only be sanctioned through proceedings established for judicial review, or as rights sounding in private law.

Prior to *Francovich*, the fact that breaches of Community law could give rise to actions for damages had been considered by the English courts in a number of circumstances. However, the first case on damages against public authorities was *Bourgoin*.[95] Indeed the proceedings in *Garden Cottage Foods*[96] concerned the activities of the Milk Marketing Board *qua* an undertaking allegedly breaching Community competition rules rather than in its quality as a statutory organisation. Against the State, the only remedy available was misfeasance in public office. In *Bourgoin*, the Court of Appeal held that the State was not required as a matter of English or Community law to compensate the victims of acts which had been found by the ECJ to be contrary to Community law, unless the Minister were shown to have acted in the knowledge that the act in question was invalid and with the intention or knowledge that it would injure the claimants. Today, the position in the English courts is that whilst it can be said that the cause of action is *sui generis*, it has the character of a breach of statutory duty.

---

94. Per Lord Denning MR in *Application dis Gaz v Falks Veritas* [1974] Ch 381 and by Lord Wilberforce in his dissenting opinion in *Garden Cottage Foods v Milk Marketing Board* [1983] 3 All ER 777 at 783 and see Usher, *op. cit.* at 392.
95. *Bourgoin v MAFF* [1986] QB 716.
96. *Op. cit.*, at fn 93.

Conclusion

This new Community remedy is as yet undeveloped and dependent on national rules. Further, much of its consequences for the different types of Community obligations are unclear, as one of the conditions is that the provision was intended to confer rights on individuals.

The ECJ case law on State liability for breach of Community law illustrates how 'the dividing line which separates interpretation and application can be perilously thin',[97] and how on occasion, the reality does not match the theory regarding the division of function established under Article 234 EC. In some cases,[98] the ECJ decided itself on conditions of liability *in concreto*, with the result that the referring national court has been left with deciding only whether the requirements of causation are met.

[97.] Craig and De Búrca, *EC Law: Text, Cases and Materials* (OUP, 1995) at p. 400.
[98.] Case 392/93, *BT, op. cit.,* at fn 77, para. 41; Case C-5/94, *Hedley Lomas, op. cit.* at fn 73, paras 27–30.

CHAPTER EIGHT

The UK courts working as Community courts

The question is whether judicial review is available for the purpose of securing a declaration that certain United Kingdom primary legislation is incompatible with Community law. . . . A declaration that the threshold provisions of the 1978 Act are incompatible with Community law would suffice for the purpose sought to be achieved by the EOC and is capable of being granted consistently with the precedent afforded by *Factortame*.[1]

Of course a British court will always be willing and anxious to conclude that United Kingdom law is consistent with Community law. Where an Act passed for the purpose of giving effect to an obligation imposed by a Directive or other instrument a British court will seldom encounter difficulty in concluding that the language of the Act is effective for the intended purpose. But the construction of a British Act of Parliament is a matter of judgment to be determined by the British courts and to be derived from the language of the legislation considered in the light of the circumstances prevailing at the date of enactment. . . . Section 2(4) of the ECA 1972 does not in my opinion enable or constrain a British court to distort the meaning of a British statute in order to enforce against an individual a Community Directive which has no direct effect between individuals. Section 2(4) applies and only applies where Community provisions are directly applicable.[2]

The manner in which UK courts discharge their duties as Community courts will be analysed through cases considered as raising the most typical difficulties.

[1]. *R v Secretary of State for Employment, ex parte Equal Opportunities Commission* [1994] 2 WLR 409 per Lord Keith at 419.
[2]. *Duke v Reliance Systems Ltd* [1988] AC 618 per Lord Templeman at 640–1.

UK courts had to solve conflicts between UK rules and Community law. They have been prepared to make a declaration that UK legislation was incompatible with Community law.[3] On occasion, they have shown willingness to interpret domestic statutes in such a way as to ensure conformity with Community law. They have also adapted remedies and procedural rules so as to satisfy Community requirements of effective protection of individual rights. Community law has also had a more pervasive influence, insofar as some of the interpretation techniques adopted to conform with Community requirements have been used in fields outside the reach of Community law. Thus the concept of objective justification applied in the context of indirect sex discrimination has percolated into the field of race discrimination law.[4]

Enforcing directives against the State: some specific difficulties

In *Foster*[5] the ECJ held that:

A body, whatever its legal form, which has been made responsible pursuant to a measure adopted by the State, for providing a public service under the control of the State and has for that purpose special powers beyond those which result from the normal rules applicable in relations between individuals, is included in any event among the bodies against which the provisions of a Directive capable of having direct effect may be relied upon.

This ruling has created much uncertainty.[6] The UK courts have been considering whether the tests laid down are alternative or cumulative, how to define public service in Community law, how much degree of control ought to be exercised by the State.

Considerations of whether the tests are alternative or cumulative illustrates the tendency of the UK courts to adopt a literal interpretation of Community law. For the ECJ the tests are clearly

---

3. See fn 1.
4. *Hampson v Department of Education* [1990] 2 All ER 25 (CA); and see J. Shaw 'European Community judicial method: its application to Sex Discrimination Law' (1990) 19 ILJ 228. See also Chapter 1.
5. C-188/89 *Foster v British Gas* [1990] ECR I-3313.
6. *Rolls Royce plc v Doughty* [1988] 1 CMLR 569.

alternative, as the underlying objective is to broaden the scope of 'vertical direct effect',[7] which is why in *Marshall I*,[8] the argument according to which the health authority was acting *qua* an employer in private law was rejected, and the directive could be relied on against a health authority, 'regardless of the capacity in which that body is acting'. Any ambiguity in the case law of the ECJ[9] has been unequivocally removed by *Kampelmann*:[10]

> An individual may rely on a precise and unconditional directive directly before the national courts as against the State and any organisations or bodies which are subject to the authority *or* control of the State *or* have special powers beyond those which result from the normal rules applicable to relations between individuals, either where the State has failed to transpose the Directive into national law within the prescribed period or where it has not done so correctly.

These problems now appear to be resolved:

> In my judgment it is *not appropriate* to apply the tripartite test in *Foster* as though it were a statutory definition. Education can be regarded as a public service. That service is under the control of the State. The Secretary of State has duties and powers in respect of the provision of education and so do LEAs. Those powers amount to sufficient control by the State for present purposes to come within the concept of control. . . . In my judgment for the purposes of the doctrine of direct vertical effect the governors of the schools must be regarded as emanations of the State and I therefore consider that this appeal must be allowed.[11]

Direct effect: an elusive concept

Griffin[12] raised the question whether Article 2 of the Collective Redundancies Directive[13] was directly enforceable against South West

---

7. See Chapter 5.
8. Case 152/84 *Marshall v Southampton & South West Hampshire Health Authority* [1986] ECR 723 (*Marshall I*).
9. See Chapter 5.
10. Cases C-253/96 to C-258/96 *H. Kampelmann and others* [1997] ECR I-6907, paras 46 and 47.
11. *National Union of Teachers and others v Governing Body of St Mary's Church of England (Aided) Junior School* [1997] 3 CMLR 630.
12. *Griffin v South West Water Services* [1995] IRLR 15.
13. Council Directive 75/129, OJ 1977 L48 amended by Directive 92/56 OJ 1992 L245.

Water Services Ltd ('SWW') – a newly privatised company – and if so, whether SWW could be required to consult with a particular trade union. The High Court approached the matter on the basis that the threefold test had to be satisfied, and finding it was so, regarded the privatised company as an emanation of the State. However, it decided that the Directive did not have direct effect. The High Court proceeded to decide upon the issue of direct effect, 'a somewhat elusive concept',[14] itself.[15] It accepted that the provisions of a directive may be unconditional and sufficiently precise notwithstanding that a difficult question of construction arises under a particular provision, a question which may warrant a reference to the ECJ. However, here no such interpretation was required. The High Court was satisfied that 'workers' representatives' did not have a Community definition since the concept refers to the laws or practices of the Member State. The Member State had a wide discretion in designating who the workers' representatives should be, and a particular trade union could not insist on being consulted on the basis of the Directive. The declaration that SWW must also consult with the trade union UNISON was not granted. In *Evans v Reading and Motor Insurers Bureau*,[16] the Court of Appeal rejected the plaintiffs' argument that they were entitled to compensation from the Motor Insurers Bureau under the terms of Directive 84/5.[17] The Court of Appeal found the provisions of the directive to be unconditional and sufficiently precise in terms of identifying the persons entitled to compensation, but not clear and precise as to the identity of the person liable to provide compensation. As a result, an interested individual could *not* rely upon the directive to ask a national court to effectuate directly a right to compensation against the Motor Insurance Bureau. However, the question of whether a Community provision has direct effect ought not to be left to national courts, since these could reach different views on this issue.

---

14. Blackburn J at p. 30, para. 126.
15. Although this question is for the ECJ alone: see Chapter 5.
16. Court of Appeal, *Times Law Reports*, 12 October 1998 [1999] CMLR 125.
17. Second Council directive on the approximation of the laws of the Member States relating to insurance against civil liability in respect of the use of motor vehicles, OJ 1984 L 8/17.

The duty of uniform interpretation

The interpretative duty provides that national courts are under the duty, stemming from Article 5 EC, to interpret domestic provisions so as to conform with the requirements of a directive, and *with the interpretation placed on it by the ECJ*, whether the national provision existed prior to or later than the directive, *i.e.* whether the national provisions do or should give effect to Community law and, by implication, irrespective of whether or not such provisions have anything whatsoever to do with the Directive other than by subject matter.

The somewhat inconsistent approach[18] of the UK courts when trying to come to terms with the 'interpretative duty'[19] is well documented,[20] and will only be briefly discussed. In the former line of authority, the House of Lords showed itself willing to interpret UK legislation in the light of a directive where such legislation was intended to implement the directive, even where it involved resorting to *Hansard*, departing from the apparently unambiguous provisions of UK regulations,[21] or even adding a few words.[22]

> If the legislation can reasonably be construed so as to conform with those obligations – obligations which are to be ascertained not only from the wording of the relevant directive, but from the interpretation placed upon it by the European Court of Justice at Luxembourg – such a purposive interpretation will be applied even though, perhaps, it may involve some departure from the strict and literal application of the words which the legislature has elected to use.[23]

However, where the legislation was found not to have been intended to implement the Directive, the interpretative duty was not discharged.[24]

18. Compare *Pickstone v Freemans* [1989] AC 66 and *Litster v Forth Dry Dock Ltd* 1989 SC (HL) 96 with *Duke v Reliance Systems Ltd* [1988] AC 618 and *Finnegan v Clowney Youth Training Programme* [1990] 2 AC 407.

19. First enunciated in Case 14/83 *Von Colson and Kamann v Land Nordrhein-Westfalen* [1984] ECR 1891 and Case 79/83 *Hartz v Deutsche Tradax* [1984] ECR 1921, the principle was further developed in C-106/89 *Marleasing v La Comercial Internacional de Alimentacion* [1990] ECR I-4135. See Curtin, 'The effectiveness of judicial protection of individual rights' (1990) 27 CMLRev 709.

20. G. De Búrca, 'Giving Effect to European Community Directives' (1992) 55 MLR 215.

21. *Pickstone v Freemans, op. cit.*, fn 18.   22. *Litster, op. cit.*, fn 18.

23. *Litster, op. cit.* 113, per Lord Oliver.

24. *Duke v Reliance Systems Ltd* [1988] AC 618; *Finnegan v Clowney Youth Training Programme* [1990] 2 AC 407; *Webb v EMO Cargo Ltd* [1992] 2 All ER 43 (CA).

What deserves closer attention is the reasoning behind this apparent contradiction. *Duke*[25] raised two separate issues. The first issue is whether UK courts are required, by virtue of the ECA section 2(4) to distort UK legislation. The second is whether the UK courts are, by virtue of Community law, required to discharge the interpretative duty where this would result in obligations being placed on private parties which they understood *Marshall* to preempt.[26] In *Duke*, the House of Lords refused to interpret the Sex Discrimination Act in the light of the Equal Treatment Directive on the grounds that it was impossible under national law, but also impossible under Community law. The duty of construction only exists in relation to rights granted by provisions which are directly effective.[27]

In *Webb*,[28] whilst *Duke* was extensively discussed, the House of Lords departed from it in one very significant way: no mention was made of 'enforceable Community rights'. The House of Lords considered itself bound by the interpretative duty even though 'Directive 76/207 does not have direct effect between a worker and an employer who is not the State or an emanation of the State'. The House of Lords was prepared to accept that directives may, through interpretation of national law, place obligations between private parties, although it did not explain why. The reluctance to apply the provisions of a directive against a private party has been recently revived:

> The effect of the decisions in *Marshall* and *Faccini Dori* is that, except in proceedings which bring into question the legal relations between the individual and the State or its emanations, directives do not give rise to rights or restrictions which without further enactment are required to be given legal effect. Accordingly, section 2(4) does not enable them to affect the validity or construction of domestic legislation.[29]

---

25. *Op. cit.*
26. If *Marshall* established that a directive could not of itself confer obligations on private parties, it did not overrule cases such as *Harz* from which it is clear that, as a matter of Community law, a directive may place obligations on private parties, through the natural effect of national law, interpreted in accordance with Community requirements.
27. ECA 1972, section 2(1), 'enforceable Community rights'.
28. *Webb v EMO Cargo Ltd* [1993] IRLR 27 (HL).
29. Per Lord Hoffmann in *R v Secretary of State for Employment, ex parte Seymour Smith* [1997] 2 CMLR 904 at 910, para. 15.

It is true that the practical effect of direct effect and of the interpretative duty are the same, as was recognised by Tesauro AG in his opinion in *Webb*: 'the dispute is between two persons governed by private law and the Court has not so far held that directives have horizontal direct effect'.[30] Still, the interpretative duty does not require the application of directives. Rather, it involves the application of *national* law construed in accordance with the objectives of the directive as interpreted by the ECJ.[31] If the ECJ held that a directive may not *of itself* impose obligations on individuals, nor be relied upon *as such* against private parties, it has consistently ensured that the duties and obligations contained in directives are available in private relationships through the medium of national law.[32] In other words, while incapable of creating private obligations directly, directives may be capable of doing so indirectly.

Reconciling the ECJ case law on the direct and indirect effect of directives has sometimes proved difficult for the UK courts.[33] If a legislative instrument is not capable of having direct effect between private parties, *i.e.* is not capable of creating obligations on private parties directly, it should not be capable of doing so indirectly either. The UK courts' refusal to place obligations on private parties through interpretation follows this logic. If a provision is not capable of imposing rights directly in certain types of litigation, why should that same provision be capable of doing so indirectly? The ECJ only said that directives could not as such impose obligations on private parties, not that they could not give rights. Furthermore, the interpretative duty ensures that directives do not create rights directly, as the rights are derived from national law.

If the reasoning followed by the UK courts may seem logical, it is wrong as a matter of *Community law*. From a Community perspective, the interpretative obligation exists, irrespective of its results on private legal relationships. The UK courts are bound by section 3(1) of the ECA as well as by section 2(4). They are instructed to follow the case law of the ECJ, which includes that on the interpretative duty.

---

[30]. Para. 6 of the Opinion.   [31]. See Chapter 5.
[32]. See Boch and Lane, 'European Community law in National courts: A Continuing Contradiction' (1992) 5 LJIL 171.
[33]. Although it was never at issue in *Pickstone v Freemans*, or *Litster*, *op. cit.*, fn 15.

The UK courts have also based their refusal on the principle of legal certainty:

> The effect – of the declaration sought – would be to give the Directive, by an easy two-stage process, the very effect which the jurisprudence of the Court says it cannot have, namely to impose obligations upon an individual. Furthermore, those obligations would be imposed arbitrarily and retrospectively, depending upon whether and when some interested person brought proceedings in public law to assert his 'right' against the State to have incompatible domestic law set aside. This seems to me inconsistent with the principle of legal certainty which is one of the fundamental doctrines of European law.[34]

There are additional objections to the placing of obligations on private parties via an interpretation of national law. In the context of employment law, Community obligations often translate into obligations placed upon individual employers and courts feel uneasy about placing costs on them.[35] The question of the fairness of placing obligations on private parties is not merely a British concern. In *Dekker*,[36] the employer's decision not to appoint Ms Dekker, was based on the Dutch legislation on social security benefits. Still, as a result of that case, the employer is ultimately the party liable[37] for a failure of the State to introduce legislation in conformity with Community obligations.

Supremacy/Remedies

As with the interpretative duty, the UK courts adopted an inconsistent approach to the requirements of primacy. In many instances, they were prepared to grant the remedy sought even though it involved a radical departure from established patterns. In other cases they decided they could not disregard the exclusive sanction Parliament had provided.

34. Lord Hoffmann, para. 13, in *Seymour Smith, op. cit.* at fn 29.
35. *Duke, op. cit.*, fn 24, at para. 35.
36. C-177/88 *Dekker v Stichting Vormingscentrum voor Jong Volwassenen (VJV-Centrum) Plus* [1990] ECR I-3941.
37. E. Traversa, 'Jurisprudence Communautaire en matière de politique sociale Année 1990', 27 RTDE 1991, p. 434 (emphasis added). See further P. Rodière, 'Sur les Effets Directifs du Droit (Social) Communautaire: à propos de deux arrêts de la CJCE', 27 RTDE 1991, p. 564; Boch (1996) 33 CMLRev 558.

In *Factortame*[38] a challenge to the validity of the Merchant Shipping Act 1988 was mounted. This Act laid down a number of restrictions to the registration of fishing vessels, as another attempt[39] to curb 'quota hopping', *i.e.* to stop Spanish vessels registered as British vessels to fish against the British quota.[40] The important question raised by the case was that of the status of an Act of Parliament until a decision is made on its validity. The Court of Appeal and the House of Lords had come to the conclusion that under the UK constitution, the UK courts had no power to disapply or suspend Acts of Parliament; there was no constitutional authority conferring upon any court such a power. Still, the House of Lords was prepared to inquire whether, as a matter of Community law, the UK courts would have jurisdiction to grant an interim injunction against the Crown, thereby, in this author's view, implying their willingness to grant such a remedy. 'Does Community law either oblige the national court to grant interim protection or give the court power to grant such interim protection?'

The ECJ dealt with the question as if there was a rule of English law which prevented a court from exercising such jurisdiction. Accordingly, it held that 'a national court which in a case before it considers that the sole obstacle which precludes it from granting interim relief is a rule of national law must set aside that rule.'[41] From the ECJ perspective, *Factortame* is just another case where the full requirements of primacy are being tested. The ruling fully conforms with the logic pursued by the ECJ. Accordingly, some criticisms of the case appear based on a misconception of the ECJ approach to primacy.[42] The ECJ was criticised[43] for dealing with

---

38. Case C-213/89 *R v Secretary of State for Transport, ex parte Factortame Ltd* [1990] ECR I-2433.
39. See a previous unsuccessful attempt in Case 3/87 *R v MAFF, ex parte Agegate* [1989] ECR 4459, R.R. Churchill (1992) 29 CMLRev 405; for a discussion of the management of the Common Fisheries Policy various issues see K.D. Magliveras, 'Fishing in Troubled Waters: The Merchant Shipping Act 1988 and the EC', 39 ICLQ 899 and C. Noirfalisse, 'The Community system of fisheries management and the Factortame case' (1992)12 YEL 325.
40. The Common Fisheries Policy (CFP) is based on a system of national quotas for fishery catches. Regulation 170/83 uses the criterion of the flag of registration of the fishing vessel to decide which national quota its catch shall count against.
41. *Factortame, op. cit.* at para. 23.
42. See Chapter 2.
43. M. Howe, *Europe and the Constitution after Maastricht* (Nelson and Pollard, 1993) p. 21.

the question in negative terms, as if there was a rule which prevented a court from granting interim relief, when in truth there was no such rule. In so doing, the ECJ bypassed the real issue, namely the absence of any constitutional authority conferring upon a UK court a power of such a nature. The question the ECJ refused to answer was whether the authority came from Community law. However, the ECJ did address this very issue right at the outset.[44] The ECJ perspective has always been that Community law takes effect in the national legal orders without reference to national law. This necessarily implies that the authority to give effect to Community rules comes from Community law.

Factortame means that since any court in the UK may be called upon to protect Community rights, any court in the UK can suspend the application of an Act of Parliament to protect putative rights in Community law. From a UK perspective, parliamentary sovereignty is said not to be questioned, for Parliament itself instructed the courts to follow the logic of supremacy.[45] In *EOC*[46] the UK courts further explored what recognition of the primacy of Community law entails, and accepted that the UK courts were competent to hear applications for judicial review of primary UK legislation,[47] and make declarations of the incompatibility of UK Acts with the Community superior norm.

Marshall II[48] raised specific questions regarding procedural rules pertaining to concepts of damages and compensation, together with some broader issues regarding the range of duties involved in national courts ensuring full and effective protection of Community-based rights. Where a Member State chooses to provide compensation as a remedy, when is it adequate? Can a national judge substitute his own assessment for that laid down by national law? How far can a UK court go – in terms of frustrating legislative intent – to ensure an effective remedy is granted?

Why Marshall II?

Ms Marshall was dismissed by her employer, a health authority, at the age of 62. Had she been a man she would have been allowed

---

44. See Chapter 2.
45. Per Lord Bridge in *Factortame (No. 2)* [1991] AC 603 at 658.
46. See *op. cit.*, fn 1.   47. See Chapter 2.
48. Case C-271/91 *Marshall v Southampton and South West Area Health Authority* [1993] ECR I-4637.

to stay in employment until she reached the age of 65. In 1980, she presented a complaint to an industrial tribunal alleging that she had been discriminated against contrary to the Sex Discrimination Act 1975 (hereafter SDA), Article 141 EC and the Equal Treatment Directive.[49] After a lengthy judicial process,[50] it was held that she had been discriminated against. Her complaint was then remitted back to the industrial tribunal to consider the question of remedy.[51] Ms Marshall was seeking compensation under the provisions of the SDA,[52] section 65 of which provided *inter alia* that if the complaint is well founded, the tribunal may choose to award compensation up to a prescribed maximum,[53] at the time £6,250. Ms Marshall challenged these provisions on the basis of Article 6 of the Equal Treatment Directive.[54]

This provision had already been interpreted by the ECJ[55] and applied by the referring national courts[56] (in this case German courts). The ECJ held that the remedy should be real and effective, have a deterrent effect, and if compensation was to be awarded, it should be adequate. Accordingly, the referring national court relying on the general rules on civil liability – rather than on the implementing legislation – awarded the plaintiff the equivalent of six months' gross salary payment (DM21,000), a figure which compares favourably with that of DM7.20, corresponding to the outlay in connection with the application for the position, which

---

49. Council Directive 76/207 on the implementation of the principle of equal treatment between men and women as regards access to employment, vocational training and promotion and working conditions, OJ 1976 L39/40.

50. Ms Marshall succeeded before the industrial tribunal; the health authority appealed and the EAT allowed the appeal; leave was given to appeal to the Court of Appeal which, in 1984, referred questions to the ECJ; in 1986, the ECJ gave its judgment, following which the Court of Appeal allowed Ms Marshall's appeal.

51. [1988] 3 CMLRev 389.   52. Sections 65 and 66.

53. Section 66(2): 'The amount of compensation awarded to a person under subsection (1)(b) shall not exceed the limit for the time being imposed by section 75 of the Employment Protection (Consolidation) Act 1978'.

54. 'Member States shall introduce into their national legal systems such measures as are necessary to enable all persons who consider themselves wronged by failure to apply to them the principle of equal treatment within the meaning of Articles 3, 4 and 5, to pursue their claims by judicial process after possible recourse to other competent authorities.'

55. See fn 19.

56. In Case 14/83, the Arbeitsgericht Hamm Urteil vom 06/09/84 – 4 CA 1076/82, Der Betrieb 1984 p. 2700 and 2701.

the plaintiff could have expected under the German legislation implementing the Directive.[57]

Ms Marshall argued that the provisions of the SDA did not provide adequate compensation as defined by the ECJ. The industrial tribunal accepted it had to interpret and apply the legislation adopted for the implementation of the Directive in conformity with the requirements of Community law, and that it had to provide an adequate remedy. After finding as a fact that the remedy available was not adequate, the industrial tribunal decided to *ignore*[58] the statutory limit, and substantially increased it so as to provide the adequate compensation required. Accordingly, Ms Marshall was awarded not the prescribed maximum of £6,250, but £11,695. An additional £7,710 interest was awarded for the period running from the date of her first application to the date of the Court of Appeal's decision allowing her claim.[59] The decision was appealed,[60] but the only ground related to interest.[61] Whether the award of a sum above the statutory limit was in excess of jurisdiction was never raised. The EAT remarked that at common law, 'save in some rare cases in the calculation of special damage, there is no power to include an element of interest when assessing damage. The power to grant interest is given by statute'.[62] Turning to the question of whether Community law provided such a power, it found that Article 6 of the Equal Treatment Directive had no direct effect, and that the duty laid down in *Von Colson* did not require a national court to construe Article 6 in order to justify an award of interest. *Von Colson* was distinguished on the ground that the purely nominal compensation available amounted, in effect, to a situation where there was *no* judicial remedy; whereas under the Sex Discrimination Act, a remedy was available. The EAT struck out the amount for interest; however, the amount awarded by the industrial tribunal, and paid by the health authority (£11,695) remained substantially above the statutory limit of £6,250.

Ms Marshall appealed against the EAT's decision to quash the award of the £7,710 interest.[63] The Court of Appeal, by a majority of two to one, dismissed it. Although the appeal only related to

[57.] D. Curtin, 'Effective Sanctions and the Equal Treatment Directive: the *Von Colson* and *Harz* Cases' (1985) 22 CMLRev 533.
[58.] [1988] 3 CMLR 389 at 402.   [59.] April 1980 to 1988.
[60.] [1989] 3 CMLR 771.   [61.] *Ibid.* at 774.   [62.] Wood J at para. 12.
[63.] [1990] 3 CMLR 425.

whether an industrial tribunal had any power to award interest in circumstances such as Ms Marshall's case, all three judges decided to address what they considered the central issue, namely whether or not Community law empowered a national judge to override a statutory limit.[64] The majority answered in the negative. All three judges were sympathetic to the argument that the statutory limit on compensation did not provide the adequate and effective remedy required by Article 6 of the Equal Treatment Directive.[65] Yet they could not agree that this finding was sufficient to found a power for a national judge to overlook a statutory limitation. UK judges cannot substitute their own appreciation for that of the UK Parliament. The Directive could not be applied in preference to national legislation since Article 6 had no direct effect. The wording of the national legislation did not have to be interpreted in the light of the Directive since its wording did not give rise to any ambiguity.[66] 'Ms Marshall and others must wait until the United Kingdom enacts legislation giving effect to Article 6 as the ECJ has construed it' (Staughton LJ, para. 60).

On appeal, the House of Lords – like the Court of Appeal – considered that beyond the question of an industrial tribunal's power to award interest lay a crucial issue, whether Community law gave national courts power to override national legislation, in order to grant the remedy sought.[67] Accordingly a reference was sent to Luxembourg.

Back in Luxembourg

Ms Marshall argued that the principle of effective protection empowered national judges to set aside where necessary any provisions of domestic law preventing such protection from being granted, so the statutory limit should be ignored. As for the award of interest, the assimilation principle was relied upon: interest should be allowed by analogy with comparable actions – *i.e.* actions for discrimination brought in the county courts and other actions in tort brought in the High Court. Where common law and statutory remedies co-exist, but the common law remedy is more

---

64. *Ibid.*, per Dillon LJ para. 16, Butler-Sloss LJ at para. 37, Staughton LJ at para. 53.
65. Dillon LJ paras 25 and 26, Butler-Sloss LJ para. 43, Staughton LJ para. 53.
66. Used again in *Webb v EMO Air Cargo (UK) Ltd* [1993] 1 CMLR 259 at 271.
67. An area which ought to have been free from doubt following *Factortame*.

in conformity with the objectives laid down in the Directive, the national judge must *prefer* it to the statutory remedy provided for under the legislation implementing the directive. In this way, the principle of institutional autonomy is respected, and the UK judge is merely asked to use a power which is available in the national legal system, although not provided for by the relevant legislation. *Marshall* thus demonstrates how the preliminary ruling procedure is used by national courts on a case by case basis; what the UK judge was told to do was precisely what the German judge did when applying the *Von Colson* ruling. The general rules on civil liability were applied, in preference to the specific provisions contained in the implementing legislation. National judges merely use a power available under national law, and they have to choose from the various sanctions the most appropriate one for the protection of Community law.

The ECJ held that Article 6 is an essential factor for attaining the fundamental objective of equal treatment for men and women, and that when financial compensation is the measure adopted in order to restore that equality, such compensation may not be limited to an upper limit fixed *a priori* in terms of amounts or by excluding an award of interest to compensate for the loss sustained by the recipient of the compensation as a result of effluxion of time until the capital sum awarded is actually paid. In contrast with *Johnston*,[68] where Article 6 was found 'not to contain, as far as sanctions for any discrimination are concerned, any unconditional and sufficiently precise obligation which may be relied upon by an individual', according to *Marshall* Article 6 may be relied upon against the State in order to set aside a national provision which imposes limits on the amount of compensation recoverable by way of reparation.

In *Griffin*,[69] one of the reliefs sought was an injunction restraining SWW from proceeding with further staff redundancy unless and until proper consultation had taken place. The High Court considered that where a directive leaves Member States the choice of remedy for breach of the directive, it cannot be interpreted so as to require the Member State to select one mode of sanction for breach of the directive in preference to another, at any rate where the sanction selected is capable of guaranteeing real and effective

---

[68]. Case 222/84 *Johnston v Chief Constable of the RUC* [1986] ECR 1651.
[69]. *Griffin v South West Water Services* [1995] IRLR 15.

judicial protection and a real deterrent effect. The sanction selected by Parliament was a complaint to the industrial tribunal, empowered, if it finds the complaint well founded, to make a declaration to that effect and make a protective award. Blackburn J held:

> Whilst, therefore, there may be a question, as there was in Case C-383/92, as to the adequacy of the award which the industrial tribunal is empowered to make having regard to some feature of the legislation which provides for the sanction, I *do not consider that it is open to me to disregard the exclusive sanction which Parliament has selected for giving effect to the duty to consult,* where it arises, and to grant to the plaintiffs a form of relief for which the 1992 Act makes no provision. Even if it were open to me in appropriate circumstances to disregard the exclusive sanction which Parliament has provided and grant injunctive relief of the kind sought, I am not persuaded that I would have any sufficient grounds for doing so. It seems to me that an order restraining an employer from effecting any redundancies unless he has 'consulted with' his employees' representatives 'with a view to reaching an agreement', which is what the plaintiffs seek, is one which is fraught with practical difficulties . . . I can well see, therefore, why Parliament has chosen to provide for breaches of the duty to consult and inform under s 188, by leaving it to an industrial tribunal which is particularly well equipped to consider such matters.[70]

In *EOC*,[71] the House of Lords decided that the Equal Opportunities Commission had a 'sufficient interest in the matter' within the meaning of RSC, Ord. 53, r 3(7) to have *locus standi* to apply for a declaration that UK legislation on the threshold conditions for redundancy pay was incompatible with the Equal Treatment Directive. However, individuals who assert that they are directly affected by failure to implement a directive have no *locus standi* to apply for a similar declaration.

---

70. *Ibid.*, at para. 63 (emphasis added).
71. *R v Secretary of State for Employment, ex parte Equal Opportunities Commission* [1995] 1 AC 1.

General principles of law and the UK courts

The general or fundamental principles applying in the Community legal order cannot be used to assess the lawfulness of national legislation which lies outside Community law. The legislation of the Member States may be assessed on the basis of the fundamental rights in two sets of circumstances: first, where the national legislation implements Community rules; secondly, but more indirectly, where a Treaty provision derogating from the principle of freedom of movement is relied upon by a Member State in order to justify a restriction of freedom of movement stemming from that Member State's legislation. In such cases the ECJ uses the fundamental rights in order to give a restrictive or extensive interpretation of the derogations laid down in the Treaty.[72]

As with other Community law requirements, the approach of the UK courts has been inconsistent. Sometimes they have applied the general principles, on occasion they have refused to do so.

The first objection to reference to general principles of law before the UK courts is that such matters are entirely domestic, to be solved by reference to national law alone. In *Hamble*,[73] the objection was vigorously rejected, as 'unreal', but it was found valid in *First City Trading*.[74] However, given the factual background of both cases, the connection with Community law should have been approached in a comparable fashion.

Hamble concerned a change[75] instituted by the British Government in the licensing regime relating to the conditions under which fishing for pressure stocks was to be permitted, within the context of the Community fisheries policy. Under the new regime, some fishermen would not qualify for a licence. Some of these fishermen made an application for declaratory and prerogative relief to secure a licence entitling their vessel to fish by beam trawl for pressure stocks in the North Sea. They argued they had a legitimate expectation that any change in the licensing policy would not be such as to frustrate the completion of the process of licence aggregation. In *First City Trading*, an application for judicial review of the Beef Stocks Transfer Scheme was brought by six meat

---

[72.] Gulmann AG's Opinion in Case C-2/92 *Bostock* [1994] ECR I-955, para. 31.
[73.] [1995] 2 All ER 714.
[74.] *R v MAFF, ex parte First City Trading Ltd and others* [1997] 1 CMLR 250.
[75.] Before the policy promoted capacity aggregation by transfer of licences.

exporters. Following the Commission decision[76] banning exports of British beef, the beef industry suffered considerable loss. The UK Government introduced a scheme for emergency financial aid to the slaughtering industry. The scheme was open *only* to those who operated their own slaughterhouses or cutting plants, whether or not they were also beef exporters. The legality of the scheme was challenged as violating a fundamental principle of Community law, that of equality or non-discrimination. In *Hamble* the High Court considered that:

> although the exercise is the formulation of policy within a discretion conferred entirely by domestic legislation, the purpose of legislation and policy alike is to permit the UK, under the principle of subsidiarity, to exercise its powers for the purposes of implementing the common fisheries policy of the European Community.

Sedley J further remarked that, if each Member State carried out its part of this joint exercise in accordance with its own domestic law, a major objective of the policy would be frustrated. The availability of eventual recourse to the ECJ from and against all Member States in relation to the carrying out of the common agricultural policy confirmed that domestic courts had to have full regard to the case law of the ECJ. By contrast, in *First City Trading*, Laws J questioned the precise status of general principles of law given that they were not provided for under the Treaty, but had been developed by the ECJ:

> It is by no means self-evident that their contextual scope must be the same as that of Treaty provisions relating to discrimination or equal treatment – which are statute law taking effect according to their own, express terms.[77]

This approach is in direct contradistinction to that of the ECJ. The ECJ never determined the boundaries of Community law differently according to the nature of the Community rules involved.[78] Rather, on numerous occasions,[79] it held that the various references to non-discrimination throughout the Treaty or the

---

76. Decision 96/239 on emergency measures to secure protection against disease in humans, OJ (1996) L78/47.
77. At para. 39.
78. S. Boyron, 'General principles of law and national courts: applying a *Jus Commune*?' (1998) 13 ELR 171 at 175.
79. Case C-13/94 *P v S and Cornwall City Council* [1996] ECR I-2143.

secondary legislation were simply the expression, in the relevant fields, of the principle of equality, one of the fundamental principles of Community law.

Laws J further declared:

> It is of the first importance to notice that falling within the scope of the Treaty is by no means the same thing as acting under powers or duties conferred or imposed by Community law – such as giving effect to a Directive. . . . The power of the Court of Justice, as it seems to me, to apply (whether on an Article 177 reference or otherwise) principles of public law which it had itself evolved cannot be deployed in a case where the measure in question, taken by a Member State, is not a function of Community law at all. . . . There is no legal space for the application of the general principles of law to any measure or decision taken otherwise than in pursuance of Treaty rights or obligations. No court can expand the Treaty provisions. The position is altogether different where a measure is adopted *pursuant* to Community law; this is the second situation. Then, the internal law of the Court of Justice applies.

In this instance, although the applicants relied on a regulation by virtue of which support was given to the British beef market in the wake of the ban, and pointed out that the Scheme had been notified as a State aid,[80] the interdependence of the Scheme with the Community regime was not recognised. The scheme was neither authorised nor required by Community law, hence the principle of equal treatment – through whatever medium[81] – could not be relied upon.

The application of general principles of law requires national judges to make difficult choices, and to take on board roles and responsibilities they might not be ready or willing to discharge. Besides, applying general principles can on occasion become an exercise in comparative law, and national courts may prefer to rely on national standards or refer to their own domestic experience to construe the meaning of a specific general principle and apply it. Identifying the meaning of general principles of law by comparing them to national law should be avoided, otherwise they may get affected (or infected) by national references,[82] and the uniform application of Community law might thus well be compromised.

---

80. Pursuant to Article 93(3) EC.
81. *I.e.* as a general principle or under Article 39 EC.
82. S. Boyron, *op. cit.*, p. 178.

Still, it hardly seems possible to iron out different understandings, assumptions and perceptions about the nature and function of public law throughout the Community.

In *Hamble*, the High Court was prepared to consider fully the case law of the ECJ on legitimate expectation, and to quote the doctrine:[83]

> For the principle of the protection of legitimate expectations to be applicable, an objective basis must exist for this principle in the shape of an *expectation* which is *worthy of protection*. Because of the *broad freedom of action enjoyed by the legislature*, the mere existence of a legal rule is not normally a suitable basis for a legitimate expectation which must be taken into account. Adequate grounds for a solid expectation can be provided on the one hand by the fact of having entered into certain obligations towards the authorities, or on the other hand by a course of conduct on the part of the authorities giving rise to specific expectations – which in certain circumstances may arise out of a commitment entered into by the authorities.

Sedley J held:

> The legal alchemy which gives an expectation sufficient legitimacy to secure enforcement in public law is the obligation to exercise powers fairly which permits expectations to be counterposed to policy change, not necessarily in order to thwart it but – as in the present case – in order to seek a proper exception to the policy. While policy is for the policy-maker alone, the fairness of his or her decision not to accommodate reasonable expectations which the policy will thwart remains the court's concern (as of course does the lawfulness of the policy). . . . It is the court's task to recognise the constitutional importance of ministerial freedom to formulate and to reformulate policy; but it is equally the court's duty to protect the interests of those individuals whose expectation of different treatment has a legitimacy which in fairness outtops the policy choice which threatens to frustrate it . . . Legitimacy was a function of expectations induced by government and of policy considerations which militated against their fulfilment. The balance in the first instance was for the policy-maker to strike; but if the outcome was challenged by judicial review, the court's criterion was not the bare rationality of the policy-maker's conclusion and its task was not only to recognise the constitutional importance of

---

83. J. Schwarze, *European Administrative Law* (Nomos, 1992), pp. 1134–5.

ministerial freedom to formulate and to reformulate policy, but also to protect the interests of those individuals whose expectations of different treatment had a legitimacy which in fairness outweighed the policy choice which threatened to frustrate it.

In the circumstances, it was not found unfair, in the light of the government's legitimate policy imperatives and objectives, to exclude from the policy's transitional provisions enterprises in the position of the applicant.

Laws J in *First City Trading*, considering the principle of equality, insisted on the need to travel within the boundaries of proper judicial authority:

> There must remain a difference between the approach of the court in arriving at a judicial decision on the question whether a measure is objectively justified, and that of the primary decision-maker himself in deciding upon the measure in the first place. . . . The decision-makers enjoy a political authority and carry a political responsibility, with which the courts are not endowed. . . . Although I am being asked to apply the principle of equal treatment as a domestic judge, I must decide whether to do so having regard to the lawful confines of the power of the Court of Justice.[84]

Laws J also highlighted differences and similarities between Wednesbury[85] and European review.

> In the former case the legal limits lie further back. [. . .] The limits of domestic review are not, as the law presently stands, constrained by the doctrine of proportionality. The European rule requires the decision-maker to provide a fully reasoned case. The Court will test the solution arrived at, and pass it only if substantial factual considerations are put forward in its justification: considerations which are relevant, reasonable, and proportionate to the aim in view. But the Court is not concerned to agree or disagree with the decision. Wednesbury and European review are different models – one looser, one tighter – of the same juridical concept, which is the imposition of compulsory standards on decision-makers so as to secure the repudiation of arbitrary power.

This statement echoes that of Sedley J, for whom the real question

---

84. Paras 68, 39 and 47.
85. *Associated Provincial Picture Houses v Wednesbury Corporation* [1947] 2 All ER 680.

with legitimate expectation is one of 'fairness in public administration'. Still, the two cases display different approaches regarding the judiciary's inclination to be involved in adjudication of policy issues. Judicial reluctance to be involved in adjudication of policy issues has limited the acceptance of the principle of proportionality.[86]

In *First City Trading*,[87] the High Court held that a Community context was not sufficient for the application of the general or fundamental principles of law identified by the ECJ. This was also applied in *Lunn Poly*,[88] where differential rates of insurance premium tax were challenged as violating the general principles of non-discrimination and proportionality. The Divisional Court held that application of these principles to insurance premium tax would involve a wholly unwarranted encroachment on the sovereign powers of the UK. First, under Article 93 EC, the Member States had yielded sovereignty *only* to the extent that harmonisation of legislation concerning turnover taxes, excise duties and other forms of indirect taxation had been imposed, and Article 33 of the Sixth Directive implicitly recognised the continuing sovereignty of Member States. Accordingly, Parliament was not purporting to act within the scope of a Community enabling provision in introducing insurance premium tax. Secondly, while the ECJ had identified general or fundamental principles, such as non-discrimination and proportionality, 'principles not wholly apparent from a perusal of the Treaty', the ECJ was a court of limited jurisdiction. Where action was taken under domestic law, which fell within the scope of the Treaty's application, then the ECJ could require that the Treaty be adhered to, but no more. But since these principles are elaborated on by the ECJ rather than included in the Treaty, there was no legal space for their application to any measure taken otherwise than in pursuance of Treaty rights or obligations.

General principles of law are part of Community law and, as such, should be accorded immediate and direct supremacy. It is hard to understand how the fact that they are, in the words of Laws J 'the common law' of the Community could have any bear-

---

86. Usher, *General Principles of EC Law* (Longman, 1998), pp. 152–6.
87. *R v Ministry of Agriculture, Fisheries and Food, ex parte First City Trading Ltd* [1997] 1 CMLR 250 at 267–9.
88. *R v Customs and Excise Commissioners, ex parte Lunn Poly Ltd and another* [1998] STC 649.

ing on their recognition by the UK courts. Of all Member States' courts, UK courts should be most familiar with the prominence of case law as a source of law. Furthermore, UK judges are instructed by the UK Parliament to accept Community law not only on the terms it is made, but also as interpreted by the ECJ.[89] Yet, general principles of law seem to be forming a new pocket of resistance for the English courts.[90]

By contrast the Scottish courts have taken bold steps in their use of the general principles of law. *Booker*,[91] was an application for judicial review of legislation and certain actings of the Secretary of State for Scotland. The petitioners sought reduction of Regulation 7 of the Diseases of Fish (Control) Regulations 1994 and of a letter of the Secretary of State rejecting a claim for compensation of the loss incurred through the destruction of their fish stock, following a compulsory slaughter order issued by the Secretary of State in pursuance of EC provisions for the control of fish diseases. The Lord Ordinary granted a *declarator* to the effect that 'in failing to provide either by legislative or administrative measures for payment of any compensation where slaughter orders are made under Regulation 7 of the Diseases of Fish (Control) Regulations 1994, the respondent was acting illegally'. The Regulations were considered to fall within the scope of EC law. Accordingly, a national court overseeing their application had ro consider *all* the rules of EC law, including fundamental rights, *in casu* that of respect for freedom of property.

Booker raises important issues. In particular, can one deduce from general Community law principles for the protection of fundamental rights an obligation for the Member States to protect the economic interests of economic agents affected by the national implementation of Community measures? And if so, to what extent, and under what conditions, may an obligation be inferred from Community law to introduce compensation schemes? At present, the legal consequences of judicial review based on general principles of law, for the most part, still need to be worked out. The case was under appeal at the time of writing.

[89] See Chapter 2.
[90] S. Boyron, *op. cit.* at fn 74, p. 178.
[91] *Booker Aquaculture Ltd v the Secretary of State for Scotland* [1999] 1 CMLRev 35.

CHAPTER NINE

Community law and criminal law

Nothing in Community law would for example materially affect the general principles of our criminal law.[1]

Article 177, which is worded in general terms, draws no distinction according to the nature, criminal or otherwise, of the national proceedings within the framework of which the preliminary questions have been formulated.[2]

Where criminal proceedings are brought by virtue of a national measure which is held to be contrary to Community law, a conviction in those proceedings is likewise incompatible with Community law.[3]

This chapter will focus on the influence of Community law on national criminal law and procedure. The ways in which Community law can serve as a defence to a criminal charge, as the source of the creation of a new legal offence, and as a way to limit the choice of penalty in the event of conviction, together with the broader implications for national criminal policy, will be discussed.

Introduction

In principle, criminal legislation and criminal procedure are matters for which the Member States are still responsible.[4] At present,

[1.] *Legal and Constitutional Implications of United Kingdom Membership of the European Communities*, Cmmd.3301 (1971), para. 25, cited by Guldenmund, Harding and Sherlock in Harding et al. (eds) *Criminal Justice in Europe* (OUP, 1995) p. 107.
[2.] Case 82/71 *Sail v Pubblico Ministerio Italiano* [1972] ECR 119, para. 5.
[3.] Case 21/81 *Bout* [1982] ECR 381.
[4.] Case 203/80 *Casati* [1981] ECR 2595.

there is no explicit mandate in the EC Treaty for the harmonisation of such rules.[5] However, it has long been recognised that harmonisation in this field might be necessary in order to avoid disparities between penalties for breaches of Community law as between the different Member States.[6] As Advocate General Jacobs AG has suggested, it would not be impossible for the Community to exercise powers to harmonise the criminal laws of the Member States if that were necessary to attain one of the objectives of the Community.[7] In addition, even if traditionally criminal law and criminal justice are symbols of State sovereignty, there is no reason why, from a Community perspective, they should be treated differently from any other obstacles to the realisation of Community objectives; this branch of national law like any other may be affected by Community law[8] as 'the effectiveness of Community law cannot vary according to the various branches of national law which it may affect'.[9] Finally, it is recognised that the opening of national borders throws up problems which call for a closely co-ordinated approach – a number of rules have already been adopted in relation to money-laundering and drugs-trafficking.

Concerns for the police and crime control agencies are contained in Article K.1 of the Treaty on European Union (TEU). The TEU gave the Union competence to initiate policy in the field of home affairs and criminal law enforcement,[10] but only provided for intergovernmental mechanisms of co-operation[11] in 'matters of common interest' for the Member States. These include *inter alia* combating drug addiction, fraud on an international scale, judicial co-operation in criminal matters, police co-operation, asylum and immigration policy. The Amsterdam Treaty adds new tasks to the

---

5. For developments in this area see Chapter 11 and Com (95) 162, Communication from the Commission to the Council and the European Parliament, *The role of penalties in implementing Community internal market legislation.* For arguments for and against harmonisation, see H. Sevenster, 'Criminal law and EC law' (1992) 29 CMLRev 29.
6. See, even before accession, the government's views, in Guldenmund, Harding and Sherlock, *op. cit.,* p. 108.
7. In Case C-240/90 *Germany v Commission* [1992] ECR I-5383. The case is further discussed in Chapter 11. The issue of Community competence to make criminal law will not be addressed further here.
8. Case C-226/97 *Lemmens* [1998] ECR I-3711.
9. Case 82/71 *Pubblico Ministerio Italiano v Sail* [1972] ECR 119, para. 5.
10. Article K–K9; the third pillar, see Chapter 1.
11. Outside any democratic or judicial control.

EU action list, including combating child pornography and illicit arms trading. It also provides for new objectives for the Union:

> to maintain and develop the Union as an area of freedom, security and justice, in which the free movement of persons is assured in conjunction with appropriate measures with respect to external borders controls, asylum, immigration, and the prevention and combating of crime[12]
>
> . . . to provide citizens with a high level of safety within an area of freedom, security and justice by developing common action among the Member States in the fields of police and judicial co-operation in criminal matters and by preventing and combating racism and xenophobia.[13]

Title VI of the TEU is replaced by a new Title: 'Provisions on police and judicial co-operation in criminal matters.' Under this Title, prevention and fight against crime is organised through closer co-operation between police forces, customs authorities and other competent authorities, and through Europol, closer co-operation between judicial authorities and approximation of rules on criminal matters.[14] The ECJ will have jurisdiction to give preliminary rulings on the validity and interpretation of framework decisions, decisions and conventions established under this new Title, and on the validity and interpretation of the measures implementing them.[15] But this jurisdiction is subject to various restrictions.[16] One of the substantive changes made by the Amsterdam Treaty is the incorporation of a large part of the 'third pillar'[17] in the EC Treaty;[18] however, the UK and Ireland have an opt-out from some of its provisions.[19]

Despite an explicit competence in this field, Community law has had a very pervasive influence on domestic criminal law.[20] As early as 1972 it was clear that Community law would influence the application of national criminal laws. The Community impact has been incremental, from the recognition that Member States may

---

12. Article 2 TEU.   13. Article 29 TEU.   14. Article 29 TEU.   15. Article 29 TEU.
16. Laid down in Article 35TEU.   17. Justice and Home Affairs. See Chapter 1.
18. New EC title on the free movement of persons covering visas, asylum, immigration and judicial co-operation in civil matters.
19. See Protocol on the application of certain aspects of Article 7 of the Treaty, although provision is made for an 'opt-in'.
20. T.C. Hartley, 'The Impact of European Community Law on the Criminal Process', (1981) Crim LR 75.

decide to provide criminal sanctions for a breach of Community law,[21] to more precise constraints.

First, as a direct result of primacy, a criminal prosecution founded on a provision of national law found incompatible with Community law would itself be contrary to Community law. Thus, it is possible to resist the application of national criminal law by relying on Community law. Secondly, national authorities must enforce Community law by national methods, including the use of criminal penalties.[22] Accordingly, if fraud is a criminal offence under national law, criminal proceedings must also be used to combat fraud against the Community.[23] Finally, the Community has developed a number of principles[24] which influence the level of sanctions or impact on the way in which the criminal procedure unfolds. Community law has reached the national criminal law systems. In the UK, criminal practitioners have, on occasions, submitted that domestic rules were in conflict with Community law. Many EC law provisions have the potential to alter or nullify the criminal law of the Member States. In the UK, the most frequent points of contact have been in respect of free movement of goods[25] and persons,[26] agriculture,[27] fisheries[28] and road traffic cases.[29]

---

21. Case 50/76 *Amsterdam Bulb v Produktschap voor Siergewassen* [1977] ECR 137, para. 32.
22. Case C-68/88 *Commission v Greece* [1989] ECR 2965.
23. A Member State which fails to prosecute fraud against the Community budget can be found guilty of breach of its Treaty obligations.
24. J. Biancarelli, 'Les principes généraux du droit communautaire applicable en matière pénale' (1997) *Revue de Science criminelle* pp. 131–67.
25. Case 83/78 *Pigs Marketing Board v Redmond* [1978] ECR 2347, subsequent proceedings [1979] 3 CMLR 118; Case 34/79 *R v Henn and Darby* [1979] ECR 3795; Case 121/85 *Conegate v HM Customs and Excise Commissioners* [1986] ECR 1007.
26. Case 30/77 *Bouchereau* [1977] ECR 1999; Case 175/78 *R v Saunders* [1979] ECR 1129; Case 131/79 *R v Secretary of State for the Home Department, ex parte Santillo* [1980] ECR 1585; Case 157/79 *R v Pieck* [1980] ECR 2171.
27. In particular cases of frauds on Intervention Boards which make payments in accordance with the Common Agricultural Policy.
28. Breach of TAC or size of mesh for fishing nets.
29. Tachograph regulations or driver's hours regulations.

175

Influence of Community law on rules of criminal procedure

Rules of criminal procedure are matters for which the Member States are responsible, but the ECJ has consistently held that Community law sets limits to that power. In particular, legislative provisions may not discriminate against persons to whom Community law gives the right to equal treatment. The ways in which the assimilation principle influenced rules of criminal procedure is illustrated by the following cases. In *Mutsch*[30] questions arose on the interpretation of Article 293 EC in the context of criminal proceedings brought in Belgium against a Luxembourg national. Belgian law, in certain circumstances, authorises Belgian nationals to request the use of German in proceedings before Belgian courts:

> The benefit of legislation in a Member State intended to promote the use of the language of a group of nationals of that State, especially in courts, must be extended without discrimination to nationals of other Member States who fulfil all the conditions laid down for the use of a particular language by the members of the population group concerned.[31]

Community law also prevents a Member State from making compensation for harm caused in that State to the victim of an assault resulting in physical injury subject to conditions which amount to discrimination on grounds of nationality.[32] So a British tourist, a recipient of services, cannot be refused criminal injuries compensation[33] because he is not a French national[34] or does not hold a residence permit.[35]

The principle of non-retroactivity of penal sanctions applies in the field of Community law. The UK has been held not to have the power to adopt an Order restricting Danish vessels from fishing within 12 miles of the UK coast.

---

30. Case 137/84 *Ministère Public v Mutsch* [1985] ECR 2681 and Case C-274/96 *Criminal proceedings against H.O. Bickel* [1998] ECR I-7637.
31. *Mutsch*, para. 7.
32. Case 186/87 *Cowan v le Trésor Public* [1989] ECR 195.
33. Article 706-15 of the Code de Procédure Pénale (French Code of Criminal Procedure).
34. Direct discrimination.   35. Indirect discrimination.

In the field of fisheries policy, the powers of the Member States to take conservation measures find their limits in the respect of general principles of law. Without embarking upon an examination of the general legality of the retroactivity of Article 6(1) of that Regulation, it is sufficient to point out that such retroactivity may not, in any event, have the effect of validating *ex post facto* national measures of a penal nature which imposes penalties for an act which, in fact, was not punishable at the time at which it was committed. The principle that penal provisions may not have retroactive effects is one which is common to all the legal orders of the Member States and is enshrined in Article 7 of the European Convention for the Protection of Human Rights and Fundamental Freedoms as a fundamental right; it takes its place among the general principles of law whose observance is ensured by the Court of Justice. Consequently the retroactivity provided for in Article 6(1) of Regulation 170/83 of 25 January 1983 authorising, as from 1 January 1983, the retention of the derogation regime defined in Article 100 of the 1972 Act of Accession cannot validate *ex post facto* national measures of a penal nature which at the time of their implementation were incompatible with Community law.[36]

Community law recognises the principle according to which persons can be penalised only in respect of facts which can be imputed to them personally,[37] but it does not prevent Member States from setting the principle aside.[38] Member States may penalise infringements of a regulation by means of a system of strict criminal liability. A system which permits a person to be convicted without any proof of fault or negligence on his part does not come into conflict with the principle *nulla poena sine culpa*.[39]

Neither Community law nor the principle of non-retroactivity of penal sanctions prevent national courts from applying the provisions of a directive, even where the offence took place before the date set for compliance with that directive, if this leads to the retroactive effect of a more favourable provision of criminal law. Accordingly, an individual who holds a valid Community model driving licence issued by one Member State, and who has taken up residence in another Member State, but has not exchanged his

---

36. Case 63/83 *R v Kirk* [1984] ECR 2689.
37. Cases 187 and 190/83 *Nordbutter and Bayerische Milchversorgung v Germany* [1984] ECR 2553.
38. Case C-326/88 *Anklagemyndigheden v Hansen* [1990] ECR I-2911.
39. Van Gerven AG in *Hansen, op. cit.*

driving licence within the one-year period prescribed by Directive 80/1263, is entitled to rely directly on Directive 91/439 in order to challenge the imposition, in the Member State in which he has established his new residence, of a term of imprisonment or a fine for driving without a licence even where the offence took place before the date set for compliance with Directive 91/439.[40] This begs the question whether *Ratti*[41] is still good law. In that case Mr Ratti was denied the possibility to resist criminal prosecution on the ground that although his products were in conformity with the requirements laid down in a particular directive, the implementation period had not yet expired and the directive could not have direct effect.

Community Law and the materiality of the infraction

Community law can have both a positive and a negative influence in this field. Thus, it may prohibit certain activities and make it a criminal offence to carry them out, whilst in other instances, it may neutralise national criminal law.

Community law may be the source of a new legal offence

Many prosecutions involve the enforcement of Community law. Article 280 EC provides that Member States shall take the same measures to counter fraud affecting the financial interests of the Community as they take against fraud affecting their own financial interests. EC legislation too may impose a duty on Member States to include criminal sanctions in their measures for implementing EC obligations. The degree to which individual measures are likely to do so depends on the status of the legislation. A number of regulations have insisted that Member States should impose criminal sanctions for breaches of the regulation.[42] On the other hand, directives by their nature[43] cannot prescribe a specific sanction.

---

40. Case C-230/97 *Criminal proceedings against Ibiyinka Awoyemi* [1998] ECR I-6781.
41. Case 148/78 *Ratti* [1979] ECR 1629, paras 42–7.
42. Bridge, 'The European Community and Criminal Law' (1976) CrimLR 88. See also Chapter 11, and Harding et al. (eds), *op. cit.*, fn 1.
43. By virtue of Article 249 EC, directives leave Member States the choice of ways and means to achieve a prescribed result.

Thus, the obligation to impose criminal sanctions contained in the Draft of the Money Laundering Directive had to be deleted in the final text. In the end, the Member States made a declaration that they would undertake to punish breach of the Directive by the imposition of criminal sanctions,[44] and money laundering was assimilated to a criminal offence in all twelve Member States.[45]

Whatever the current state of the doctrine, Member States have in fact chosen to attach criminal sanctions to breaches of directives in legislation implementing a number of directives.[46] This is rather paradoxical, since Member States often insist that criminal law is an attribute of State sovereignty.[47] Yet by choosing to impose a criminal penalty, Member States accept that that penalty is subject to Community scrutiny and Community standards. If Member States remain free to choose a particular sanction for breach of a Community obligation, the ECJ has nevertheless made it clear that sanctions must be effective, have a deterrent effect and be proportionate to the offence committed.[48] Accordingly, if a Member State chooses a criminal penalty that penalty must achieve the Community standard. These Community law principles could aggravate the sanctions attached to a particular criminal offence for persons who act in contravention of Community provisions, which have been implemented in national law through the imposition of criminal penalties. This suggestion is based on the premise that the directive has been implemented in national law, and that all the conduct which the directive seeks to prohibit has been made a statutory offence, yet the penalty attached to this offence falls short of the Community standard. In such circumstances, national courts could impose a penalty which is effective, proportionate to

---

44. J. Dine, 'European Community Criminal Law?' (1993) Crim LR p. 247.
45. Eight of which have criminalised the laundering of the proceeds of any criminal activity or serious criminal offence, and not just the proceeds of drug trafficking. See Com 95(98) *Protecting the Community financial interests: the fight against fraud*, Annual Report 1994, p. 19. This study was carried out before the last enlargement.
46. A. Missir di Lusignano, 'La protection des intérêts financiers de la Communauté', *Journal des Tribunaux* (1996) pp. 73–8. Also the Food Safety Act 1990: powers of enforcement in relation to offences have been considerably strengthened and new offences have been introduced together with more serious criminal sanctions.
47. A paradox noted by A. Missir di Lusignano, *op. cit.*
48. Joined Cases C-58, 75, 112, 119, 123, 135, 140–1, 154 and 157/95 *Gallotti and Others* [1997] 1 CMLR 32, para. 14; C-382/92 *Commission v United Kingdom* [1994] ECR I-2455, para. 55; C-383/92 *Commission v United Kingdom* [1994] ECR I-2479, para. 40.

the offence committed and which will have a deterrent effect, as at stake is the judicial discretion as to sentencing rather than determination or aggravation of the liability in criminal law of persons who act in contravention of a non-implemented or badly implemented directive.

The next section will examine in detail the limits placed on the duty of national courts to construe national criminal law in conformity with Community law where a directive has not been implemented or has been implemented wrongly.

The duty of interpretation in the context of criminal proceedings

A Member State cannot rely on non-implemented directives against individuals, as 'a directive may not of itself impose obligations on an individual and . . . a provision of a directive may not be relied upon as such against such a person'.[49] Criminal proceedings cannot be brought in respect of conduct not clearly defined as culpable by law, and if a Member State has not transposed a directive, the national authorities cannot rely on its provisions against an individual who acts in breach of the directive. Furthermore, national courts cannot interpret national law in such a way as to make it compatible with the requirements laid down in the directive.

In applying national law, and in particular national law specifically introduced in order to implement a directive, national courts are required to interpret their national law in the light of the wording and the purpose of the directive in order to fulfil the result it seeks to achieve and thereby comply with Article 249(3) EC. However, this obligation on the national court to refer to the content of the directive is limited. National criminal law must be construed in accordance with *the principles and criteria of interpretation specific to that field of law*, a marked feature of which is the concern for safeguarding the principle of legality.[50] The ECJ upholds the principle of legality in criminal law – *nullum crimen, nulla poena*

---

49. Case 14/86 *Pretore di Salo v Persons unknown* [1987] ECR 2545, paras 19–20; Case 80/86 *Kolpinghuis Nijmegen* [1987] ECR 3969.
50. Colomer AG in Cases C-74/75 and C-129/95 *Criminal proceedings against X* [1996] ECR I-6609 at para. 62 of his Opinion.

sine lege – by virtue of which conduct will lead to criminal liability *only* if it contravenes a national provision which defined it before-hand as an offence. The ECJ has repeatedly held[51] that a directive cannot, of itself, and independently of a national law adopted by a Member State for its implementation, have the effect of determin-ing or aggravating the liability in criminal law of persons who act in contravention of the provisions of that directive. In other words, individuals cannot be prosecuted for acts which, although unlaw-ful under Community rules, are not punishable under national law. This case law, developed in relation to situations where a directive has not been incorporated in national law has been ex-tended to cases where the directive has been implemented, but wrongly.[52] So criminal liability cannot be incurred in respect of conduct which has not been made a statutory offence, although it ought to have been, had the directive been properly implemented.[53] In sum, no one may be punished by virtue of an extensive interpre-tation of national criminal law to bring it into conformity with a Community directive, if the conduct is not punishable under national law, and no one may be punished on the basis of the pro-visions of a directive.

Where a Member State has decided to attach a criminal sanc-tion to breach of a directive, the fact that it has not defined conduct which, under the directive, ought to be considered unlaw-ful can only be treated as a failure to fulfil Community obligations for which an action will have to be brought by the Commission. It cannot be corrected by national courts following the interpretative duty. 'The principle of legality in criminal law forms the same in-superable barrier to the effectiveness of directives and to the need to interpret national law in conformity with them.'[54] Apart from constituting 'an inherent limit to the effectiveness of Community directives',[55] this situation brings to light some of the paradoxes in-volved in leaving to Member States a discretion in the choice of sanctions. Indeed, if a Member State chooses to penalise breaches

51. Case 14/86 *Pretore di Salò v Persons unknown* [1987] ECR 2545; Case 80/86 *Kolpinghuis Nijmegen* [1987] ECR 3969; Case C-168/95 *Arcaro* [1996] ECR I-4705, para. 36.
52. Cases C-74/75 and C-129/95 *Criminal proceedings against X* [1996] ECR I-6609.
53. Cases C-74/75 and C-129/95 *Criminal proceedings against X* [1996] ECR I-6609, para. 72.
54. Colomer AG in Case C-74/95 and 129/95, *op. cit.*, at para. 75 of his Opinion.
55. *Loc. cit.*, at para. 54.

of a directive by means of a civil liability regime, then liability might ensue for types of conduct not listed in the implementing legislation but listed in the directive, if the national court is prepared to discharge its interpretative duty.[56]

There are other ways in which Community law may help resist a conviction.

Defence to a criminal charge

In the UK there have been numerous prosecutions relating to the tachograph required to be installed in certain vehicles by Community legislation.[57] Criminal proceedings have also been brought on the ground of infringement of fisheries legislation.[58] However, the contravention of a provision in a UK statute implementing Community legislation may not be an offence if it can be shown that the Community source has not been properly implemented or interpreted. Thus, Community law may be the foundation of an objection to the competency of the charge.[59] Where Community law is the basis for an offence, the offence can be held invalid, if it can be shown that the Community instrument which formed the basis of the offence has not been properly interpreted or implemented. It is also possible to argue that the domestic provision is unlawful, not because it implements Community law badly, but because the Community legislation on which it is based is itself invalid.[60] In other words, a challenge to the validity of Community legislation itself may be a defence to a criminal charge.

Community law defences have been mounted in a number of criminal prosecutions brought before national courts against traders alleged to have breached production or marketing regulations. Article 28 EC was used, in some instances successfully, as a defence to such criminal charges. Many leading judgments regarding Article 28 have been delivered in the course of references made by national courts in the context of criminal proceedings

---

56. See Chapter 5.
57. See Case 133/83 *R v Thomas Scott & Sons Bakers Ltd* [1985] 1 CMLR 188; Case C-47/97 *Criminal proceedings against E. Clarke & Sons (Coaches) Ltd* [1998] ECR I-2147; Case 79/86 *R. T. Hamilton v Whitelock* [1987] ECR 2363.
58. *Wither v Cowie* 1994 SLT 963; *Walkingshaw v Marshall* 1991 SCCR 397.
59. Case 79/86 *R.T. Hamilton v Whitelock, op. cit.*
60. For such an attempt (albeit unsuccessful) see *P.F. (Stranraer) v Marshall* [1988] 1 CMLR 657.

following prosecutions for selling goods improperly labelled[61] or without a particular certificate of origin,[62] for selling goods at a loss,[63] or below a prescribed minimum price,[64] and for canvassing at private dwellings for the purpose of selling educational material.[65]

Community law has supremacy over national criminal law.[66] Accordingly, no conviction may be obtained on the basis of a national legislative measure contrary to Community law[67] as the following cases show.

Some provisions of the legislation under which the Pigs Marketing Board was established and operated were found incompatible with Articles 28 and 29 EC. Accordingly, the Board could not rely upon this legislation to support the scheme for the marketing of pigs, and no pig producer in Northern Ireland could be required by law to market any of his pigs through the agency of the Board.[68]

The compatibility of certain provisions of UK customs legislation with Community law has also been challenged before UK courts in criminal proceedings concerning the seizure by the United Kingdom customs authorities of various consignments of goods imported from other Member States, regarded as 'indecent or obscene' articles whose importation into the UK is prohibited. One such case was *Conegate*.[69] Conegate argued that the forfeiture of the goods in question constituted an infringement of Article 28 EC which could not be justified on grounds of public morality within the meaning of Article 30 EC. In a previous judgment,[70] involving the importation of obscene publications into the UK, the ECJ had recognised that the prohibition on the importation of goods might be justified on grounds of public morality by virtue of Article 30 EC, and that each Member State remained free to determine, in accordance with its own scale of values and in the form selected by it, the requirements of public morality in its territory. Conegate

61. Case 27/80 *Criminal Proceedings against Anton Fietje* [1980] ECR 3839.
62. Case 8/74 *Procureur du Roi v Dassonville* [1974] ECR 837.
63. Cases C-26–8/91 *Criminal proceedings against Keck and Mithouard* [1993] ECR I-6097.
64. Case 82/77 *Openbaar Ministerie v Van Tiggele* [1978] ECR 25.
65. Case 382/87 *Ministère Public v Buet and EBS* [1989] ECR 1235.
66. Case 82/71 *Pubblico Ministerio Italiano v Sail* [1972] ECR 119.
67. Case 269/80 *R v Tymen* [1981] ECR 3079, paras 15–17.
68. Case 83/78 *Pigs Marketing Board v Redmond* [1978] ECR 2347, [1979] 3 CMLR 118.
69. Case 121/85 [1986] ECR 1007.
70. Case 34/79 *Henn & Darby* [1979] ECR 3795.

contended that, since in the UK the manufacture of erotic articles was not subject to any restriction, and that their marketing was subject only to prohibitions regarding transmission by post and display in public places,[71] no recourse could be had to standards concerning public morality. This argument was found convincing. The ECJ held that if Member States are free to determine the requirements of public morality in their territory, the operation of such a prohibition would constitute arbitrary discrimination[72] where a lawful trade in the same goods existed in the Member State concerned. In other words, a Member State may not apply to imported goods restrictions which are stricter than those applicable to the manufacture and marketing of the same products within its territory. Whilst Member States remained entitled to make their own assessments of the indecent or obscene character of certain articles, the fact that goods cause offence could not be regarded as sufficiently serious to justify restrictions on the free movement of goods, where the Member State concerned did not adopt, with respect to the same goods manufactured or marketed within its territory, penal measures or other serious and effective measures intended to prevent the distribution of such goods in its territory. In short, a Member State may not rely on grounds of public morality in order to prohibit the importation of goods from other Member States when its legislation does not prohibit the manufacture of the same goods on its territory, and only contains certain marketing restrictions. Member States, however, remain free to apply to those goods, once imported, the same restrictions on marketing which are applied to similar products manufactured and marketed within the country. The UK could rely on Article 30 EC even if the manufacture and marketing of the products whose importation had been prohibited were not prohibited in all the constituent parts of its territory, if the national court was able to conclude from the applicable rules, taken as a whole, that their purpose was, in substance, to prohibit the manufacture and marketing of those products.

---

71. Other restrictions were in force in certain of the constituent parts of the UK.
72. Prohibited by Article 30 EC.

Injunctions in aid of the criminal law

Enforcement powers may be exercised at the local level by local authorities which may institute proceedings in their own name for the promotion or protection of the interests of the inhabitants of their area.[73] The English courts have jurisdiction to grant injunctions in aid of criminal law, and local authorities may bring an action to protect public rights, as illustrated by the Sunday trading saga. In *Kirklees*,[74] Lord Goff considered the basis upon which an interim injunction should be granted in order to ensure compliance with criminal law. Even where the defendant in such an action alleges that national legislation which the local authority is trying to enforce is in breach of Community law, the local authority will not be required to give an undertaking in damages.

The enforcement of Community law by public authorities may also take the form of a civil action.[75] Thus the Attorney-General, pursuant to his general power to enforce public rights or duties owed to the public at large may, for example, seek an injunction to require an undertaking to admit inspectors sent by the EC Commission to investigate an alleged breach of the Community competition rules.

A word must be said about powers granted to the Commission in relation to the enforcement of competition law, since it can be regarded as a public interest matter and since national courts have on occasion become involved. The Commission has the power to search premises and to take away relevant documents. On occasion, it would have to seek the assistance of national courts to gain access to premises and even to obtain search warrants. In the same way, national courts may seek the assistance of the Commission when enforcing Community policies. A national court hearing proceedings on the infringement of Community rules and seeking the production of information concerning the existence of the facts constituting these infringements can require the Commission to produce documents and Commission officials to give evidence.[76]

It has been shown how Community law may be the source of a

---

73. Local Government Act 1972, section 222(1)(a).

74. *Kirklees BC v Wickes* [1992] 3 All ER 717, [1992] 2 CMLR 765.

75. See J.A. Usher, 'The Legal Framework for Implementation in the United Kingdom' in T. Daintith (ed), *Implementing EC Law in the United Kingdom* (Wiley, 1995).

76. Case C-2/88 *Imm Zwartveld* [1990] ECR I-4405.

creation of a new legal offence, and that it may affect the definition of a crime or offence meriting prosecution. Community law
may also determine what is a permissible sanction in the event of
conviction.

The punishment must fit the crime

Community law provisions are capable of imposing duties directly
on individuals. A corresponding duty is imposed on the Member
States to adopt measures to ensure compliance by individuals.
However, Community law sets limits as regards the control
measures which Member States are allowed to maintain in connection with the free movement provisions. Control procedures must
not be conceived in such a way as to restrict the freedom guaranteed by the Treaty and they must not be accompanied by a penalty
so disproportionate to the gravity of the infringement that it creates an obstacle to the exercise of that freedom. In short, penalties
must be compatible with the principle of proportionality.

So, where in certain circumstances a Member State may require
an importer to indicate the origin of its products, the fact that the
importer did not comply with the obligation to declare the real
origin of the goods cannot give rise to the application of penalties
which do not take account of the purely administrative nature of
the contravention. Accordingly, penalties such as seizure of the
goods or any pecuniary penalty fixed according to the value of the
goods would be incompatible with Community law.[77] Challenges
to the validity of Community legislation may be mounted on the
same grounds. Article 6(3) of Regulation 1880/83 is invalid inasmuch as it prescribes forfeiture of the entire security as the penalty
for failure to comply with the time limits imposed for the sub-
mission of applications for export licences.[78]

In relation to provisions governing the free movement of persons, similar principles apply. The right of Community workers to
enter the territory of a Member State may not be made subject to
the issue of an entry clearance certificate by the authorities of that
Member State. The Treaty allows Member States to lay down restrictions on freedom of movement in their territory on grounds of

[77.] Case 41/76 *Donckerwolcke* [1976] ECR 1921, paras 35–7.
[78.] Case 181/84 *Man Sugar* [1985] ECR 2889, para. 31.

public policy, public security or public health.[79] However these do not constitute a pre-condition to the acquisition of the right of entry and residence, they merely provide for the possibility, in individual cases, of imposing restrictions on the exercise of a right derived *directly* from the Treaty. Therefore administrative measures requiring formalities at a frontier other than simply the production of a valid identity card or passport are not justified. The issue of a special residence document[80] has only a declaratory effect and it cannot be assimilated to a residence permit. Member States cannot require possession of a general residence permit instead of the document provided for by Community law[81] or impose disproportionate penalties for the failure to obtain such a permit. Accordingly, failure by an individual to obtain a special residence permit may not be punished by a recommendation for deportation or by measures which go as far as imprisonment.[82]

The proportionality principle affects the sanctions attached to a criminal offence. Proportionality has to be determined either in the light of the mischief it is meant to correct,[83] or in the light of the nature of the contravention.[84] In this way, Member States' competence to prohibit or restrict certain types of criminal conduct or behaviour is limited by Community law.

In sum, where the exercise of one of the fundamental freedoms is restricted by an excessive penalty, that penalty must be reduced.

Community law and immigration law

EC law imposes limits on the powers of criminal courts to make recommendations for the deportation of the beneficiaries of the free movement provisions following criminal convictions. In this way, the extent of the Member State's discretion to implement those recommendations and to deport offenders on its own initiative may be circumscribed.[85]

---

79. Article 39 EC.   80. Directive 68/360, Article 4.
81. Directive 68/360, Article 4 and Annex.
82. Case 157/79 *R v Pieck* [1980] ECR 2171.
83. Case 30/77 *Bouchereau* [1977] ECR 1999, para. 35.
84. Case 118/75 *Criminal Proceedings against Watson and Belman* [1976] ECR 1185.
85. C. Vincenzi, 'Deportation in Disarray: The Case of EC Nationals' (1994) Crim LR pp. 163–75.

Article 39 EC ensures freedom of movement for workers within the Community, *subject to restrictions justified on grounds of public policy, public security or public health*. Nationals of Member States can move freely in the territory of Member States and stay in a Member State to take up a post there in accordance with the laws, regulations and administrative provisions governing the employment of national workers. Directive 64/221[86] defines the scope of the reservation concerning public policy, public security or public health and lays down procedural safeguards[87] for persons subject to measures restricting their freedom of movement or rights of residence. It also restricts the grounds for deportation or for refusing a worker leave to enter a Member State.[88]

Criminal offences as a ground for expulsion

Article 3 of Directive 64/221 is relevant to expulsions following a criminal conviction:

> Measures taken on grounds of public policy or public security *shall be based exclusively on the personal conduct of the individual concerned*. Previous criminal convictions *shall not in themselves* contribute grounds for the taking of such measures.[89]

In *Bouchereau*,[90] the ECJ considered the question whether a criminal conviction could be sufficient in itself to justify a recommendation for deportation. It held that the terms of the Directive required national authorities to carry out a specific appraisal from the point of view of the interests inherent in protecting the requirements of public policy. Such an appraisal might not necessarily coincide with the appraisal which formed the basis

---

86. On the co-ordination of special measures concerning the movement and residence of foreign nationals which are justified on grounds of public policy, public security or public health, OJ (English Special Edition) 1962–1964, p. 117.
87. Article 6 provides that the person concerned shall be informed of the grounds of public policy, public security or public health upon which the decision taken in his case is based, unless this is contrary to the interests of the security of the State involved. Article 7 provides *inter alia* that the person concerned shall be notified of any decision to refuse the issue or renewal of a residence permit and to expel him from the territory. Article 8 gives the person concerned access to the same legal remedies as are available to nationals in respect of acts of the administration.
88. Articles 3 and 4.   89. Article 3(2) (emphasis added).
90. Case 30/77 *Bouchereau* [1977] ECR 1999.

of a criminal conviction. The existence of a previous criminal conviction could only be taken into account in so far as the circumstances which gave rise to that conviction are evidence of *personal conduct* constituting *a present threat* to the requirement of public policy.[91] The ECJ added that recourse by a national authority to the concept of public policy presupposes the existence, in addition to the perturbation of the social order which any infringement of the law involves, of a genuine and sufficiently serious threat to the requirements of public policy affecting one of the fundamental interests of society. When applying the preliminary ruling to the facts of the case, the magistrates' court considered that the possession of a small amount of drugs by Mr Bouchereau did not make him a sufficiently serious threat to the requirements of public policy. Accordingly, a recommendation for deportation was not made and a fine of £35 was imposed.

In *Bouchereau*, the ECJ also remarked that a finding of a threat to the requirements of public policy implies the existence in the individual concerned of a propensity to act in the same way in the future, and that past conduct alone may constitute such a threat to the requirements of public policy. Whether this runs counter to the express words of Article 3(1) of the Directive is a matter of some debate.[92] Still, past conduct alone without a propensity of further misconduct has been found 'to be sufficient to constitute a present threat to public policy.'[93]

In *Santillo*[94] past criminal convictions were considered. Mr Santillo had been convicted of buggery, rape, indecent assault and assault occasioning actual bodily harm. On 21 January 1974 he was sentenced to a total of eight years' imprisonment for these four offences. When passing sentence, the criminal court made a recommendation for deportation. On 10 October 1974 the Court of Appeal (Criminal Division) refused the applicant leave to appeal against the prison sentence and the recommendation for deportation. On 28 September 1978 the Secretary of State made a deportation order against him to take effect when his prison sentence was completed. Having completed his prison sentence on

---

91. *Loc. cit.*, paras 27 and 28.
92. Craig and De Bùrca, p. 787; Vicenzi, *op. cit.*, fn 85.
93. *R v Secretary of State for the Home Department, ex parte Marchon* [1993] 2 CMLR 132 (CA) at 137.
94. Case 131/79 *R v Secretary of State for the Home Department, ex parte Santillo* [1980] ECR 1585.

3 April 1979 – after remission of one-third for good behaviour – he was due to be released but remained in detention under the Immigration Act. On 10 April 1979, he applied to the High Court to set aside the deportation order on the ground that, as it had been made more than four years after the recommendation for deportation, Article 9(1) of Directive 64/221 had been infringed. A reference was made to the ECJ, which ruled that:

> a lapse of time amounting to several years between the recommendation for deportation and the decision by the administration is liable to deprive the recommendation of its function as an opinion within the meaning of Article 9. It is indeed essential that the social danger resulting from a foreigner's presence should be assessed at the very time when the decision ordering expulsion is made against him as the factors to be taken into account, particularly those concerning his conduct, are likely to change in the course of time.

Back in the referring court,[95] it was held that the requirement[96] that the opinion from a competent authority must be sufficiently proximate in time to the expulsion order is satisfied where the 'opinion' was that of a trial court sentencing the alien to imprisonment. Although the expulsion order was made over four years later, no new factors had supervened such as to invalidate the opinion of the trial court and the alien had received full remission of his sentence for good conduct in prison. Where a Community national has been sentenced by an English court to imprisonment for a criminal offence and the trial court has recommended that he be deported after serving his sentence, the recommendation is an 'opinion from a competent authority' within the meaning of the Directive. Where there is a four and a half year interval between the 'opinion' and the deportation order, the burden of proof lies on the individual to show that his personal circumstances have changed sufficiently to deprive the 'opinion' of its efficacy through lapse of time.

95. [1981] 1 CMLR 569, Court of Appeal.
96. Article 9(1) of Directive 64/221.

Policing the police

The Amsterdam Treaty provides that the new TEU Title on police and judicial co-operation in criminal matters shall not affect the exercise of the responsibilities of Member States with regard to the maintenance of law and order and the safeguarding of internal security.[97] Yet such an effect has already been felt in the Community law Title, as will now be shown.

The exercise of a Member State's responsibility for law and order and internal security is not beyond the reach of Community law, since Member States must ensure proper policing of operations which might endanger the free movement of goods.[98] By failing to adopt all necessary and proportionate measures in order to prevent the free movement of fruit and vegetables from being obstructed by actions by private individuals, the French Government failed to fulfil its obligations under Article 28 EC in conjunction with Article 10 EC:

> As an indispensable instrument for the realisation of a market without internal frontiers, Article 30 therefore does not prohibit solely measures emanating from the State which, in themselves, create restrictions on trade between Member States. It also applies where a Member State abstains from adopting the measures required in order to deal with obstacles to the free movement of goods which are not caused by the State. The fact that a Member State abstains from taking action or, as the case may be, fails to adopt adequate measures to prevent obstacles to the free movement of goods that are created, in particular, by actions by private individuals on its territory aimed at products originating in other Member States is just as likely to obstruct intra-Community trade as is a positive act.[99]

Article 10 EC not only requires Member States to abstain from adopting measures or engaging in conduct liable to constitute an obstacle to trade, but also requires them to take all necessary and appropriate measures to ensure that free movement is respected on their territory. Thus, Community law creates both a negative and a positive obligation on the Member States, with far-reaching consequences and a potential for judicial review of police operations.

---

97. Article 33 TEU, Article 64 EC.
98. Case C-265/95 *Commission v France* [1997] ECR I-6959.
99. Case C-265/95, *op. cit.*, paras 30 and 31.

Unless a Member State can show that action on its part would have consequences for public order with which it could not cope by using the means at its disposal, it must adopt all appropriate measures to guarantee the full scope and effect of Community law so as to ensure its proper implementation in the interests of all economic operators. In this way, the proportionality of operations carried out by the police or law enforcement agencies is subject to judicial review and Member States will have to justify *inter alia* low prosecution rates,[100] levels of intervention by the police,[101] or a decision to limit police escort.[102]

So if Member States retain exclusive competence as regards the maintenance of public order and the safeguarding of internal security and unquestionably enjoy a margin of discretion in determining what measures are most appropriate to eliminate barriers to the importation of products in a given situation, the exercise of this discretion is subject to judicial scrutiny. Such review may take place in the national courts[103] as well as before the ECJ,[104] and whether both would reach the same conclusions when deciding whether all appropriate measures to guarantee the full scope and effect of Community law so as to ensure its proper implementation in the interests of all economic operators have been taken, is a matter of speculation.

Limits

There are limits to the usefulness of Community law within the context of criminal proceedings, as the following cases illustrate.

The *Saunders* case concerned the consequences flowing from a breach of an undertaking given by a British national, on a plea of guilty in criminal proceedings, to proceed to Northern Ireland and not to return to England or Wales for a period of three years. Ms Saunders tried to rely on Article 39 EC – which entails the right of a worker, subject to limitations justified *inter alia* on grounds of public policy and public security, to move freely within the territory of Member States so as to accept offers of employment actually made and to stay there for the purpose of employment –

---

100. *Ibid.*, paras 18 and 50.   101. *Ibid.*
102. *R v Chief Constable of Sussex, ex parte International Traders Ferry Ltd* [1997] 2 CMLR 164 (CA), [1998] 3 WLR 1260 (HL).
103. *Ibid.*   104. Case C-265/95, *op. cit.*

for the purpose of opposing the application of measures restricting her freedom of movement within the UK. However, in such circumstances Community law is of no avail:

> Although the rights conferred upon workers by Article 48 may lead the Member States to amend their legislation, where necessary, even with respect to their own nationals, this provision does not however aim to restrict the power of the Member States to lay down restrictions, within their own territory, on the freedom of movement of all persons subject to their jurisdiction in implementation of domestic criminal law.[105]

This case applies the established principle according to which the provisions of the Treaty on freedom of movement for workers cannot be applied to situations which are wholly internal to a Member State, in so far as there is no factor connecting them to any of the situations envisaged by Community law.

> The application by an authority or court of a Member State to a worker who is a national of that same State of measures which deprive or restrict the freedom of movement of that worker within the territory of that State as a penal measure provided for by national law by reason of acts committed within the territory of that State is a wholly domestic situation which falls outside the scope of the rules contained in the Treaty on freedom of movement for workers.[106]

In one of the many cases[107] where the compatibility of the Shops Act 1950 with Article 28 EC was considered, the Article 28 EC defence was rejected together with the request for a preliminary ruling as the High Court was 'satisfied that the defendants' real concern is to obtain a two-year delay so that they may continue to trade in infringement of the criminal law and at a very great profit to themselves, in the hope that the answers to these theoretical questions can be long delayed.'[108] Accordingly the injunction in aid of criminal law requested by the local authority was granted and the defendants restrained from using land as a retail market contrary to the provisions of the Shops Act.

[105]. Case 175/78 *R v Saunders* [1979] ECR 1129, para. 10.
[106]. *Loc. cit.*, para. 12.   [107]. See Chapter 1.
[108]. *Wychavon District Council v Midland Enterprises (Special Events) and another* [1988] 1 CMLR 397, per Millet J at 409; and also see P. Diamond, 'Dishonourable Defences: the Use of Injunctions and the EEC Treaty – Case Study of the Shops Act 1950' (1990) 54 MLR 72.

Another unsuccessful (albeit inventive) use of Community law was tried in relation to the consequences to be attached to the failure to notify a technical regulation on breath-analysis apparatus. The ECJ held that technical regulations are not excluded from the notification procedure laid down in Directive 83/189, even though they fall within the scope of criminal law. However, failure to notify a technical regulation on breath-analysis apparatus did not have the effect of making it impossible for evidence obtained by means of such apparatus to be relied upon against an individual charged with driving while under the influence of alcohol.[109]

Conclusion

So Community law has the capacity to prescribe or prevent enforcement at national level. But its impact is not limited to the emergence of 'Euro-defences' and the enactment of new regulatory offences. Community law has a say in what is a permissible sanction, and Community or national legislation laying down excessive penalties may be challenged. There are also broader implications for domestic criminal justice policy. As the Community relies heavily on domestic enforcement machinery, this has consequences for allocation of resources and priorities for law enforcement agencies.[110] 'The outcome is axiomatic: the fact of an expanding body of criminal law, some of which is at the service of the Community, as distinct from national policies, inevitably complicates the operation of Member States' systems of criminal law enforcement.'[111]

109. Case C-226/87 *Criminal proceedings against Lemmens* [1998] ECR I-3711.
110. *R v Chief Constable of Sussex, ex parte International Traders Ferry Ltd* [1997] 2 CMLR 164 (CA), [1998] 3 WLR 1260 (HL).
111. Guldenmund, Harding and Sherlock, *op. cit.*, fn 1, pp. 125–6.

CHAPTER TEN

Enforcing Community law against Community institutions

In cases where national authorities are responsible for administrative implementation of Community regulations, the legal protection guaranteed by Community law includes the right of individuals to challenge, as a preliminary issue, the legality of such regulations before national courts and to request those courts to refer questions to the Court for a preliminary ruling.[1]

That right would be compromised if, pending delivery of a judgment of the Court, which *alone has jurisdiction* to declare a Community regulation invalid, individuals were not in a position, where certain conditions are satisfied, to obtain a decision granting suspension of enforcement which would make it possible for the effects of the disputed regulation to be rendered inoperative as regards them.[2]

The combined provisions of Articles 178 and 215 of the Treaty only give jurisdiction to the Court to award compensation for damage caused by the Community institutions or by their servants in the performance of their duties, or in other words for damage capable of giving rise to non-contractual liability on the part of the Community. Damage caused by national institutions, on the other hand, can only give rise to liability on the part of those institutions, and the national courts retain sole jurisdiction to order compensation for such damage. Where, as in this case, the decision adversely affecting the applicant was adopted by a national body acting in order to ensure the implementation of Community rules, it is necessary, in order to establish the jurisdiction of the Court, to determine whether the unlawful conduct alleged in support of the

---

[1.] Cases C-143/88 and C-92/89 *Zuckerfabrik Suderdithmarschen AG v Hauptzollamt Itzehoe* [1991] ECR I-415, para. 16.
[2.] C-465/93 *Atlanta Fruchthandelsgesellschaft mbH e.a.* [1995] ECR I-3761, para. 20.

application for compensation is in fact the responsibility of a Community institution and cannot be attributed to the national body.[3]

This book is not concerned with the limited right of access of individuals before the Court of First Instance or the ECJ.[4] However, alongside direct actions under Article 230, there are instances where Community law can be challenged indirectly before national courts. The purpose of this chapter is to explain how individuals can defend themselves before their domestic courts for violations of Community law by the Community institutions.

Where national administrations apply Community legislation, Community law can be challenged before national courts. Article 234 provides for a means to review the validity of Community legislation or action against a superior norm of Community law. The role of Article 234 and that of national courts in challenging the validity of Community acts and the conditions to the granting of interim relief pending a preliminary ruling on validity will be examined. The fact that Community policies are for the most part implemented by national authorities places further duties and responsibilities on national courts. Indeed, on occasion, loss can be caused to individuals as a result of concurrent activities on the part of the Community and national authorities. In such cases of concurrent liability, the normal course of action is for the individual to seek redress before domestic courts.

Article 234 as a means of securing a declaration of invalidity of Community law

References for preliminary rulings on the validity of a measure, like actions for annulment, allow the legality of acts of the Community institutions to be reviewed.[5]

Article 234 provides that the Court of Justice shall have jurisdiction to give preliminary rulings concerning the validity of acts of the institutions of the Community. This, in turn, presupposes that

---

3. Case 175/84 *Krohn* [1986] ECR 753, paras 18–19.
4. Since 1993, the Court of First Instance has jurisdiction to hear and determine at first instance *any* action brought by a natural or legal person against an act of a Community institution: Decision 94/149, OJ 1994 L66/29.
5. Case 314/85 *Foto-Frost v Hauptzollamt Lübeck-Ost* [1987] ECR 4199.

such challenges can be mounted before national courts. Thus, the validity of a Regulation[6] fixing total allowable catches (TAC) for certain fish stocks was challenged in judicial review proceedings in the High Court of Justice in the context of the decision of the Department of Agriculture for Northern Ireland allocating to the Northern Ireland Fish Producers' Organisation (NIFPO) its catch quotas for cod and whiting in the Irish Sea.[7] The distribution of quotas was challenged as being unlawful, inasmuch as the allocation of TAC for the UK in Regulation 3362/94 was itself alleged to be contrary to Community law.

If challenges to the validity of Community legislation can be mounted before national courts, the latter may not of themselves rule upon the validity of Community law. Unlike where matters of interpretation are concerned, where a question of validity is raised, *all* national courts and tribunals are under a *duty* to refer the question to the ECJ. In *Foto-Frost v Hauptzollamt Lübeck-Ost*[8] the ECJ, in effect, rewrote the words of Article 234 and held that it was not open to national courts to make a finding of invalidity. Where a challenge to validity is mounted, the national court has no discretion, it *must* refer to the ECJ which has exclusive jurisdiction to declare Community acts invalid. The rule in *Foto-Frost* was soon after followed and applied in *R v MAFF and another, ex parte FEDESA*[9] in relation to a challenge to the validity of a statutory instrument implementing a directive, even though the directive itself was already the subject of a direct challenge before the ECJ.[10] The requirement that national courts refer questions of validity to the ECJ reduces the litigants' dependence on national courts' willingness to refer.

6. Regulation 3362/94, OJ 1994 L 363/1.
7. Case C-4/96 *NIFPO and Northern Ireland Fishermen's Federation v Department of Agriculture for Northern Ireland* [1998] ECR I-681.
8. Case 314/85, [1987] ECR 4199 para. 20; and Cases C-143/88 and C 92/89 *Zuckerfabrik Suderdithmarschen AG v Hauptzollamt Itzehoe* [1991] ECR I-415.
9. [1988] 3 CMLR 207.
10. In Case 68/86 *United Kingdom v Council* [1988] ECR 855.

Assessing the validity of Community legislation or action, against which norms?

The validity of Community legislation or action can only be judged in the light of Community law itself. The grounds on which a Community measure may be annulled under Article 230 include lack of competence, infringement of an essential procedural requirement, misuse of power and infringement of the Treaty or any rule of law relating to its application. The latter is of particular relevance, since it is on this ground that litigants may base claims that Community measures or actions are in breach of general principles of law such as proportionality, equality, legal certainty, or in breach of principles governing respect for fundamental rights.

Challenges to the validity of Community legislation or action, which relate mostly to the Common Agricultural Policy (CAP) and to fisheries, are rarely successful. This is partly explained by the fact that the ECJ has recognised that implementation by the EC Council of the Community's agricultural policy often necessitates the evaluation of a complex economic situation. Thus the Community institutions must be allowed a wide margin of discretion. This discretion is not limited solely to the nature and scope of the measures to be taken but also to the nature of the facts relied upon, as it is open to the Council to rely, if necessary, on general findings. In reviewing the exercise of this discretionary power, the ECJ confines itself to examining whether there has been a manifest error or misuse of power or whether the authority in question has clearly exceeded the bounds of its discretion.[11] This background also influences the way in which the ECJ applies the principle of proportionality.

> In order to establish whether a provision of Community law complies with the principle of proportionality, it must be ascertained whether the means which it employs are suitable for the purpose of achieving the desired objective and whether they do not go beyond what is necessary to achieve it. Furthermore, whilst a measure's patent unsuitability for achieving the objective which the competent institution seeks to pursue may affect its legality, the Community institutions must nonetheless be recognised as having a broad discretion in regard to agricultural policy which reflects the responsibilities which the Treaty imposes on them.[12]

11. Case C-122/94 *Commission v Council* [1996] ECR I-881, para. 18.
12. Case C 4/96, para. 57.

The same approach is adopted in relation to the principle of equality. The prohibition of discrimination laid down in Article 34(3) of the Treaty requires that comparable situations should not be treated in a different manner unless the difference in treatment is objectively justified. Conversely the principle of equality of treatment requires that different situations must *not* be treated in the same way unless such treatment is objectively justified.

In sum, if it is possible, in judicial review proceedings against UK regulations implementing a Community instrument, to challenge the validity of the Community instrument itself, and base such challenges on *inter alia* infringement of the principles of legal certainty, equality, proportionality, and the objectives of the CAP, violation of Article 253 EC[13] or infringement of an essential procedural requirement, such challenges are rarely successful. In relation to the CAP, the legality of a measure can be affected only if the measure is *manifestly inappropriate* having regard to the objective which the competent institution is seeking to pursue.[14]

The validity of Community legislation cannot be assessed against national standards, including provisions of national constitutions intended to protect fundamental rights.[15] This is a requirement of primacy. Conflicts between Community legislation and fundamental rights as protected by the national constitution have not yet arisen in the UK, but have caused problems in Germany, raising the prospect of a direct threat to the supremacy of Community law. In the end, the crisis was avoided by the ECJ holding that Community law recognised analogous principles protecting fundamental rights. However, there is always the possibility of a crisis, as the German Supreme Court has maintained that it retains its jurisdiction to decide on the compatibility of Community law with fundamentals of the German Constitution. It is conceivable that once the UK incorporates the European Convention for the Protection of Human Rights and Fundamental Freedoms (hereafter the Convention), the validity of some Community action or legislation will be challenged in the UK courts as being incompatible with the Convention. Even if the Union respects fundamental rights and freedoms such as that contained in

---

13. Statement of reasons on which the measures is based.
14. Case 265/87 *Schraeder* [1989] ECR 2237, paras 21–2.
15. Case 11/70 *Internationale Handelsgesellschaft GmbH v Einfuhr- und Vorrasstelle für Getreide and Futtermittel* [1970] ECR 1125.

the Convention,[16] given the real possibility of diverging interpretations between the Luxembourg and Strasbourg courts,[17] such challenge to the validity of Community law could also be mounted before UK courts. In this way new challenges to the supremacy of Community law in the UK may arise. To take a practical example, the inviolability of commercial premises is approached differently by the Strasbourg and Luxembourg courts. By virtue of Article 10 EC national courts have a duty to co-operate with the Community institutions. Such duty includes providing assistance to the Commission when it investigates alleged infringement of competition rules, and might involve providing assistance to gain access to premises. A company might argue that the national court ought not to give assistance to the Commission on the grounds that the Commission's action is in breach of the Convention.

The relationship between Article 234 and Article 230

The possibility that natural or legal persons can challenge the validity of Community legislation before domestic courts in some ways offsets their fairly restricted access under Article 230. However, in cases raising complex issues of fact and law, proceedings before national courts present serious disadvantages as an alternative to a direct action. Such limits were outlined in *Extramet*.[18] By virtue of the division of function established under Article 234, the fact-finding power lies principally with the national courts making the reference, but only a full exchange of pleadings as in direct actions is likely to be adequate if all the issues raised are to be properly considered.[19]

For some time it was unclear whether a natural or legal person could challenge the validity of a Community measure in proceedings under Article 234, where it was open to it to challenge the

16. Article 8 TEU.
17. R. Lawson, 'Confusion and Conflict? Diverging Interpretations of the European Convention of Human Rights in Strasbourg and Luxembourg' in R. Lawson and M. de Blois (eds), *The Dynamics of the Protection of Human Rights in Europe* (Kluwer, 1994) p. 252.
18. Case C-358/89 *Extramet v Council* [1991] ECR I-2501.
19. Jacobs AG in *Extramet v Council*: and again in Case C-188/92 *TWD Textilwerke Deggendorf GmbH* [1994] ECR I-883.

measure in question directly. The ECJ has held that Article 234 should not be used as a way to remedy the failure of a natural or legal person to challenge a Community act under Article 230(4).[20] In *TWD*, the ECJ ruled on the time-barring effects of the expiry of time limits for bringing a direct action:

> A national court is bound by a Commission decision adopted under Article 93(2) of the Treaty where, in view of the implementation of that decision by the national authorities, the recipient of the aid to which the implementation measures are addressed brings before it an action in which it pleads the unlawfulness of the Commission's decision and where that recipient of aid, although informed in writing by the Member State of the Commission's decision, did not bring an action against that decision under the second paragraph of Article 173 of the Treaty, or did not do so within the period prescribed.

This ruling was strongly influenced by the facts of the case: the applicant was fully aware of the Commission's decision and of the fact that it could *undoubtedly* have challenged it under Article 230 EC. 'In such factual and legal circumstances, the definitive nature of the decision taken by the Commission pursuant to Article 93 of the Treaty *vis-à-vis* the undertaking in receipt of the aid binds the national court by virtue of the principle of legal certainty.'

That *TWD* only laid down limited and well-defined restrictions was confirmed in *Accrington Beef*.[21] In spite of the expiry of the time limits under Article 230 EC, the ECJ plea of illegality was accepted. The ECJ stressed that where the contested provisions were contained in a Community regulation, it was not obvious that an action by the applicants challenging that regulation under Article 230 would have been admissible.[22] The same result was reached in *Eurotunnel*,[23] where the ECJ held that Eurotunnel could challenge the validity of directives[24] in preliminary-ruling proceedings even where it did not challenge those directives by means of

20. Case C-188/92, *op. cit.*
21. Case C-241/95 *R v Intervention Board for Agricultural Produce, ex parte Accrington Beef Co. Ltd and others* [1996] ECR I-6699.
22. At para. 14.
23. Case C-408/95 *Eurotunnel SA and others v SeaFrance* [1997] ECR I-6315.
24. Directive 91/680 supplementing the common system of VAT, amending Directive 77/388 with a view to the abolition of fiscal frontiers, and Article 28 of Directive 92/12 on the general arrangements for products subject to excise duty and on the holding, movement and monitoring of such products.

an action under Article 230, as it was unclear whether such an action would have been admissible. The fact that another national court had already given judgment in separate proceedings was also dismissed as irrelevant.

The need for interim protection

The delay in obtaining a preliminary ruling from the ECJ underlines the growing importance of interim protection. The ECJ has developed a fully-fledged system of interim protection at national level.[25] Pending a preliminary ruling from the ECJ on the validity of a regulation, national courts are entitled to suspend enforcement of a national administrative measure based on that regulation. They also have the power to order interim measures which may create a new legal position for the benefit of the person seeking legal protection.

In *Zuckerfabrik*,[26] the Court considered the question for the first time. The case concerned an application for suspension of the enforcement of a national measure based on a Community regulation,[27] the validity of which was challenged. In *Atlanta*,[28] the applicant sought an order similar to that of specific performance, and the ECJ was asked whether national judges had any power to take positive interim measures which would create a new legal regime for the litigant.[29] The question arose in proceedings between German importers of bananas (the Atlanta companies), and the Federal Office of Food and Forestry on the allocation of import quotas for third-country bananas. This case belonged to a series of actions before the ECJ and the German courts concerning the common organisation of the market in bananas[30] and a common import regime replacing the various national arrangements whereby, in trade with third countries, imports of bananas would be subject to a Community levy. The Regulation under challenge

---

25. E. Sharpston, 'Interim relief in the national courts' in Lonbay and Biondi (eds), *Remedies for Breach of EC Law* (Wiley, 1995) pp. 47–54.
26. Cases C-143/88 and C-92/89 *Zuckerfabrik Suderdithmarschen AG v Hauptzollamt Itzehoe* [1991] ECR I-415.
27. Regulation 1914/87, OJ 1987 L183/5, introducing a special elimination levy in the sugar sector.
28. C-465/93 *Atlanta Fruchthandelsgesellschaft mbH e.a.* [1995] ECR I -3761.
29. R. Medhi, 'Le droit communautaire et les pouvoirs du juge national de l'urgence' (1996) 32 RTDE pp. 77–100.
30. Regulation 404/93, OJ 1993 L 47/1.

discontinued the annual duty-free import quota for bananas enjoyed by Germany. Both the action for annulment of the Regulation[31] and the application for interim relief[32] brought by the German Government failed. The Atlanta companies, importers of third-country bananas, were allocated by the German authorities – in application of the Regulation – a provisional import quota for third-country bananas. They challenged the quota on the ground that the Regulation limited their freedom to import. They also sought interim relief in the form of an order to grant additional import licences, for third-country bananas over and above the number already allocated, pending the ECJ ruling on the question of validity. The German court ordered the administration provisionally to grant the applicants additional import licences,[33] and at the same time it asked the ECJ whether a distinction ought to be drawn, with respect to the requirements for making an interim order, between an interim order intended to preserve the *status quo* and one intended to create a new legal regime. As the German court pointed out, the granting of additional import licences called into question the uniform application of the Regulation in all the Member States. As to whether the grant of positive measures would, as such, have radical consequences for the Community legal order the ECJ held that 'the consequences of the interim measure, whatever it may be, for the Community legal order must be assessed as part of the balancing exercise between the Community interest and the interests of the individual'.[34]

The principle of interim protection

Interim protection requires that national courts should have the power to grant interim remedies. In the context of actions for annulment under Article 230 EC, the Court has the power to order interim suspension of the contested act,[35] and it also has the power to prescribe any necessary interim measure.[36] Accordingly, the interim legal protection which national courts must be in a position to afford individuals under Community law must be the same,

---

31. Case C-280/93 *Germany v Council* [1994] ECR I-4973.
32. Case C-280/93R *Germany v Council* [1993] ECR I-3667.
33. Subject to conditions destined to ensure that if the applicants lost their case, the additional quotas allocated to them could be set off against the quota entitlement for the following year.
34. *Atlanta*, para. 29.   35. Article 240 EC.   36. Article 243 EC.

whether they seek suspension of enforcement of a national administrative measure or the grant of positive interim measures. Accordingly:

> the interim legal protection which the national courts must afford to individuals under Community law must be the same, whether they seek suspension of enforcement of a national administrative measure adopted on the basis of a Community regulation or the grant of interim measures settling or regulating the disputed legal positions or relationships for their benefit.[37]

Where the compatibility of national legislation with Community law was challenged,[38] the ECJ held that the national court which had referred questions of interpretation for a preliminary ruling in order to enable it to decide that issue of compatibility had to be able to grant interim relief and to suspend the application of the disputed national legislation until such time as it could deliver its judgment on the basis of the interpretation given in accordance with Article 234. Community law is a single system; even if Community law is formulated at Community level and applied at national level, individuals are entitled to a coherent and consistent system of judicial protection both at national and Community level:

> The interim legal protection which Community law ensures for individuals before national courts must remain the same, irrespective of whether they contest the compatibility of national legal provisions with Community law or the validity of secondary Community law, in view of the fact that the dispute in both cases is based on Community law itself.[39]

Pending the outcome of a ruling by the ECJ, interim relief may be granted by UK courts to protect Community rights, whether these have been breached following the adoption of a UK statute said to be in conflict with Community law, or whether they have been breached following the application by UK administrative authorities of an allegedly invalid Community act.

In the context of requests for interpretation, the national court is asked to suspend the application of a piece of domestic legis-

---

37. *Atlanta*, para. 28.
38. Case C-213/89 *R v Secretary of State for Transport, ex parte Factortame and others* [1990] ECR I-2433.
39. *Zuckerfabrik, op. cit.* fn 26, para. 20, see also *Atlanta, op. cit.*, fn 28, para. 24.

THE NEED FOR INTERIM PROTECTION

lation allegedly in conflict with Community law. However, in proceedings where validity is at issue, the national judge is asked to
suspend the application of a Community act the validity of which
is contested, thereby questioning the presumption of validity in favour of Community legislation. It has been said that, whilst in the
first instance interim protection ensures the immediate supremacy
of Community law, in the latter primacy is set aside, suspended,
albeit provisionally, insofar as interim protection calls into question the presumption of validity attached to a Community
regulation:

> The judicial protection of individuals relying on Community law
> goes as far as allowing a national court to suspend temporarily the
> application of Community law. That judgment . . . places the
> protection of the individual in the foreground, even in front of
> the question of priority.[40]

In reality, primacy is not set aside. In both sets of circumstances,
primacy is safeguarded, for the validity of Community legislation
or action can only be assessed against a superior Community
norm. In other words, challenges to the validity of Community
legislation are only concerned with upholding the primacy of
Community law.

The conditions for the grant of interim relief: national or Community conditions?

When they apply Community law, national judges are part of the
Community judicial architecture. However, in most cases, given
the regrettable absence of Community rules, the national/Com-
munity judge has to apply the domestic rules.[41] As these differ
from one jurisdiction to another, the uniform application of Community law is jeopardised. Since the right to interim protection is
based on Community law, national judges asked the ECJ whether
specific Community rules existed which ought to be applied in
preference to their own domestic rules governing the granting of
interim protection.

Are UK courts obliged to apply domestic rules governing interim protection in order to prevent irreparable damage or are

---

40. Opinion of Leger AG in Case C5/94 *R v MAFF, ex parte Lomas* [1996] ECR
I-2553, para. 62.
41. See above, Chapter 6.

there Community rules dealing with this situation? The House of Lords had already referred this question to the ECJ in *Factortame*,[42] but it remained unanswered until the *Zuckerfabrik* and *Atlanta* judgments. The ECJ followed its traditional approach:[43] the suspension of enforcement of administrative measures based on a Community regulation, whilst governed by national procedural law in particular as regards the making and examination of the application, must in all the Member States be subject, at the very least, to conditions which are uniform so far as the granting of such relief is concerned.[44] Further, since the power of national courts to order interim relief corresponds to the jurisdiction reserved to the ECJ by Article 243 in the context of actions brought under Article 230 of the Treaty, national courts may grant such relief only on the same conditions as apply when the ECJ deals with an application for interim measures.[45]

A national court can order interim relief if four conditions are met. First, it must entertain serious doubts as to the validity of the Community act and state them in its decision; secondly, if the validity of the contested act is not already before the ECJ, it must make a reference; thirdly, there must be urgency, in that the interim relief is necessary in order to avoid serious and irreparable damage being caused to the party seeking the relief; and finally, due account must be taken of the Community interest. The ECJ did not rule out the possibility of the national court requiring a cross-undertaking in damages, 'if the grant of interim relief represents a financial risk for the Community, the national court must be able to require the applicant to provide adequate guarantees, such as the deposit of money or other security'.[46]

In *Zuckerfabrik* the ECJ had already set out the conditions governing suspension of enforcement of a national administrative measure adopted in implementation of a Community regulation. In *Atlanta* the ECJ confirmed the same conditions were applicable where a national court orders a positive measure rendering the regulation whose validity is challenged provisionally inapplicable. However, the powers of national courts to grant such relief [47] was limited further. The ECJ stressed how the primary duty of national

---

42. *Op. cit.*, fn 38.   43. *Ibid.*
44. Cases C-143/88 and C-92/89, *Zuckerfabrik, op. cit.*, fn 26, paras 25 and 26.
45. *Atlanta, op. cit.*, fn 28, para. 39.
46. *Atlanta*, para. 45; and see *Zuckerfabrik*, para. 32.
47. Medhi, *op. cit.*, fn 29, p. 95.

courts called upon to apply Community law is to ensure that full effect is given to Community law: 'regulations should not be set aside without proper guarantees.'[48] The ECJ emphasis is placed on the need and importance of upholding the validity of the Community regulation.[49]

Serious doubts must exist as to the validity of the Community regulation on which the contested administrative measure is based. Only the possibility of a finding of invalidity can justify the grant of interim relief. The national court cannot restrict itself to referring the question of the validity of the regulation to the ECJ, it must set out, when making the interim order, the reasons for which it considers that the Court should find the regulation to be invalid.[50] This requirement is puzzling, given the ECJ insistence that a finding that a regulation is invalid is a matter reserved exclusively to itself. When setting out these reasons the national court must pay due regard 'to the extent of the discretion which the Community institutions must be allowed in the sectors concerned'.[51]

'Taking account of the Community interest' has been further clarified. The national court must examine whether the Community act in question would be deprived of all effectiveness if not immediately implemented, and it must have regard to the damage which the interim measure may cause the legal regime established by that regulation for the Community as a whole.[52] In practice, the national judge must consider the cumulative effect which would arise if a large number of national courts were also to adopt interim measures for similar reasons. Whether national courts could assess such a 'legal domino effect'[53] remains to be seen. Interim protection is intended to protect a special situation of the plaintiff, accordingly the national judge must balance the Community interests against that of the applicant by considering 'those special features of the applicant's situation which distinguish him from the other operators concerned'.[54] Again it is not certain that the national judge is best placed to weigh the need for individual protection against the Community interest.

The Court also clarified the meaning of urgency. 'The damage relied on by the applicant must be such as to materialise before the

---

48. *Zuckerfabrik*, para. 30; and see *Atlanta*, para. 42.
49. E. Sharpston, 'Interim relief in the national courts' in Lonbay and Biondi (eds), *op. cit.* fn 24, pp. 47–54.
50. *Atlanta*, para. 36.   51. *Atlanta*, para. 37.   52. *Atlanta*, para. 44.
53. Bebr (1996) 33 CMLRev, p. 802.   54. *Atlanta*, para. 44.

Court of Justice has been able to rule on the validity of the contested Community act.'[55]

The national court must consider whether immediate enforcement of the contested measure would be likely to result in irreversible damage to the applicant which could not be made good if the Community act were to be declared invalid. Purely financial damage cannot be regarded in principle as irreparable.

Concurrent liability issues

Community law and policies are implemented principally by national administrations. National agencies, particularly in the fields of the Common Agricultural Policy and fisheries, are responsible for applying Community regulations or decisions. This involves *inter alia* carrying out inspection checks, making compulsory slaughter orders, collecting levies, making compensation payments, giving subsidies, and granting import and export licences. It is also incumbent upon national agencies to recover sums lost as a result of irregularities or negligence. Sometimes national administering of Community measures causes damage to individuals. This may be so because even where national authorities act within the framework of Community law, they may themselves have committed some wrongful action for which they may be held liable; such is the case where the national administration misapplied the Community rule, or misunderstood the Community instructions, or went beyond the margin of discretion recognised by the Community authorising measures. However, if the Community authorities have approved the national scheme putting into operation wrongly the relevant Community policy, one might be led to regard the Community as the true author of the conduct causing the damage. Damage may also be caused by the national administration applying an invalid Community regulation or following an unlawful Commission instruction; in such circumstances, although carried out by national administrations, the wrongful conduct can in fact be attributed to the Community institutions. Sometimes damage is caused by national authorities implementing badly a Community act which is itself unlawful; in such cases, given that both the Community and the Member States have acted unlawfully are they

---

55. *Atlanta*, para. 41.

jointly and severally liable for damages caused to individuals, and which courts are competent to hear the action for damages? The purpose of the next sections is to examine the role of national courts in dealing with claims arising out of concurrent liability.[56]

The nature of the problem: national and Community institutions are 'accountable under different legal orders'[57]

On the one hand, an individual or a company cannot bring an action for damages against the Community in national courts. The appropriate forum for this type of action is the Court of First Instance,[58] who alone has jurisdiction, to the exclusion of national courts, in actions brought by natural or legal persons based on Articles 235 and 288(2) EC relating to compensation for damage caused by the Community institutions. On the other hand, an individual or a company cannot bring an action for damages against a Member State before the Court of First Instance; only national courts are competent to hear such claim, since co-operation between Community and national authorities cannot make the Community responsible for reviewing the legality of administrative acts of Member States applying Community law. Yet an individual or a company may suffer damages as a result of joint action. Is there any forum where they can bring their claims? And if so, what is the appropriate forum? Must the Member State be sued before a national court for its share of the damages and the Commission before the Court of First Instance for its share? Is the action against the Community only accessible after all national rights of action have been exhausted? And if so, how is this compatible with the principle of effective judicial protection? When national and Community administrations are jointly involved in actions resulting in damage caused to individuals, it may be difficult to decide whether the alleged illegality on which to found the action emanates from the Community institution or whether it must be

---

56. C. Harding, 'The Choice of Court Problem in cases of Non-Contractual Liability under EEC Law' (1979) 16 CMLRev 389; W. Wils, 'Concurrent Liability of the Community and the Member States' (1992) 17 ELR 191.

57. C. Harding and A. Sherlock, *European Community Law: Text and Materials* (Longman, 1995), p. 289.

58. Article 225 and Council Decision 88/591, OJ 1988 L319/1; as amended by Decision 93/350, OJ 1993 L144/21, and by Decision 94/149, OJ 1994 L66/29. Most of the cases discussed in the next section were decided by the ECJ prior to the transfer of jurisdiction.

attributed to the national body. In a complex system where Community and national administrations are so intertwined, the division of jurisdiction between the Community judiciary and national courts constitutes a serious obstacle to the effective judicial protection of individuals.

Cases of joint and several liability ought to be distinguished from more straightforward matters such as claims for recovery of sums unduly paid over, or claims for subsidies withheld, both types which can easily enough be claimed from the relevant national authority responsible for such payments or collection of money.[59]

The solutions

The principles which can be derived from the case law of the ECJ[60] will now be discussed. However, these were developed largely prior to the establishment of the principle of State liability for breach of Community law. The ECJ insistence on the need to base the liability of the Member States for breach of Community law on the same principles as the liability of the Community institutions may presage a change of approach[61] to the issue of concurrent liability, and may be the straightforward application of principles of joint and several liability, the option considered as the most desirable[62] but involving radical reform, since national and Community institutions are each responsible in separate legal orders.

An action based on the non-contractual liability of the Community institutions has a 'subsidiary nature'[63] vis-à-vis the remedies available under national law. Thus in principle the recommended course of action is to claim compensation from the implementing national authority in a claim before the relevant national court, and if necessary to remind the national court it has a duty to refer the question of the validity of the Community

59. C. Harding and A. Sherlock, op. cit., fn 56, at pp. 285–90; and Warner AG in Case 126/76 Dietz v Commission [1977] ECR 2431.
60. The cases discussed were all decided before the transfer of jurisdiction of such actions to the Court of First Instance.
61. J. Shaw, Law of the European Union, 2nd ed. (MacMillan, 1996), p. 364.
62. See Harding, op. cit. fn 55, and W. Wils, 'Concurrent liability of the Community and the Member States' (1992) 17 ELR 191.
63. Darmon AG in Case C-55/90 Cato v Commission [1992] ECR I-2533; J. Rideau and J.-L. Charrier, Code de procédures européennes (Litec, 1990), pp. 183–6.

measure under Article 234. However, where it is not possible for an individual to obtain redress before national courts, an application under Articles 235 and 288 may be declared admissible.

The ECJ is not competent to examine under Article 288 the validity of decisions taken by national agencies implementing Community policies.[64] Claims for payment of amounts allegedly due, but withheld, fall within the exclusive jurisdiction of national courts.[65] Yet it may be that payment was withheld because the Community regulation providing for such payments has been unlawfully withdrawn. In the absence of a Community provision authorising the national bodies to pay the amount claimed, an application under Articles 235 and 288 will be admissible. Indeed, in such cases, even if the applicants had succeeded in convincing the national court of the invalidity of the Community measures which had caused them damage, they still could not have obtained from the national administration the benefit to which they claimed to be entitled without the prior intervention of the Community legislature.[66] Equally, where an applicant is seeking to benefit from an advantage unlawfully refused to him by a provision of secondary Community law, an action to establish liability will be declared admissible in so far as the applicant would have been unable to secure the advantage which he seeks by instituting proceedings before the national courts, such as is the case when the national administration has merely followed express instructions from the Community institutions.[67]

Claims for recovery of sums levied under invalid Community measures must be brought before the national courts against the national body which levied the charge, even where authorities have merely and correctly applied Community rules, and/or even though the sum in question may have been paid into EU funds. 'Only national courts have jurisdiction to entertain actions for recovery of amounts wrongfully charged by national administrations on the basis of Community rules subsequently declared invalid'.[68]

64. Case 12/79 *Wagner v Commission* [1979] ECR 3657.
65. Case 133/79 *Sucrimex and Westzuker v Commission* [1980] ECR 1299.
66. Case 90/78 *Granaria v Council and Commission* [1979] ECR 1081.
67. Case 175/84 *Krohn v Commission* [1986] ECR 753, and also Case 5/71 *Zuckerfabrik Schoeppenstedt v Council* [1971] ECR 975; judgment in Joined Cases 9 and 11/71 *Compagnie d'Approvisionnement v Commission* [1972] ECR 391; Case 74/74 *CNTA v Commission* [1975] ECR 533.
68. Case 96/71 *Haegeman v Commission* [1972] ECR 1005; Case 20/88 *Roquette* [1989] ECR 1533; Case C-282/90 *Vreugdenhil v Commission* [1992] ECR I-1937.

Exhaustion of national remedy

It is recognised in the case law of the Court that there may be concurrent liability on the part of a Member State and on the part of a Community institution. In its judgment in *Kampffmeyer*[69] the ECJ, after recognising the liability in principle of a Community institution, went on to request the applicants to await the outcome of national proceedings concerning the possible liability of the Member State in question in order 'to avoid the applicants' being insufficiently or excessively compensated'. The ECJ held that the national court should decide matters first of all, allowing the ECJ to postpone judgment until it knew how much compensation had been awarded at national level. Therefore in the majority of cases, actions should be brought first against the Member State in the national courts,[70] according to an application of a principle of an exhaustion of effective national remedies, and then brought before the CFI.

This principle of exhaustion of national remedies has been the subject of much criticism. First, in most instances of concurrent liability, the Community institution should in fact bear the primary responsibility as it acts as the senior or authorising partner with a supervisory role. Criticisms have also been made in terms of the fair and sound administration of justice.[71]

The principle of exhaustion of national remedies has been set aside where national rights of action are not capable of resulting in compensation for the damage allegedly suffered,[72] and where the measures which originally caused the damage are measures adopted by a national authority pursuant to express instructions from the Community institutions, or invalid Community provision.

An established body of the case law of the Court of Justice shows that the action for damages, pursuant to Articles 178 and 215 of the Treaty, was set up as an independent action, having its own

---

69. Joined Cases 5, 7 and 13 to 24/66 *Kampffmeyer and others v Commission* [1967] ECR 245.
70. P. Oliver, 'Joint liability of the Community and of the Member States' in Heukels and McDonnell (eds), *The Action for Damages in Community Law* (Kluwer, 1997), p. 285.
71. For both see Harding and Sherlock, *op. cit.*, fn 58, p. 289.
72. J. Boulouis and R.-M. Chevallier, *Grands Arrêts de la Cour de Justice des Communautés européennes*, Vol. 1 (Dalloz, 1991), p. 412 *et seq.* and *Krohn op. cit.*, para. 27.

particular place in the system of means of redress and subject to conditions for its use formulated in the light of its specific purpose. It must nevertheless be viewed in the context of the entire system established by the Treaty for the judicial protection of the individual. When an individual considers that he has been injured by the application of a Community legislative measure that he considers illegal, he may, when the implementation of the measure is left to the national authorities, contest the validity of the measure, when it is implemented, before a national court in an action against the national authorities. That court may, or even must, as provided for in Article 177, refer the question of the validity of the Community measure in dispute to the Court of Justice. However, the existence of such a means of redress will be capable of ensuring the effective protection of the individuals concerned only if it may result in making good the alleged damage.[73]

Still, it might not be straightforward to ascertain whether the initiation of proceedings before a national court would enable the applicant to obtain a 'satisfactory outcome'. Further, attribution of liability may be difficult where the individual act which gave rise to the damage suffered is taken pursuant to national general rules, adopted following approval by the Community authorities. An illustration of the issues involved in such cases and of the hurdles faced by litigants in such circumstances is provided by the case of *Cato*.[74] In *Cato*, the individual decision which gave rise to the damage was not taken on the express order of the Commission, but on the basis of a national scheme allegedly wrongly approved by the Community authorities as being in accordance with a Community provision. Mr Cato brought an action for non-contractual liability of the Community requesting compensation for the damage resulting from the non-payment, in respect of his fishing vessel, of the final cessation premium provided for under Community legislation.[75] Under Directive 83/515 Member States were required to take the necessary measures to ensure that vessels for which final cessation premiums have been paid were permanently barred

---

73. Case 281/82 *Unifrex v Commission and Council* [1984] ECR 1969, para. 11.
74. Case C-55/90 *Cato v Commission* [1992] ECR I-2533.
75. In order to encourage a reduction of production capacity in the fisheries sector, Directive 83/515 authorises Member States to introduce a system of financial aid for measures reducing such capacity and provides for financial contributions by the Community to the aid thus granted.

from fishing in Community waters, and to forward information to the Commission. On the basis of the information provided, the Commission had to examine whether the measures proposed fulfilled the conditions for financial contributions from the Community. The UK submitted to the Commission the draft measures which it intended to adopt in implementation of the Directive, and the Commission adopted a decision[76] concluding that they fulfilled the conditions for financial contributions from the Community. Accordingly, the UK introduced a system of decommissioning grants payable to the owners of fishing vessels permanently withdrawn from operation within the fishing industries.[77] Grants are made on the basis of an application which must specify the means by which the permanent withdrawal is to be effected. Mr Cato, a fisherman, sold his fishing vessel to a couple who intended to use it as a houseboat and expected to qualify for a decommissioning grant in the amount of £22,144. In the contract of sale, the purchasers stated that they were aware that the vendor had applied for a decommissioning grant and that, should the vessel once more be used for fishing in Community waters under the flag of a Member State, the new owner of the vessel might be obliged to repay the amount of the grant. Mr Cato tendered his application for a decommissioning grant. His vessel was struck off the register of fishing vessels.

The vessel was in fact resold to two Irish nationals, who had expressed an interest in the vessel's engine. The purchasers declared in the contract of sale that they were aware that the vessel was to receive a decommissioning grant and that they might be required to repay the amount of that grant if the vessel was once again used for fishing within Community waters under the flag of a Member State. Notwithstanding that declaration, they subsequently requested the Irish authorities to register the vessel as a fishing vessel. The latter having been informed by their British counterparts that the decommissioning grant had not yet been paid, registered the vessel and issued a fishing licence. In the light of those developments, the British Minister, who had waited for proof of the final use to which the vessel had been put, rejected Mr Cato's application for a grant. An application for judicial review

[76]. Decision 84/17, concerning the implementation by the UK of certain measures to adjust capacity in the fisheries sector pursuant to Council Directive 83/515: OJ 1984 L 18/39.
[77]. The Fishing Vessels (Financial Assistance) Scheme 1983, SI 1983 No 1883.

of that decision was refused on the grounds, first, that the application had been made after the expiration of the limitation period of three months; secondly, that the applicant was in any case not entitled to the grant as the Minister was not satisfied that the vessel had been withdrawn from all activity in the fishing industry. Mr Cato brought a second private law action against the Minister which was dismissed by the High Court, a judgment which was affirmed by the Court of Appeal. The House of Lords refused leave to appeal. Mr Cato then brought a claim for damages against the Commission, alleging that the damage was the consequence of the Commission's decision approving the UK scheme. The ECJ rejected it, considering that no relevant connection existed between the Commission's conduct and the individual decision taken by the national authorities. The non-payment of the decommissioning grant was in substance a claim for payment of amounts allegedly due, which ought to have been brought before the national courts. The ECJ also found that in approving the UK scheme the Commission did not act unlawfully in such a way as to entail liability on the part of the Community.

> The object of the Directive is to encourage temporary or permanent reduction of production capacity in the fisheries sector. In order to attain that objective, the Directive authorises Member States to introduce a system of financial aid for measures reducing such capacity and provides for financial contributions by the Community to the aid thus granted under the conditions set out in the Directive. It follows that the Directive leaves it to Member States to choose whether or not to introduce such an aid scheme and to determine its form and details, provided that the latter are not at variance with the objectives of the Directive.[78]

The argument that the UK scheme imposed an impossible evidential burden, since no one can prove that a vessel intended to be used for other purposes will not, prior to its destruction, be used once again in the unforeseeable future for fishing within Community waters, was rejected. The ECJ held that 'the fact that the actual conduct of the United Kingdom authorities in the course of events may not be entirely free of blame cannot, no matter how regrettable, be attributed to the Commission in the exercise of its power of prior verification'.[79]

[78.] *Cato, op. cit.*, fn 73, 78, paras 21 and 22.   [79.] *Ibid.*, para. 2.

The Commission's power of verification is intended solely to determine whether the schemes proposed by Member States for reducing production capacity satisfy the conditions for financial contributions from the Community laid down in the Directive. A decision adopted by the Commission pursuant to this power of verification, and approving a national scheme in conformity with the objectives of the Directive, cannot be regarded as unlawful and hence as entailing liability on the part of the Community. Even if Mr Cato had secured judicial review, the UK courts would have been led to verify the compatibility of the scheme with the Directive and therefore with the Commission decision which approved the scheme. Pursuant to *Foto-Frost* these issues would have had to be referred to the ECJ. Such a reference, however, would serve no purpose other than delaying the assessment that the national court will have to make of the conduct of the national authorities. As indeed, for the ECJ the approval of the scheme by the Commission only constitutes a declaration of compatibility with the objectives of the Common fisheries policies.

Conclusion

Community institutions are principally controlled by the ECJ.[80] Still, given that Community law is largely applied and administered at national level, national courts may hear claims that a Community act is unlawful. A challenge to the validity of Community legislation can be mounted indirectly in the national courts. It involves a plea that the national administrative act is unlawful and cannot be applied because it is based on a parent Community act which is invalid. However, the power to declare a Community act invalid is reserved to the ECJ. Accordingly a national court seised with such a claim must ask for a preliminary ruling and having referred the question of validity of the Community act, may in *exceptional circumstances* grant interim protection in the form of suspension of the national implementing measure or an order for specific performance. Often, damage is caused to individuals as a result of joint action by the Community and national authorities, and in most instances claims for compensation for unlawful action are best brought before national courts.

80. Articles 230, 232, 241, 235 and 288 EC.

CHAPTER ELEVEN

Specific Community rules for the enforcement of Community law

The problem can be simply stated. On the one hand, the Community system is a decentralised one, in that it operates primarily through the legislature, executive and judiciary of the Member States . . . On the other hand, Community law has to be interpreted and applied uniformly in all the Member States.[1]

The benefits of the internal market will not flow unless its rules are applied effectively and consistently throughout the Community . . . At the same time it is important that in this market, local, regional and national diversity be retained. The acceptance of such diversity is politically and culturally important to Europe, but it risks being in conflict with the effective operation of an internal market.[2]

Community law establishes rights and obligations, and Member States have, by virtue of Article 10 EC, a duty to take all and appropriate measures to ensure the full application of Community law. But generally the Community does not prescribe any particular methods or sanctions designed to ensure that these rights are effectively protected or that these obligations are properly adhered to. The applicable procedures and remedies for the enforcement of Community law are, in principle, a matter governed by national law, provided that certain basic standards are observed.[3] Still, in a number of areas, the question of the remedies available to affected parties in national courts has been dealt with by specific Community legislation.

[1.] Jacobs, 'Remedies in national courts for enforcement of Community law' in *Liber Amicorum for Don Manuel Diez de Velasco* (1993) p. 969.
[2.] The Sutherland Report: *The Internal Market after 1992: Meeting the Challenge,* Report to the EEC Commission by the High Level Group on the operation of the internal market.
[3.] See Chapter 6.

This chapter looks at the various fields where courts in the UK have to follow Community-established rules. Further, it will discuss the likelihood of future developments, given that the Community legislature has been invited to play a more significant role in establishing rules to enforce the rules.[4] Finally the problems linked with leaving the harmonisation of remedies in the judicial sphere will be analysed.

The present

In a number of areas UK courts have to follow already established Community rules. For some time a number of Community directives[5] have specifically required Member States to adopt measures to enable individuals to enforce by judicial process the rights which the directive is intended to confer. However, Community influence in the field of remedies and procedural rules has become more precise.

The Community Customs Code[6] incorporates all the basic principles of existing Community Customs legislation[7] in relation to trade with third countries. It provides for the right to repayment of duties not legally owed to the customs authorities and establishes a two-phase right of appeal against the decision taken by customs authorities in the Member States. Claims for repayment have to be made within three years. It lays down the various circumstances which would or might give rise to repayment together with the criteria attaching to their exercise. The code applies only to taxes charges, levies and duties created by Community provisions or collected by the Member States on behalf of the Community. It does not apply to any national tax, charges and duties which may be levied contrary to Community law.[8]

---

4. C. Boch, 'Rules to enforce the rules: Subsidiarity v Uniformity in the implementation of the Single European Market Policy' in Mayes (ed), *The Evolution of Rules for a Single European Market, Part II: Rules Democracy and the Environment* (Office for Official Publications of the European Communities, Luxembourg, 1995) p. 1.
5. *Inter alia* Directive 64/221 and Directive 76/207.
6. Council Regulation 2913/92 establishing the Community Customs Code: OJ 1992 L302/4.
7. The definitions of 'import duties' and 'export duties' are drawn in broad terms to include agricultural levies and monetary compensatory amounts.
8. See Chapter 6.

In areas that directly affect the Community's financial interests[9] such as: the Common Agricultural Policy[10] and fisheries,[11] the Community legislator has attempted to harmonise the imposition of sanctions by Member States.[12] There is also a new generation of legislation dealing with the functioning of the internal market.[13] The main provisions of the Official Control of Foodstuffs Directive[14] are concerned with the scope, manner and frequency of inspections of food-processing premises as a means of enforcing EC regulations on foodstuffs, with the overall aim of providing verification of compliance with these;[15] Article 23 of the Television Without Frontiers Directive[16] ensures a right to reply; the Community Trade Mark Regulation[17] requires *inter alia* that some national courts are designated as Community trademarks courts and that these shall have jurisdiction over actions for infringement and counterclaims for revocation and invalidity.

Partial harmonisation of collective actions has occurred in a number of fields: the Misleading Advertising Directive[18] requires the availability of means to combat misleading advertisements and that 'such means shall include legal provisions under which persons *or* organisations *regarded under national law* as having a legitimate interest in prohibiting misleading advertising' may seek certain remedies.[19] Article 12(1) of the Directive on Advertising of Medicinal Products provides likewise.[20]

9. OJ 1995 L312/1, OJ 1995 C315/48.
10. Regulation 3887/92, OJ 1992 L391/36.
11. *E.g.* Regulation 2847/93, OJ 1993 L261/1.
12. B. Swart, 'From Rome to Maastricht and Beyond: The Problem of Enforcing Community Law' in Harding and Swart (eds.), *Enforcing European Community Rules: Criminal Proceedings, Administrative Rules and Harmonisation* (Dartmouth, 1996).
13. G. Betlem and C. Joustra, 'The Draft Consumer Injunctions Directive' [1997] 5 Consum L.J pp. 8–18.
14. Directive 89/39, OJ 1989 L186/23.
15. N. Burrows and H. Hiram, 'The Official Control of Foodstuffs' in T. Daintith (ed), *Implementing EC Law in the United Kingdom* (Wiley, 1995), pp. 139–164.
16. Council Directive 89/552 on the co-ordination of certain provisions laid down by law, regulation or administrative action in Member States concerning the pursuit of television broadcasting activities: OJ 1989 L298/23.
17. Council Regulation 40/94, OJ 1994 L11/1, Articles 90–104.
18. Council Directive 84/450, OJ 1984 L250/17.
19. Article 4(1); however it does not require any specific remedies. Whilst the French implementing legislation uses criminal sanctions, German law has adopted civil remedies for redressing unlawful advertisements.
20. Council Directive 92/28, OJ 1992 L113/13.

Article 7(2) of the Unfair Contract Terms Directive[21] contains a similar rule in that 'persons *or* organisations having a legitimate interest under national law in protecting consumers, may take action according to the national law concerned before the competent authority to seek declaratory relief'. These provisions therefore leave it up to national law to decide under what conditions consumer groups will have standing or title and interest to sue. The criteria for establishing such legitimate interest have not been harmonised. Furthermore, the Directive does not explicitly require that the national implementing legislation should lay down the criteria to identify those having a legitimate interest, and it does not seem to prevent countries with an independent public enforcement authority from conferring on such a public body the sole right to mount a legal challenge. This is an issue which has given rise to litigation in the UK. The Unfair Contract Terms Directive was implemented in the UK by the Unfair Terms in Consumer Contracts Regulations 1994.[22] The Regulations provided that the Director General of Fair Trading 'shall consider any complaint made to him about the fairness of any contract term drawn up for general use, and that he may seek an injunction to prevent the continued use of that term'. The Consumers' Association and *Which* magazine sought[23] a declaration that the Secretary of State for Trade and Industry had acted *ultra vires* and unlawfully by failing to give organisations such as them with a legitimate interest under national law to protect consumers, a right to take legal action under English law to obtain a ruling as to whether contractual terms drawn up for general use are unfair. It was submitted that the Directive required Member States first, to ensure that their national law adopts criteria to define the persons or organisations who have such legitimate interest in protecting consumers, and second, to allow such persons or organisations to bring legal proceedings to establish that contractual terms drawn up for general use are unfair. The High Court asked the ECJ[24] whether Article 7(2) of the Unfair Contract Terms Directive imposes obligations on Member States to ensure that national law (i) states criteria to

---

21. Council Directive 93/13, OJ 1993 L95/29.
22. SI 1994 No 3159, which came into force on 1 July 1995.
23. *R v Secretary of State for Trade and Industry, ex parte The Consumers Association*, 11 December 1995, see LEXIS CO/656/95 (Transcript: John Larking).
24. Case C-82/96 was in fact withdrawn on 7 October 1998.

identify private persons or organisations having a legitimate interest in protecting consumers, and (ii) allows such private persons or organisations to take action before the courts or before competent administrative bodies for a decision as to whether contractual terms drawn up for general use are unfair. However, the case was withdrawn before being heard.

The Regulations are currently being amended so as to give organisations with a legitimate interest in protecting consumers the right to bring legal proceedings to establish that contractual terms drawn up for general use are unfair. The Directive on Injunctions for the Protection of Consumers' Interests[25] will approximate the laws, regulations and administrative provisions of the Member States relating to actions seeking an injunction aimed at the protection of the collective interests of consumers for a range of consumer protection directives.[26] It addresses some of these difficulties by providing a definition of the entities which must be recognised as qualified to seek an injunction. Trans-frontier consumers' protection should also be enhanced by this new Directive, as Member States must be prepared to grant *locus standi* to qualified entities outside their territory.

A case study: the public procurement rules

An example of a comprehensive EC legislative framework dealing with remedies and procedural law is provided by the 'Remedies Directives' in the field of public procurement: Directive 89/665[27] and Directive 92/13.[28] The existing directives on public works and public supplies contracts laid down rules for advertising, tendering and the award of public contracts above a certain value, but had

---

25. Directive 98/27 on injunctions for the protection of consumers' interests: OJ 1998 L166/51.
26. The directives listed in the Annex are: Directive 84/450 (misleading advertising), OJ 1984 L250/17; Directive 85/577 (contracts negotiated away from business premises), OJ 1985 L372/31; Directive 87/102 (consumer credit), OJ 1987 L42/48, last amended by Directive 98/7, OJ 1998 L101/17; Directive 89/552 (television broadcasting activities), OJ 1989 L298/23, as amended by Directive 97/36, OJ 1997 L202/60; Directive 90/314 (package travel, holidays and tours) OJ 1990 L158/59; Directive 92/28 (advertising of medicinal products for human use), OJ 1992 L113/13; Directive 93/13 (unfair terms in consumer contracts), OJ 1993 L95/29; Directive 94/47 (timeshare), OJ 1994 L280/83; Directive 97/7 (distance contracts), OJ 1997 L144/19.
27. OJ 1989 L395/33.   28. OJ 1992 L176/14.

left it to the Member States to ensure that these rules were complied with. The Commission found that compliance with the directives was very poor, as the authorities awarding contracts in the Member States largely ignored the rules set out in the directives. Given the limited resources available to it, it was impossible for the Commission to seek to police the existing framework itself.[29] Accordingly, the Community legislature took steps to ensure that effective remedies in the field of procurement should be available, including in the national courts. The next section briefly describes the rules laid down and discusses the extent to which the Remedies Directives strengthened the existing enforcement mechanisms.

The directives provide for a conciliation procedure,[30] so that disputes may be settled without recourse to the courts. They also regulate certain issues regarding the ways in which individuals may seek redress before their national courts, on issues such as *inter alia* the interest in bringing an action,[31] burden of proof,[32] interim measures including suspension,[33] setting aside of decisions taken unlawfully,[34] and award of damages.[35] Before the introduction of the Remedies Directives in England, alleged illegalities in awards of public contracts could be challenged in the UK courts by an action for breach of statutory duty. In the absence of a contract between the disappointed tenderer and the procuring authority, the only remedy open was an action for judicial review of the award of the contract, for which the complainant had to obtain leave of the court and show title and interest. Awards for damages were rare. The United Kingdom chose to implement the Remedies Directives as part of the framework of secondary legislation governing procurement in the field of public works, public supplies and public services.[36] The implementing Regulations designated the forum for relief.[37] The UK, rather than creating a set of special-

---

29. Although the Commission did pursue a number of Article 226 EC actions in this field.
30. Utilities Remedies Directive, 92/13 OJ 1992 L176/14, Articles 9–11.
31. *Ibid.*, Article 1.   32. Article 2(7).   33. *Ibid.*, Article 2(1)(a).
34. *Ibid.*, Article 2(1)(b).   35. *Ibid.*, Article 2(1)(d).
36. For an analysis see L. Gormley, 'Remedies in Public procurement: Community Provisions and the United Kingdom' in Lonbay and Biondi, *op. cit.*, pp. 155–164; S. Weatherill, 'Enforcing the Public Procurement Rules in the UK' in S. Arrowsmith (ed), *Remedies for Enforcing the Public Procurement Rules* (Earlsgate Press, 1993), pp. 271–304.
37. Regulation 26(3) of the Public Supply Contract Regulations, Regulation 31(4) of the Public Works Contract Regulations.

ist review bodies to review decisions of contracting authorities or entities, opted for the solution of using the normal courts, which have no real expertise in public procurement. Under this system, litigants are immediately in the High Court or the Court of Session, where the costs of litigation will act as a deterrent and not just to those who may seek to abuse such a right for an oblique motive.[38] The Remedies Directives empower the High Court or the Court of Session (i) to take interim measures to correct alleged infringement or prevent further damages, for example to make an interim order suspending the award of a contract; (ii) to set aside unlawful decisions taken by the contracting parties, for example the removal of discriminatory technical specifications in the invitation to tender, and (iii) to award damages to aggrieved suppliers or contractors.

At present not enough data appears available to assess the enthusiasm of UK courts for suspending award procedures and/or awarding damages.[39] It is also too early to comment upon whether the Remedies Directives have significantly improved compliance with the public procurement directives. However, some limitations of the system are already apparent. First, some breaches of the substantive rules are difficult to prove in legal actions. Failure to publish a notice is easy to show, but it is not simple to demonstrate that a local authority has been motivated by unlawful considerations in awarding a contract to a particular firm.[40] Secondly, the lack of detailed rules governing the amount of damages to be awarded by the national courts undermines the uniform application of the rules. The Commission[41] found that in some Member States, compensation is minimal, covering only the costs incurred in the course of submitting a bid, whereas in other Member States, it covers the firm's loss of earnings, *i.e.* loss of the profit which it would have made if awarded the contract. The Com-

---

38. The fear of abuse of the review procedures by cowboy claimants was evident in the negotiations leading up to the adoption of the Directives. See Gormley, *op. cit.*, pp. 157 and 159.

39. C. Bovis, *EC Public Procurement Law* (Longman, 1997) pp. 102–8, in particular at p. 107.

40. See Sue Arrowsmith, 'Public Procurement: an example of a developed field of national remedies established by Community law' in Micklitz and Reich (eds), *Public Interest Litigation before European Courts* (Nomos Verl, 1996), pp. 125–52 at p. 128.

41. COM (95) 162, Communication on the role of penalties in implementing Community internal market legislation, p. 5.

mission commented that such significant difference in compensation arrangements affects how awarding authorities and firms behave, which the Commission opined can lead to distortion of competition. Such findings suggest that, to be effective, harmonisation of remedies must be as detailed as possible.[42] In other words, reference to national rules must be kept to a minimum. Thirdly, the effectiveness of a regime does not rest solely on the existence of a framework for enforcement; it is also dependent upon the quality of the substantive rules themselves. This point was made when the Remedies Directives were proposed – some evidence was adduced to the effect that the lack of effectiveness of the regime was due to the inferior quality of the substantive rules themselves. The Public Procurement Directives were criticised for not taking sufficiently into account the prevailing commercial realities.[43] Finally, it is doubtful whether rules on remedies could ever improve compliance with the substantive rules, given that undertakings would be reluctant to institute proceedings against contracting authorities as this may damage a valuable commercial relationship, actual or potential.[44]

Why Community rules for the enforcement of Community law?

Legislative intrusions in the field of remedies are essential for a number of reasons. In the field of protection of the financial interests of the Community, developments were justified by the concern to see that Community law is applied properly, that the Common Agricultural Policy instruments achieve their aims and that the Community budget be only used to finance legitimate expenditure. In other fields Community-harmonised measures are meant to secure a level playing field and also to ensure judicial protection of Community rights. To secure a level playing field for undertakings, the mere creation of a uniform regulatory framework is not sufficient – an homogeneous system of application and enforcement

---

[42]. But this jeopardises the political and practical feasibility of harmonisation. See below.

[43]. See House of Lords Select Committee on the European Communities, Session 1988–89, 12th Report.

[44]. *Ibid.*, and also see C. Bovis, *op. cit.*, fn 39.

must also be put in place. It is also desirable, as it would ease the monitoring of the application of Community law by the Commission. Where Member States are merely required to establish adequate, equivalent and effective sanctions for breach of Community law, the system of sanctions varies between the Member States, reflecting different legal and social traditions.[45] Evaluating the adequacy, effectiveness and comparability of these sanctions is an uphill task. Thus Article 6 of the Timeshare Directive[46] requires the Member States 'to prohibit any advance payments by a purchaser before the end of the period during which he may exercise the right of withdrawal.' Does this simply mean that individual consumers affected by infringement of that prohibition by a company have the right to be reimbursed, or does it require additional sanction in order to dissuade companies from infringing this prohibition? This raises issues of principle in relation to the availability of damages and their nature, *i.e.* whether enhanced, aggravated or punitive. The UK, Austria, Ireland and Sweden foresaw fines, other Member States have used traditional civil remedies: reimbursement with interest.[47] Are these sanctions equivalent? To what extent do consumers enjoy a comparable system of protection under the same Community regime? And to what extent are companies operating in this sector on a level playing field?

Political feasibility

For a long time, there was hardly any Community legislation dealing specifically with remedies or procedural rules for breach of Community law. The Community legislator was more preoccupied by the adoption of substantive rules rather than by issues relating to their implementation and enforcement. The European Parliament was the Community institution which initiated formal reporting on the monitoring of the application of Community

---

[45]. The tension between uniform application and diversity of application mechanisms was explored in Chapter 6.

[46]. Directive 94/47 on the protection of purchasers in respect of certain aspects of contracts relating to the purchase of the right to use immovable properties on a timeshare basis, OJ 1994 L280/83.

[47]. Commission's Working Paper on enforcement of European Consumer legislation, available from http://europa.eu.int/comm/dg24/policy/developments/enfo/enfo01_en.pdfp.5.

law.[48] Today it is widely acknowledged that the mechanisms available at national level for ensuring compliance with Community law are all too often inadequate and all Community institutions declare their willingness to address this problem, *inter alia* by way of the Declaration on the Implementation of Community law,[49] and the Resolution on Effective Penalties.[50] In some specific areas steps have been taken:[51] a new provision combating fraud against the budget[52] has been inserted in the Treaty; and a new intervention mechanism to safeguard free trade in the Single Market[53] has been adopted. There is also widespread support for the proposition that market integration requires a high degree of legal uniformity. The European Parliament adopted Resolutions[54] for the harmonisation of European private law, the European Contract Law Commission infers the need for European private law from the interests of trade: legal diversity means higher costs, uncertainty and greater risks.[55] However progress in this area is slow, and is likely to remain so, given the problems of political and practical feasibility which will now be addressed in turn.

First, the Member States do not have the same attachment to compliance in relation to each and every one of their Community obligations.[56] Secondly, there is an inherent conflict in the Community system, ensuring effectiveness of rules, and also ensuring uniformity of interpretation and application of rules in a decentralised framework for application and enforcement. How can the Community institutions legislate to harmonise procedures and

48. 'Resolution of 9 February 1983 on the Responsibility of the Member States for the application of Community Law', OJ 1983 C68/32, and also the 'Resolution on the monitoring of application of Community law by the Member States', OJ 1985 C 343/8, in particular points 2 and 12 of the latter; OJ 1993 C21/513, Opinion of the EcoSoc, OJ 1993 C 201/59, Council Resolution OJ 1992 C334/1.
49. TEU, Final Act, Part III: Declarations, Declaration No 19, 'Declaration on the Implementation of Community Law.'
50. Council Resolution on the effective uniform application of Community law and on the penalties applicable for breaches of Community law in the internal market, OJ 1995 C188/1.
51. See above.   52. Article 279 EC.
53. COM (97) 619, and Regulation 2679/98, OJ 1998 L337/8.
54. OJ 1989 C158/400; OJ 1994 C205/518.
55. R. van den Bergh, 'Subsidiarity as an Economic Demarcation Principle and the Emergence of European Private Law' (1988) 5 MJECL 129.
56. Witness the difficulties surrounding the adoption of the Directive on the burden of proof in cases of discrimination based on sex, Directive 97/80 EC, OJ 1998 L14/6, for which a proposal was first submitted to the Council in May 1988 COM (88) 269.

remedies when the assumption underlying the system established by the Treaties is that the national remedies enforced by national courts, in accordance with national procedural rules must be respected? 'The underlying premise is that States based on the rule of law will organise their national legal systems in such a way as to ensure proper application of the law and adequate legal protection of their subjects'.[57]

The main obstacle to the adoption of common rules in the field of remedies stems from the fact that the Community institutions do not have general competence, but may act only within the limits conferred upon them. In other words, for the Community to be able to act, there must be a legal basis in the Treaty. This limit on Community competence has been further exacerbated by the principle of subsidiarity, that decisions must be taken as closely as possible to the citizens. For the Community to be able to act, the Commission has to demonstrate that the objective of the action envisaged can be better achieved by the Community. Furthermore, the Treaty[58] makes it incumbent on the Community not to go beyond what is necessary to achieve the objectives of the Treaty. Accordingly, the specific features of national legal systems must be taken into account to every extent possible by leaving a wide scope for national decisions. Reliance on national systems is the norm; defining common penalties, sanctions and remedies must remain the exception. 'Clearly, and taking into account the subsidiarity principle, the Community legislator's rules pertaining to remedies cannot but be exceptional.'[59]

Still, respect for the integrity and diversity of national legal systems is capable of harming the achievement of Community objectives. The Sutherland Report[60] clearly showed how the risk of fragmentation of the Single European market arises just as much from divergent interpretation and enforcement of Community law as from the introduction of national obstacles to trade: 'Subsidiarity does not and cannot be interpreted as permitting such

---

57. Jacobs AG's Opinion in Cases C-430 and 431/93, *Van Schijndel et al v SPE* [1995] ECR I-4705, para. 30.
58. Articles 1 EC, Art 5 TEU and see the protocol on the application of the principle of subsidiarity and proportionality.
59. For a discussion of how Community legislation in the field of procedural remedies developed and the question of its legal basis, see COM (93) 576, *Green Paper on Access to Justice*.
60 *Op. cit.*, fn 2.

developments.' Accordingly, the Report called for greater equivalence of legal procedures and sanctions and urged the Community institutions 'to make some progress on long outstanding issues about practical recourse to Community law'.

The limits of referral to national systems

The existence of different national rules in the field of procedures and remedies can only be maintained insofar as these rules are capable of securing compliance with the Community substantive rules. Only effective and consistent rules are capable of ensuring fair competition. Indeed, compliance with Community legislation imposes direct or indirect costs on businesses. Where some national rules on remedies are deficient, compliance is not secured, and in turn this undermines the conditions of fair competition. Furthermore, Community law is not only concerned with economic operators producing, exchanging, and selling goods or relocating themselves. In the words of the Commission, ensuring compliance extends far beyond economic issues; the internal market rules require the attainment of a high level of protection with regard to health, safety, the environment and consumers. Community law needs to be complied with, otherwise the very credibility of common legislation would be damaged as it would 'expose the Union's citizens and their environment to risks that are unacceptable to the individual and to Society as a whole'.[61]

Some contributions of the Community legislator in the field of remedies and procedural rules were motivated[62] by the need to guarantee the effective application of Community law,[63] and the opportunity for 'any person whose legitimate interest has been damaged to effectively exercise such right or remedy'.[64] So harmonised rules are needed to ensure that the functioning of the internal market is not disrupted, and that economic operators' and consumers' confidence in the internal market is not undermined. It is suggested that the Commission will have increased difficulties in demonstrating that rules pertaining to remedies are necessary to

61. COM (95)162, *op. cit.*, p. 3.
62. COM (93) 576, *Green Paper on Access to Justice*, and also COM (96) 13, Action Plan on consumer access to justice and the settlement of consumer disputes in the internal market.
63. Directives 84/450, 89/665, 92/13, and 92/28.
64. Directive 93/7.

prevent distortion of competition or to ensure the proper functioning of the internal market, as can be seen in the debate
surrounding the proposal for the introduction of a system of civil
liability for damage to the environment. It was argued that a level
playing field could not stem from the mere adoption of a system of
civil liability, but would require harmonisation of all the rules of
civil procedure as well. What this debate shows[65] is that Community harmonisation measures cannot successfully achieve their
objectives unless they are as detailed as possible and encompass
the whole of European public and private law. It can therefore be
seen how the Community system carries obvious contradictions.

There are other issues of practical feasibility, in particular
when further enlargement is being contemplated. The challenge for
the Community institutions is not merely to consider whether to
do less in order to do better, but also to reflect on whether and to
what extent the uniform application paradigm is realistic. Harmonisation may be desirable from an efficiency perspective, or to
bring about legal certainty, but divergent legal rules are better able
to satisfy the heterogeneous preferences of a large and diverse
population and might have to remain in an enlarged Union. In this
respect, it is important to note that intra-State differences exist as
well as an inter-State dimension, which the inter-jurisdictional differences within the UK serve to highlight. The question whether
harmonisation of domestic laws carries with it the necessity for
consequential adjustment within the domestic jurisdiction coin-
cides, ironically, with the time when Scotland at least wishes to
expand its sphere of autonomy.[66]

The ECJ has a significant role to play in helping to buttress the
case for the Community harmonisation programme. In certain
areas, although the Community legislator carefully avoided indicating the legal nature of these new Community sanctions and
penalties, attempts at harmonisation have met with resistance on
the ground that the Community has no competence in criminal
law matters. By adhering to the view that the Community is competent to prescribe sanctions that have a punitive character
without being criminal, the Court made harmonisation of the
sanction system easier. Indeed, after the judgment of the ECJ legit-

---

65. And see the discussion of the experience of the Remedies Directives in the field
of public procurement, above.
66. C. Himsworth, 'Things fall apart: the harmonisation of Community judicial
procedural protection revisited' (1997) 22 ELR 291–311, p. 305.

imating the power of the Commission to adopt anti-fraud sanctions,[67] the Commission came forward with a set of proposals for regulations introducing far-reaching measures to combat fraud.[68]

Whether or not the Community legislator manages to adopt harmonised rules in the field of remedies, such rules will continue to be needed and claims will come before national courts. So courts will have to continue to influence national rules, on a case by case basis. However, leaving the development of Community law in this area to the hazards of private litigation has a number of drawbacks.

The limits of the decentralised enforcement model

These have been explored throughout the book, and will be summarised only briefly here. First, reliance on private litigation may not be an option. Complaints go to the Commission because individuals are unable to secure compliance with Community law at national level,[69] because for a variety of reasons[70] access to the judicial process at national level is threatened. Secondly, private litigation is particularly inadequate as a means of enforcing Community law in specific fields. In the area of public procurement, firms might never be willing to use judicial remedies – however effective and easy to use – because of the fear of losing future government business: 'Thou shalt not bite the hand that feeds you.' In the field of environmental protection, establishing title and interest may be difficult, and even where it is not, in most cases no identifiable material loss exists. Thirdly, the ECJ can only ensure an adequate standard of judicial protection on a case by case basis.[71] Such an approach is evidently haphazard, and the ECJ might never be called upon to adjudicate on the most important obstacles in the way of adequate enforcement. Fourthly, the guidelines laid down by the ECJ regarding the manner in which national courts must evolve national rules are neither clear nor precise, and in turn invite litigation. Finally, if the ECJ rationale for influencing the workings of national legal systems is that the same Community right should be afforded the same degree of protection, then the

---

67. Case C-240/90 *Germany v Commission* [1992] ECR I-5381.
68. See above on the regulations adopted in relation to PIF (Protection des intérêts financiers).
69. COM (96) 600, *op. cit.*, at p. 84.   70. See Chapter 3.
71. See Chapter 6.

non-discrimination or assimilation principle is of very little help. Indeed this principle only requires that a remedy be available on conditions no less favourable than those applied to a similar right of action in purely domestic matters. It does nothing to address and correct the variety in national practices. [72]

Legislative harmonisation or judicial intervention?

In matters where Community law arises, national courts must adopt the interpretative techniques developed by the ECJ. National courts must ascertain the purpose of national legislation, assess its compatibility with the Community superior norm, and award compensation in appropriate circumstances. But the same national rules when falling outside the reach of Community law do not evolve; they remain the same, even though they are dealing with the same type of issue. This possibility of the emergence of a double standard for the protection of individual rights, depending on whether claims are based on national or on Community law, has been a matter of debate for some time. 'The insistence in the Court's case law on an effective judicial remedy for the enforcement of Community rights may result paradoxically in a new form of discrimination in the national courts against those whose rights arise on the basis of national law alone'. [73]

When, in order to protect a Community right, national courts evolve national rules governing remedies, the result is the co-existence of two sets of rules, one governing purely internal situations and the other governing Community-related domestic situations. This paradox is difficult to justify, given that there is no separate national court structure to apply Community law which might allow two separate bodies of law to grow within the same jurisdiction.

A 'variable speed system of guarantees for individual rights' may arise, unless and until national courts decide on their own initiative to rectify this situation. Some of these issues, and notably whether such a double standard of protection is prohibited by Community law, were raised in *Volker-Steen*.[74] In this case, a German court inquired whether it had a duty under Community law

---

72. C. Himsworth, *op. cit.*, fn 66, pp. 291–311.
73. Jacobs, 'Remedies in national courts for enforcement of Community law' in *Liber Amicorum for Don Manuel Diez de Velasco* (1993) p. 983.
74. Case C-132/93 *Steen-Volker v Deutsche Bundespost* [1994] ECR I-2715.

to evolve national rules which, in a situation *unconnected* with any of the situations contemplated by Community law, treats national workers less favourably than nationals from other Member States. The ECJ answered that:

> Community law does not preclude a national court from examining the compatibility with its constitution of a national rule which, in a situation *unconnected* with any of the situations contemplated by Community law, treats national workers less favourably than nationals from other Member States.

In short, national judges are free to correct such an anomaly, but Community law itself does not seem to prohibit the emergence of two different systems.[75] Where national judges are not prepared to correct this discrimination, Community rights are afforded a higher level of protection, and it may be asked what is so special about Community rights to warrant this situation – an abnormality raised by Jacobs AG himself:[76] 'Rights are not, by virtue of being Community rights, inherently of greater importance than rights recognised by national law.' This of course can serve as an argument to convince national judges to extend the privileged status awarded to Community-based claims to claims based on national law. Thus Community law may lead to a higher level of protection for claims whether or not they fall within the remit of Community law. In this way, national judges preserve the homogeneity of the system,[77] and the standard of protection of individual rights is enhanced.

Conclusion

Today there are three different models of enforcement of Community rules,[78] direct enforcement, indirect enforcement and 'joint

---

75. Fernandez Esteban de la Marre, 'National Judges and Community Law: the Paradox of the Two Paradigms of Law' in (1997) 4 MJECL 143 points to a number of principles which should lead to a reconciliation of the two 'paradigms of law'.
76. In Cases C-430/93 and 431/93 *van Schijndel et al v SPE* [1995] ECR I-4705, para. 27 of Opinion.
77. In the words of Van Gerven, 'homogeneity friendly interpretation' (1995) 32 CMLRev 679.
78. A typology borrowed from R. Guldenmung and L. Westeroun van Meeteren, 'Towards an administrative sanctioning system in the Common Agricultural Policy' in Harding and Swart (eds), *Enforcing European Community Rules* (Dartmouth, 1996).

action'. Powers of direct enforcement of the Community competition rules have been entrusted to the Commission.[79] The 'joint action' model of enforcement involves procedures and remedies laid down – with a varying degree of detail – in Community instruments, but to be imposed by the Member States. Decentralised enforcement remains the norm, and through the years a body of rules and principles has emerged.[80] The spill-over of such rules and principles to matters of purely internal law has taken place in a number of areas in the UK[81] and Community law has, indirectly, improved the standards of judicial protection of individual rights.

In the absence of Community rules for the enforcement of Community law, some of the obstacles to the enforcement of Community law at national level may be alleviated by the adoption, at national level, of rules of court[82] codifying the various principles derived by the ECJ. Community law is not foreign law, and therefore the Member States must take the same care and commitment in seeing that it is properly enforced as they take to see that their own law is enforced.

[79]. Although the need for decentralisation is pressing.
[80]. See Chapters 6 and 7.   [81]. See Chapter 1.
[82]. As have been adopted for use of Article 234 EC, see for England and Wales, RSC Ord. 114, rr1–6; County Court Rules, Ord. 19, r11; Crown Court Rules 1982 (SI 1982/1109), r29; Scotland, RC 65.2–65.5; Act of Adjournal (Consolidation) 1988, rr 63–7 and 113–18; and the Sheriff Courts (Scotland) Act 1907 c51, Sch
  I, r134.

Further reading and useful sources of information

Many suggestions for additional reading can be found in the footnotes to the text. The following books offer a good starting point:

M. Brealey and M. Hoskins, *Remedies in EC Law* (2nd ed) (London: Sweet & Maxwell, 1998).

N. Foster, *Blackstone's EC Legislation* 1998–1999 (9th ed) (London: Blackstone, 1998).

J. Steiner and L. Woods, *Textbook on EC Law* (6th ed) (London: Blackstone, 1998).

S. Weatherill and P. Beaumont, *EC Law* (2nd ed) (London: Penguin, 1995).

S. Weatherill, *Law and Integration in the European Union* (Oxford: OUP, 1995).

Casebooks:

P. Craig and G. De Búrca, *EU Law: Text, Cases and Materials* (2nd ed) (Oxford: Clarendon, 1998).

Plender and Usher, *Cases and Materials on the Law of the European Communities* (3rd ed) (London: Butterworths, 1993).

S. Weatherill, *Cases and Materials on EC Law* (4th ed) (London: Blackstone, 1998).

Useful websites:

http://europa.eu.int.(main home page for the European Institutions)
http://www.europarl.eu.int (European Parliament website)
http://europa.eu.int/dj/index.htm (European Court of Justice)

A comprehensive list of websites can be found in 'Europe on the Internet' (1999), *European Access*, pp. 20–23.

Select Bibliography

Abbamonte, G.B. (1997) 'Competitors' Rights to Challenge Illegally Granted Aid and the Problem of Conflicting Decisions in the Field of Competition Law' ECLR 87.

Allan, T.R.S. (1997) 'Parliamentary Sovereignty: Law, Politics and Revolution' 113 LQR 443.

Andenas, M. (1994) *Article 177 References to the European Court, Policy and Practice* (London: Butterworths).

Anderson, D. (1995) *References to the European Court* (London: Sweet & Maxwell).

Arnull, A. (1989) 'The Use and Abuse of Article 177' 52 MLR 622.

Arnull, A. (1993) 'Owning Up to Fallibility: Precedent and the Court of Justice' 30 CMLRev 247.

Arrowsmith, S. (1996) 'Public Procurement: An Example of a Developed Field of National Remedies Established by Community Law' in H.W. Micklitz and N. Reich (eds) *Public Interest Litigation before European Courts* (Baden-Baden: Nomos).

Barav, A. (1977) 'Aspects of the Preliminary Ruling Procedure in EC Law' 2 ELR 3.

Barents, R. (1994) 'The Quality of Community Legislation: Some Observations on EC Legislation in the Agricultural Sector' 1 Maastricht Journal of Comparative Law 101.

Behrens, P. (ed), (1992) *EC Competition Rules in National Courts, Part One: United Kingdom and Italy* (Baden-Baden: Nomos).

Betlem, G. and Joustra, C. (1997) 'The Draft Consumer Injunctions Directive' 5 Consum. LJ 8.

Birkinshaw, P. (1997) 'European Integration and UK Constitutional Law' 3 European Public Law 57.

Boch, C. (1998) 'Language Protection and Free Trade: The Triumph of the Homo McDonaldus?' 4 European Public Law 379.

Boch, C. (1994) 'Home Thoughts from Abroad' in *In Search of New Constitutions*, Hume Papers on Public Policy (EUP).

Boch, C. (1995) 'Rules to Enforce the Rules: Subsidiarity v uniformity in the Implementation of the Single European Market Policy' in D. Mayes (ed), *The Evolution of Rules for a Single European Market Part II, Rules, Democracy and the Environment* (Luxembourg: Office for Official Publications of the European Communities).

Boch, C. (1997) 'The Enforcement of the EIA Directive: A Breach in the Dyke?' 9 JEL 129.

Boch and Lane (1992) 'European Community Law in National Courts: A Continuing Contradiction' 5 LJIL 171.

Boulouis, J. and Chevalier, R.M. (1991) *Grands Arrêts de la Cour de Justice des Communautés Européennes* Vol. 1, 5th ed (Paris: Dalloz).

Bovis, C. (1997) *EC Public Procurement Law* (London: Longman).

Boyron, S. (1998) 'General Principles of Law and National Courts: Applying a *Jus Commune?*' 13 ELR 171.

Brealey, M. and Hoskins, M. (1994) *Remedies in EC Law* (London: Sweet & Maxwell).

Brealey, M. and Hoskins, M. (1998) *Remedies in EC Law* (2nd ed) (London: Sweet & Maxwell).

Bridge, J.W. (1975–76) 'Community Law and English Courts and Tribunals: General Principles and Preliminary Rulings' 1 ELR 13.

Bridge, J.W. (1976) 'The European Community and Criminal Law' Crim LR 88.

Burns, T. (1996) 'Law Reform in the European Community' 16 YEL 243.

Burrows, N. and Hiram, H. (1995) 'The Official Control of Foodstuffs' in T. Daintith (ed), *Implementing EC Law in the UK* (Chichester: Wiley).

Caranta, R. (1995) 'Judicial Protection Against Member States: A New *ius commune* is Taking Shape' 32 CMLRev 703.

Collins, L. (1990) *European Community Law in the United Kingdom* (4th ed) (London: Butterworths).

Convery, J. (1997) 'State Liability in the UK after *Brasserie du Pêcheur*' 34 CMLRev 603.

Coppel, J. (1994) 'Rights, Duties, and the end of *Marshall*' 57 MLR 859.

Craig, P. and De Búrca, G. (1995) *EC Law: Text, Cases and Materials* (Oxford: Clarendon Press).

Craig, P.P. (1993) '*Francovich*, Remedies and the Scope of Damages Liability' 109 LQR 595.

Curtin, D. (1990) 'The Effectiveness of Judicial Protection of Individual Rights' 27 CMLRev 709.

Curtin, D. and Heukels, T. (eds) (1994) *The Institutional Dynamics of European Integration* (The Hague: Kluwer).

Curtin, D. and Mortelmans, K. (1994) 'Application and Enforcement of Community Law by the Member States: Actors in Search of a Third Generation Scenario Script' in D. Curtin and T. Heukels (eds) *The Institutional Dynamics of European Integration* (The Hague: Kluwer).

Curtin, D. and O'Keeffe, D. (eds) (1992) *Constitutional Adjudication in European Community Law and National Law* (London: Butterworths).

Daintith, T. (1995) 'The Indirect Administration of Community Law' in T. Daintith (ed), *Implementing EC Law in the United Kingdom* (Chichester: Wiley).

De Búrca, G. (1992) 'Giving Effect to European Community Directives' 55 MLR 215.

Diamond, P. (1990) 'Dishonourable Defences: The Use of Injunctions and the EEC Treaty – Case Study of the Shops Act 1950' 54 MLR 72.

Dine, J. (1993) 'European Community Criminal Law?' Crim LR 246.

Dumon, F. (1976) 'The Case Law of the Court of Justice – A Critical Examination in the Methods of Interpretation' (Judicial and Academic Conference 27–28 September 1976 (Luxembourg: Court of Justice of the European Communities).

Edward, D. and Lane, R. (1995) *European Community Law – An Introduction* (2nd ed) (Edinburgh: Butterworths/Law Society of Scotland).

Esteban de la Marre, Fernandez (1997) 'National Judges and Community Law: The Paradox of the Two Paradigms of Law' 4 MJECL 143.

Fletcher, L. (1996) 'Enforcement of Community Sex Equality Law' in T. Hervey and D. O'Keeffe (eds) *Sex Equality Law in the European Union* (Chichester: Wiley).

Gialdino, C.C. (1995) 'Some Reflections on the *Acquis Communautaire*' 32 CMLRev 1089.

Gormley, L. (1986) 'The Application of Community Law in the UK' 23 CMLRev 287.

Gormley, L. (1997) 'Remedies in Public Procurement: Community Provision and the United Kingdom' in J. Lonbay and B. Biondi (eds) *Remedies for Breach of EC Law* (Chichester: Wiley).

Green, N. and Barav, A. (1986) 'National Damages in the National Courts for Breach of Community Law' 6 YEL 55.

Haguenau, C. (1995) *L'Application effective du Droit Communautaire en Droit Interne* (Brussels: Bruylant).

Harding, C. (1979) 'The Choice of Court Problem in Cases of Non-Contractual Liability under EEC Law' 16 CMLRev 389.

Harding, C. and Sherlock, A. (1995) *European Community Law: Text and Materials* (London: Longman).

Harding, C. (1997) 'Member State Enforcement of European Community Measures: The Chimera of Effective Enforcement' 4 MJECL 5.

Harding, C. and Swart, B. (eds) (1996) *Enforcing European Community Rules: Criminal Proceedings, Administrative Procedures and Harmonisation* (Aldershot: Dartmouth).

Harlow, C. (1996) '*Francovich* and the Problem of the Disobedient State' 2 ELJ 199.

Hartley, T.C. (1981) 'The Impact of European Community Law on the Criminal Process' Crim LR 75.

Heukels, T. and McDonnell, A. (eds) (1997) *The Action for Damages in Community Law* (The Hague: Kluwer).

Himsworth, C. (1997) 'No Standing Still on Standing' in P. Leyland and T. Woods (eds) *Administrative Law Facing the Future* (London: Blackstone).

Himsworth, C. (1997) 'Things Fall Apart: The Harmonisation of Community Judicial Procedural Protection Revisited' 22 ELR 291.

Jacobs, F. (1993) 'Remedies in National Courts for Enforcement of Community Law' in *Liber Amicorum for Don Manuel Diez de Velasco*.

Kellermann, A.E. (1994) 'The Quality of Community Legislation Drafting' in D. Curtin and T. Heukels (eds) (1994) *The Institutional Dynamics of European Integration* (The Hague: Kluwer).

Kennedy, T. (1993) 'First Step Towards a European Certiorari' 18 ELR 121.

Lawson, R. (1994) 'Confusion and Conflict? Diverging Interpretations of the European Convention of Human Rights in Strasbourg and Luxembourg' in R. Lawson and M. de Blois (eds), *The Dynamics of the Protection of Human Rights in Europe* (The Hague: Kluwer).

Lenaerts, K. (1992) 'Interaction Between Judges and Politicians' 12 YEL 1.

Lenz, C.O. and Grill, G. (1996) 'The Preliminary Ruling and the UK' Fordham International Law Journal 844.

Lewis, C. (1997) *Remedies in Community Law* (London: Sweet & Maxwell).

Lonbay, J. and Biondi, A. (eds) (1997) *Remedies for Breach of EC Law* (Chichester: Wiley).

Mackenzie, Lord Stuart (1977) *The European Communities and the Rule of Law*, 29th Hamlyn Lectures 1.

Mancini, F. and Keeling, J. (1991) 'From CILFIT to ERT: The Constitutional Challenges Facing the European Court' 10 YEL 1.

Mayes, D. (ed) (1995) *The evolution of rules for a Single European Market* (Luxembourg: Office for Official Publications of the European Communities).

Medhi, R. (1996) 'Le droit communautaire et les pouvoirs du juge national de l'urgence' 32 RTDE 77.

Micklitz, H.W. (1996) 'Public Interest Litigation before European Courts' in H.W. Micklitz and N. Reich (eds), *Public Interest Litigation before European Courts* (Baden-Baden: Nomos).

Missir di Lusignano, A. (1996) 'La protection des intérêts financiers de la Communauté' *Journal des Tribunaux* 73.

Munro, C. (1996) 'The UK Parliament and EU Institutions – Partners or Rivals?' in E. Smith (ed) *National Parliaments as Cornerstones of European Integration* (London: Kluwer).

Murray, J. (1996) 'Arbitrability in the EU' in A.I.L. Campbell and N. Voyatzi (eds) *Essays in Honour of Lord Mackenzie Stuart* (Gosport: Trenton).

O'Keeffe, D. (1984) 'Appeals against an Order to Refer under Article 177' 9 ELR 87.

Oliver, P. (1997) 'Joint Liability of the Community and of the Member States' in T. Heukels and A. McDonnell (eds) *The Action for Damages in Community Law* (The Hague: Kluwer).

O'Neill, A. and Coppel, J. (1994) *EC Law for UK Lawyers* (London: Butterworths).

Oppenheimer, A. (1994) *The Relationship between European Community Law and National Law: The Cases* (Cambridge: CUP).

Pescatore, P. (1983) 'The Doctrine of Direct Effect: An Infant Disease of Community Law' 8 ELR 155.

Plender, R. (ed) (1997) *European Courts: Practice and Precedents* (London: Sweet & Maxwell).

Prechal, S. (1995) *Directives in European Community Law: A Study on EC Directives and their Enforcement by National Courts* (Oxford: OUP).

Reich, N. (1996) 'Judge-made "Europe à la carte": Some Remarks on Recent Conflicts Between European and German Constitutional Law Provoked by the Bananas Litigation' 7 EJIL 103.

Rideau, J. and Charrier, J.L. (1990) *Code de procédures européennes* (Paris: Litec).

Schwarze, J. (ed) (1996) *Administrative Law under European Influence* (London: Sweet & Maxwell/Nomos).

Sevenster, H. (1992) 'Criminal Law and EC Law' 29 CMLRev 29.

Sharpston, E. (1997) 'Interim Relief in the National Courts' in J. Lonbay and A. Biondi (eds) *Remedies for Breach of EC Law* (Chichester: Wiley).

Shaw, J. (1990) 'European Community Judicial Method: Its Application to Sex Discrimination Law' 19 ILJ 228.

Shaw, J. (1996) *Law of the European Union* (London: Macmillan).

Shaw, J. in P. Behrens (ed) (1992) *EC Competition Rules in National Courts, Part One, United Kingdom and Italy* (Baden-Baden: Nomos).

Siedentopf, H. and Ziller, J. (eds) (1988) *Making European Policies Work* (London: Sage).

Steiner, J. (1992) 'Drawing the Line: Uses and Abuses of Article 30 EEC' 29 CMLRev 749.

Steiner, J. (1993) 'From Direct Effect to *Francovich*' 18 ELR 3.

Steiner, J. (1995) *Enforcing EC Law* (London: Blackstone) pp. 14–27 and 42–118.

Swart, B. (1996) 'From Rome to Maastricht and Beyond: The Problem of Enforcing Community Law' in C. Harding and B. Swart (eds) *Enforcing European Community Rules: Criminal Proceedings, Administrative Procedures and Harmonisation* (Aldershot: Dartmouth).

Timmermans, C.W.A. (1996) *Compliance with Judgments of International Courts* (The Hague: Kluwer).

Tridimas, T. (1994) 'Horizontal Effect of Directives, A Missed Opportunity?' 19 ELR 621.

Usher, J.A. (1981) *European Community Law and National Law: The Irreversible Transfer?* (London: Allen & Unwin).

Usher, J.A. (1992) '*La sanction des Infractions au droit communautaire*' (FIDE).

Usher, J.A. (1995) 'The Legal Framework for Implementation in the United Kingdom' in T. Daintith (ed) *Implementing EC Law in the United Kingdom* (Chichester: Wiley).

Usher, J.A. (1998) *EC Institutions and Legislation* (London: Longman).

Usher, J.A. (1998) *General Principles of EC Law* (London: Longman).

Van den Bergh, R. (1998) 'Subsidiarity as an Economic Demarcation Principle and the Emergence of European Private Law' 5 MJECL 129.

Vandersanden, G. (ed) (1994) *La Réforme du Système Juridictionnel Communautaire* (Brussels: Etudes Européennes).

Van Gerven, W. (1995) 'Briding the Gap Between Community and National Laws: Towards a Principle of Homogeneity in the Field of Legal Remedies?' 32 CMLRev 679.

Van Gerven, W. (1996) 'Bridging the Unbridgeable: Community and National Tort Laws' ICLQ 507.

Vincenzi, C. (1994) 'Deportation in Disarray: The Case of EC Nationals' Crim LR 163.

Waelbroeck, M. (1994) 'Treaty Violations and Liability of Member States and the EC: Convergence or Divergence' in D. Curtin and T. Heukels (eds) *The Institutional Dynamics of European Integration* (The Hague: Kluwer).

Wathelet, M. and Rapenbuch, S. (1997) 'La Responsabilité des Etats Membres en Cas de Violation du Droit Communautaire: Vers un Alignement de la Responsabilité de l'Etat sur celle de la Communauté ou l'inverse?' *Cahiers de Droit Européen* 13.

Weatherill, S. (1993) 'Enforcing Public Procurement Rules in the UK' in S. Arrowsmith (ed) *Remedies for Enforcing the Public Procurement Rules* (Winteringham: Earlsgate Press).

Weatherill, S. (1995) *Law and Integration in the European Union* (Oxford: OUP).

Weatherill, S. (1996) *Cases and Materials on EC Law* (3rd ed) (London: Blackstone).

Weiler, J. (1987) 'The European Court, National Courts and References for Preliminary Rulings – The Paradox of Success: A Revisionist View of Article 177' in H. Schermers (ed) *Article 177: Experiences and Problems* (TMC Asser Instituut).

Weiler, J. (1988) 'The White Paper and the Application of Community Law' in R. Bieber and others (eds) *1992: One European Market?* (Baden-Baden: Nomos).

Wils, W. (1992) 'Concurrent Liability of the Community and the Member States' 17 ELR 191.

Index